Developing the Primary School Curriculum

R.J. Campbell
University of Warwick

HOLT, RINEHART AND WINSTON
London · New York · Sydney . Toronto

Holt, Rinehart and Winston Ltd: 1 St Anne's Road,
Eastbourne, East Sussex BN21 3UN

British Library Cataloguing in Publication Data

Campbell, R.J.
  Developing the primary school curriculum.
  1. Education, Elementary—England—Curricula
  I. Title
  372.19′0942   LB1564.G7
ISBN 0–03–910598–9

Typeset by Inforum Ltd, Portsmouth
Printed and bound in Great Britain by Mackays of Chatham Ltd.

Last digit is print number: 9 8 7 6 5 4 3 2 1

Acknowledgements

Extracts from the Plowden Report *Children and their Primary Schools*, from *Primary Education in England* and from *Mathematics Counts* are reproduced with the permission of the Controller of Her Majesty's Stationery Office, and the extract from *The Creativity of the School* is reproduced with the permission of the OECD.

I should also like to record my gratitude to the following, whose advice, encouragement and criticism have particularly influenced my thinking about primary education: those primary teachers and headteachers, necessarily anonymous, whose ideas, practices and professional judgements provided much of my basic source material; Professor Marten Shipman, who encouraged the initial research, and gave his time generously to discuss the ideas in the book, and to offer powerful, though gently expressed, criticism; Professor Denis Lawton, Mrs Ann Lewis and Mr Colin Richards, who were kind enough to read draft chapters and to offer constructive commentary on them; and Mr Derek Willmer, who has shared with me over a long professional association his shrewd judgement about developments in primary education, and the values they should embody. I am also grateful to Helen Mackay and Juliet Wight-Boycott, editors at Holt Saunders, for encouragement and advice. None of the above is responsible for errors and faults in the book.

Finally, my wife, Sarah, and our children, Florence and Victoria, have tolerated, while I have been writing the book, even more distracted and forgetful behaviour from me than they are accustomed to. A special word of appreciation to them.

Contents

Introduction

This introduction serves as a kind of prologue to the book. It attempts to do three things: to *set the scene* in which primary school curriculum development occurs; to identify the *main themes* of the book; and to offer background information on the *empirical inquiry* that provided the evidence upon which much of the analysis in the book has been based.

SETTING THE SCENE

When you are being shown round a primary school, you normally observe children in their classrooms, grouped round tables or seated at desks; you become aware of the classroom paraphernalia of felt tips, pencils, work cards, books, apparatus of one kind or another, and, nowadays, the intrusive technology of the micro-computer; and you notice the teacher, usually the sole adult inhabitant of the classroom world, in close relationship with the pupils. This classroom world is, to use a theatrical metaphor, the 'front stage' view of primary schools.

The 'backstage' view is more difficult to observe unless you become a teacher or student teacher. It is the world of the staffroom, with its motley array of allegedly easy chairs; its paraphernalia are publishers' catalogues, local-authority circulars, sets of children's books, notice boards, duty rotas, and closely observed tea bags; in it, teachers relate to other teachers, adult to adult, exchanging social gossip, fuel consumption rates of new cars, 'news from the front' about pupil behaviour, and daunting tales of attempted parental interference.

Within this informal, relaxed, behind-the-scenes world, more purposeful, more formally 'professional' activities are occasionally organised: meetings of teachers to discuss aspects of the school curriculum. They include small working parties, full staff meetings, discussions between teachers and their headteacher or local-authority advisers, and inter-school liaison groups. Such activities range from the informal consultation over lunch or coffee to the occasional day given over to in-service training for the whole school staff. These kinds of meetings, along with the implementation and evaluation of changes that follow from them, are a major mechanism for what has become known as 'school-based' curriculum development. With one or two exceptions, such as Hargreaves (1980) and Burgess (1983), teachers' meetings have not been given serious attention by researchers, or indeed by teachers themselves, sometimes understandably. But they have provided the main source of evidence for this book, both from direct observation and from interviews and discussions with participant teachers.

New significance has been given to the functioning and quality of such teacher meetings as pressure has built up on teachers to engage with colleagues in school in curriculum 'reviews', 'appraisals' and 'self-evaluations'. At their best they provide for professional encounters of a revitalising kind: at their worst they offer anecdotal inducement to institutional lethargy. However, two points about them need to be made briefly at this stage. First, teachers are not trained for the skills, knowledge and relationships that curriculum meetings entail; they are trained for classroom performance, not curriculum analysis. Second, many teachers have a disinclination bordering on distaste for meetings of any kind where 'theory' may be involved, partly because the profession still tends to believe that an interest in theory is inversely related to ability in practice.

THE MAIN THEMES: SPECIALISM, PARTICIPATION AND COLLEGIALITY

There are three main themes in this book:

(a) *specialism* and curriculum development in primary schools;
(b) *teacher participation* in curriculum decision-making;
(c) *collegial relationships* between teachers in primary schools.

There is in addition a sub-theme concerned with the significance of how teachers perceive school-based curriculum development: with *teacher perceptions*.

Specialism

Specialism is a broad concept which includes the role of 'specialist knowledge' or 'subject expertise' in curriculum development in primary schools, which have been traditionally 'generalist' in organisation and ideology. This book's treatment of specialism examines the ways in which the specialist or subject expertise of a teacher can be used to influence the curriculum practice of other teachers in a school. The analysis thus focuses on the role of the 'curriculum postholders', with major attention given to the *leadership* of school-based curriculum initiatives by them. The term 'curriculum postholder' technically refers to a teacher given a Scale 2 or 3 responsibility post, with associated salary increase, for an identified curriculum subject or area. It is used here, somewhat inaccurately, to refer to teachers exercising de facto responsibility for a subject whether or not they hold an identified scale post for it. Thus where a head, deputy or Scale 1 teacher accepts a subject responsibility, they are referred to as curriculum postholders. This simplification is not entirely justifiable, but it is a neutral description and avoids using the other common terms such as 'consultant' or 'subject adviser', which implicitly indicate how the role should be performed, as well as the responsibility. The book is therefore not about school-based curriculum development in general so much as postholder-led development, or development influenced by postholders' expertise.

Participation

Participation by teachers in decision-making about the curriculum provides the second theme. Unfortunately, the word itself, like 'collaboration' and 'collective', has a tired feel to it. None the less the notion of curriculum development underlying this book is not only one of changes in curriculum *products*, such as new guidelines or new teaching approaches; it is about the *processes* by which new guidelines are produced and new approaches adopted. It concerns the ways in which teachers who are expected to implement curriculum change contribute to its planning and evaluation.

After the publication of HM Inspectorate's *Primary Education in England* (DES 1978a) headteachers' offices across the country resounded to the noise of old syllabuses and schemes of work being dusted off and slapped onto desks to be re-examined in the light of the Inspectorate's call for greater through-school continuity in the curriculum. It is too cynical to regard this as the sound of the profession alert to the latest fashion. The survey had illustrated, in sometimes graphic and guilt-inducing detail, the fragment-ation, repetition and unconnectedness of the primary school curriculum as experienced by many pupils as they passed from one class teacher to another, few of whom seemed to have accepted, in any authentic sense, responsibility for the curriculum outside their own classrooms. Part of the explanation for such fragmentation lies in the two powerful traditions that the headteacher is responsible for the school's curriculum and that class teachers are 'autonomous'. This book examines the idea that if teachers participate in some explicitly *collaborative* action to *recreate* the curriculum in their school, rather than acting as *individuals* to *receive* it, they may move closer to accepting collective responsibility for the curriculum overall in the school, as well as for its application in their own classrooms.

Collegiality

Collegiality refers to the ethos or, as it is often called, in a strange meteorological metaphor, the atmosphere or climate of relationships, in a school. Collegiality is an adaptation of an old idea of a college: a society of scholars, equal to one another in status, with a common purpose, but with distinctively different knowledge. Adapted to primary schools, it stresses colleague relationships that *combine* commitment to the two ideas of specialist expertise and collaboration. Leadership of curriculum-development groups made up of subject 'experts' who engage in the collective examination of each other's professional practice may turn out to be an unsettling experience for primary school teachers who have conventionally 'done their own curricular thing'. The process therefore has to be based on relationships that are both supportive and critical, respectful of specialist expertise and the authority it may confer, but insistent upon its subjection to the scrutiny of professional colleagues.

There is no shortage of rhetoric about such relationships, but Alexander (1984) has created a useful analytic framework for them. He identifies three 'pre-existing characteristics' of schools in which they might occur:

(a) a concern for *intellectual autonomy* among staff including 'receptivity to new ideas', 'scepticism towards authoritative statements' and 'a commitment to intellectual engagement';

(b) *mutual accountability*, which requires teachers to see themselves as 'equally accountable to each other for their particular contributions to the educational process';

(c) *positive leadership* by the headteacher in goal setting and encouraging participation.

The atmosphere in a school is as pervasive in practice as it has been conceptually amorphous, but this book examines the role of the head and the other teachers in creating and sustaining the kind of collegial relationships that school-based curriculum development requires.

Teacher perceptions of curriculum development

An important sub-theme in the book concerns ways in which teachers *perceive* curriculum development and their role in it. Teachers in the same school, invited to participate in the same curriculum-development initiative, may none the less define their situation differently. Anyone involved in discussing a student teacher's lesson after observing it will be aware of the potential for the same situation to be defined very differently by those involved. Likewise with curriculum development, subjective interpretations of its worth, the motivation of its initiators, and its significance will vary. What a head sees as 'enthusiastic leadership' by a curriculum postholder may be viewed as sycophantic ambition by other demoralised or jaundiced teachers.

This is a critical issue in respect of what counts as being 'professional' in primary schools in the 1980s. If we consider again involvement in the range of teacher meetings outlined earlier it becomes clear that teachers may see them in at least one of two ways. For some teachers they will be opportunities to develop their professionalism outside the classroom and into the field of school policy making and rational curriculum planning with colleagues. They will define their own job in the school as 'extended professionalism', to use Hoyle's (1975) terms. Other teachers, 'restricted professionals', may define curriculum meetings as a distraction from the 'real' job of teaching, which lies within a classroom practice that is intuitive and preferably unanalysed. Such teachers may perceive voluntary curriculum-development meetings, which are usually held after teaching finishes, as valuable only for those of their colleagues who have full ambitions or empty private lives. There is no separate chapter in this book devoted to teacher perceptions of curriculum development, because it emerges as an issue in each one. There are, of course, some objective realities of the situation, such as staffing and resources, but a major thread in the argument of the book is that how realities are perceived by teachers is more critical to the effectiveness of school-based curriculum development than are the realities themselves.

THE WARWICK INQUIRY: METHODS, SCHOOLS AND CURRICULUM DEVELOPMENT PROGRAMMES

Over an eighteen-month period during 1980–82 I carried out an inquiry into ten school-based curriculum development programmes in eight primary schools in a Midlands county. (Two schools provided two programmes each.) Very little was known about this kind of programme in English primary schools, compared with secondary schools, and most of the US research into curriculum development had implied that curriculum change assumed the acceptance of innovation from outside the individual school — what Henderson and Perry (1981) called the 'top-downwards operation'. Since most curriculum research did not seem directly relevant to the situation faced by English primary schools in the early 1980s, the aim of the Warwick inquiry was, at its simplest, to find out, record and analyse what was involved for primary school teachers when they engaged in programmes designed to develop the curriculum from within the school.

For this reason I adopted an approach influenced by what social scientists call the case-study method. I should make it clear, however, that my approach was less intensive than normal case studies, which tend to be produced by long-term participation in the life of an institution. My own case studies were built up in collaboration with the teaching staff, and relied heavily upon discussions and interviews with teachers, observation of teachers' meetings of different kinds, and the analysis of school documents. A useful discussion of case-study method for reporting curriculum practice is that by Stenhouse (1982), whose notion of a 'case record' illustrates my approach. His case record, although incorporating the use of documents and observation, depends heavily upon a 'reflective' interviewing style:

> The people I interview are participants and they are observers of themselves and others; my object is to provide in interview the conditions that help them to talk reflectively about their observations and experience. It is their observations I am after, not mine.

Although there were small variations from school to school, a typical procedure for constructing a case study was as follows:

(a) identification of the school and initial approach by letter, explaining the purpose of the inquiry;

(b) visit to the school to discuss the inquiry with the head, identify the particular development programme, and obtain relevant documents and factual data about the school;

(c) visits to the school to discuss the development with the participating members of staff;

(d) observation of some aspects of the development in practice, e.g. staff meetings, working parties of staff, classroom activities;

(e)   first draft written up and presented to school staff for comments;
(f)   meeting staff involved to discuss the comments on the first draft;
(g)   final draft written up and degree of confidentiality negotiated.

In every case study accounts from teachers with different roles in the development were obtained. Thus the views of the headteacher, the teacher with a special-responsibility post, and some of the other teachers involved were obtained. This variety of viewpoints was intended as a protection against my receiving only an 'official version' of the programme from the viewpoint of the initiators (usually the head and the special-responsibility postholder); it also enabled me to take some account of disagreement and differing perceptions among the teachers.

The schools and their context

Eight schools were invited to participate in the inquiry because of their known involvement in curriculum development. The schools were not representative, in any accepted statistical sense, of schools in the local authority or elsewhere. Indeed a statistical sample of schools would not have been appropriate, since the inquiry was concerned not with the *extent* of school-based curriculum development in primary schools, but with the *nature* of it.

In the local authority concerned there were a variety of primary schools, including infant (5–7), first (5–8), junior (7–11) and middle (8–12) schools as well as combined schools (5–11 or 5–12). The authority was administered in four divisions, two of which fed into selective secondary schools, while the other two fed into comprehensive schools. In one of the selective divisions transfer into secondary schools was at age 11+, while in the other three divisions transfer was at 12+. Within the latter three divisions, children in some voluntary schools transferred at 11+. Thus administrative arrangements within the authority reflected in microcosm the unstandardised character of provision nationally, as indicated by Her Majesty's Inspectorate (DES 1977), in so far as there was no uniform age of transfer from primary school and no entirely uniform pattern of provision for pupils aged 5–16. The schools collaborating in the inquiry came from the divisions transferring children at 12+, although one of the schools (School 1) that provided two case studies was, at the time of the inquiry, in the process of changing from a 7–11 junior school to an 8–12 middle school. One case study for this school relates to the time when it was a 7–11 school while the other relates to the first year of its existence as an 8–12 school. Brief characteristics of the schools are given in Table I.1.

Three of these characteristics require brief comment. First, no very large or very small schools were included: they were all Group 5 or Group 6. Second, there was considerable variety in the nature of the schools' catchment areas, three being predominantly working class, two predominantly professional class, and three of more socially mixed composition. Third, three schools (2, 3 and 8) had been allocated staffing under Section 11 of the Local Government Act 1966. The three allocations were 0.5, 2.5 and 2.5 respectively. Even after subtracting these allocations there was substantial variation in staffing, with pupil:teacher ratios between 26.7:1 (School 1) and 21.7:1 (School 8).

Table I.1 *Some characteristics of the participating schools*

School	Age-range	Status	Catchment area	Number on roll	Full-time equivalent staff	Pupil:teacher ratio (PTR)
1	7–11 (then 8–12)	Voluntary controlled	Small town, socially mixed	321 (328)	12 (13)	26.7 (25.2)
2	8–12	County	Small town, mainly working class	380	16.5	23.0
3	8–12	County	Large town, multi-ethnic, working class	350	18.4	19.0
4	8–12	County	Small town, mainly professional	324	13.6	23.8
5	5–12	County	Small town, mainly professional	280	11.9	23.5
6	8–12	Voluntary controlled	Suburban/village, socially mixed	252	11.0	22.9
7	8–12	County	Suburban, socially mixed	400	16.5	24.2
8	8–12	Voluntary aided	Urban, multi-ethnic, working class	239	13.5	17.7

Three other features of the schools were particularly relevant to the inquiry. They are summarised here, but fuller details are given in the Appendix. First, all were *primary* in the sense that they were organised on the principle of class teaching. This was true even though all the schools had specialist facilities for science and craft, and most used specialist teachers (often part-time) for French and music. Second, seven of the eight schools were *semi-open-plan*, with some parts of the school designed to provide class areas with three walls linked to a similar area by what would otherwise be a corridor. Thus co-operation between teachers at classroom level was more feasible than in most primary schools. Third, in respect of staffing policy, *curricular expertise* had played an untypically significant role in the allocation of responsibility posts, with an unusually good match between the postholders' training and the curriculum areas for which they held responsibility (at least in respect of the programmes considered in the inquiry).

TEN SCHOOL-BASED CURRICULUM DEVELOPMENT PROGRAMMES IN OUTLINE

Case study A

The postholder with a Scale 2 responsibility post for social studies in School 1 led a working group of five staff revising an existing scheme of work. The process included organising and recording the meetings of the working group, providing reports for meetings of the whole staff, attending liaison meetings with staff of the receiving secondary school and other primary schools, and participating in in-service courses and conferences. The revised scheme comprised identified criteria for evaluation and an agreed sequence of concepts and skills, and was adopted as the school's policy document on social studies. Chapter 7 examines this case more fully.

Case study B

The deputy head had responsibility for developing combined studies, a co-operative teaching arrangement in the fourth year at School 1. She led a group of four staff implementing the arrangement for the first time. The process included regular meetings of the four staff involved to plan new units of work in detail, and to evaluate the programme as it progressed. In the course of these meetings, as well as general support for the programme, some professional disagreements emerged and were confronted.

Case study C

The postholder with a Scale 3 responsibility post for language in School 2 led a working group of five staff revising a school-wide policy on language across the curriculum. The process had included producing agenda, minutes and working papers for the staff group, reporting back to a meeting of the whole staff and (for the postholder) advising staff on the implementation of the new policy and monitoring its progress. The latter aspect of her role had become problematic, and the head had taken over responsibility for it.

Case study D

The postholder with a Scale 3 responsibility post for language in School 3 led an in-school training programme for ten staff, designed to increase their awareness of language problems encountered by children in the course of routine classroom assignments. This involved the teachers as a group in planning, observing and evaluating how well individual pupils coped with aspects of language, and in reporting their observations back to the group. The postholder had also attended a pre-programme course at the Open University, and liaised with another school and with the local-authority adviser. She prepared material for each staff meeting, managed the planning and discussion sessions and produced an evaluation report. Chapter 8 examines this case more fully.

Case study E

The headteacher of School 4 planned and organised an enrichment programme for fourth-year pupils, involving a group of five teachers and three local-authority advisers to provide a range of short, specialist options tutored in unusually small groups in order to extend children's work. He had been involved in consultation with a university researcher, had prepared a summary paper on able children for the staff, had managed the planning sessions, and evaluated the programme by staff and pupil questionnaires.

Case study F

The postholder with a Scale 2 responsibility post for science in school 5 had revised the scheme of work in science throughout the school, had co-ordinated its implementation, and organised a staff meeting at the end of the first year to evaluate its progress. He had been involved in discussing his ideas for the scheme with the local-authority adviser, had led staff meetings to examine the revised scheme before its implementation, had prepared resource materials for use by other teachers, and had occasionally taught alongside them. Chapter 9 examines this case more fully.

Case study G

The postholder with a Scale 3 responsibility post for art and craft in School 6 had attempted to incorporate craft, design and technology into the existing scheme. He had provided a working definition of design education for the staff, with a scheme illustrating ways in which appropriate work could be planned and implemented. He led staff discussion groups, and worked alongside other teachers to demonstrate techniques.

Case study H

The postholder with a Scale 3 responsibility post for environmental studies in School 7 had developed a scheme of work to provide more structure and sequence in the school's 'topic' work. She had provided a justification for the approach embodied in the scheme, a description of the skills and concepts involved and reference to supporting resources in the school. She led the staff discussions of the scheme and established close links with the school resources materials and with the school's art specialist.

Case study I

The postholder with a Scale 3 responsibility post for art and craft in School 7 was used as a specialist teacher in order to maintain influence over the quality of work in art/craft throughout the school. Her role included developing a scheme of work, identifying links with other subjects, and the appropriate use of materials and media. She also advised other teachers and exercised responsibility for display and for monitoring work throughout the school.

Case study J

The part-time music teacher in School 8 had developed and maintained a multicultural approach to music in the school, particularly, but not exclusively, through the establishment of steel bands. She had to develop justifications for adopting this approach and maintain its social and educational value as it became very popular with the pupils. It also involved her in liaison with other schools.

Even in the brief form presented here, the case studies serve to illustrate two points. First, they show the variety of practices included in the term 'school-based curriculum development'; they include review and planning exercises (e.g. A), implementation and evaluation activities (B), monitoring change (C), staff development programmes (D and E), syllabus reform (G and H), and specialist teachers being used to raise standards and innovate (I and J). Second, they illustrate in practice two of the themes identified earlier — specialism and teacher participation or collaboration — for, despite variations from school to school, these programmes were characterised by curriculum postholders leading groups of staff working together to develop aspects of the school's curriculum. Since two of the postholders were used as specialist teachers, some examination of the role they played, compared with that of postholders who were class teachers, became possible.

THE STRUCTURE OF THE BOOK

So far the main themes of the book and the empirical inquiry that provided evidence for them have been presented. The book itself falls into three parts, each of which is broadly different from the others in respect of the status of its material and approach.

Part 1 (Chapters 1–6) provides an *analysis* of curriculum development in primary schools. It includes the political background, theories of school-based curriculum development, the role of postholders and conflicts they may experience, approaches to in-school evaluation, and the role of the headteacher and others in supporting school-based curriculum development.

Part 2 provides *empirical* evidence from three fuller case studies of school-based curriculum development in particular settings. There is brief commentary on them to link problematic issues arising in them to the analysis developed in Part 1.

Part 3 is more *speculative*, offering an ideal image of the values of the 'collegial' primary school and considering obstacles to their realisation. These include the teachers' perceptions of their role relationships and the conditions in which primary teachers work.

PART ONE

SCHOOL-BASED CURRICULUM DEVELOPMENT IN PRIMARY SCHOOLS

1

The Political Context of Curriculum Development in Primary Schools

TEACHER AUTONOMY AND CURRICULUM DEVELOPMENT

When primary teachers meet in their staffrooms to review the curricular practice in their schools, external political control upon their decision-making may seem remote. From 1944 until recently, the central and local authorities exercised relatively weak control over what was taught in primary schools, and for this reason, if for no other, primary school teachers worked on the assumption that the potential for developing the curriculum in their schools was restricted only by resources and by the talents, commitment and energies of individual teachers. Kogan (1980), while noting that this apparent autonomy could be exaggerated, summarised the position in the following way:

> after 1945, the convention that schools create their own curriculum became part of the established wisdom of British education. It was announced to be the right way of doing things.

In the early 1980s it would seem that many primary school teachers still operated within that convention, if the following excerpt from an interview is typical. A primary teacher is explaining how she had introduced a particular change into the curriculum — in this case a change in the approach to teaching music:

> I'd been responsible for music here since we opened. The head was keen on having a strong musical, kind of, strand in the school and so I got a lot of support. Initially, normal activities were started — you know, building up an orchestra, school concerts, teaching singing and recorders — and we always had specialist peripatetic help with strings. Then about six years ago — it was a lot of coincidences really — a number of things happened. Some of the teachers said that the West Indian boys were always drumming on the desks in their lessons and doing it almost in an absent-minded way — you know — disrupting lessons but not meaning to. Then we had a visitor from the Commonwealth Institute who did an assembly for us using steel drums and this had a tremendous impact on the pupils. It made us realise what interest and excitement there was for steel band music. The county adviser said he

could find some of the money to start a school steel band. Then the band played in a local event — the town pancake race actually — and got a lot of publicity and from there it went on by leaps and bounds . . . As a matter of fact, although I was in charge of music, I was the one who wasn't keen. I thought it was a gimmick and because it was obviously, well, popular, the pupils would lose interest in more conventional music.

To English primary school teachers, the fact that a curricular change started off in this rather opportunistic, and even accidental, way is probably not surprising. The idea that the curriculum should be responsive to children's interests, and that the cultural interests of ethnic groups should be incorporated into it, is familiar, even routine, to the extent that it often evokes, as it did in this case, a little self-conscious suspicion of trendiness. But what is startling to teachers trained for other educational systems is the apparent lack of official regulation over such changes, and the ease with which primary school teachers appear to be able to decide to change the curriculum in their own classes and schools with little or no reference to anyone else. By visiting educationalists from countries where the curriculum is prescribed in detail at local or state level, the English primary teacher has been seen as a model either of curricular autonomy or of irresponsibility, depending upon the visitor's point of view. Fisher (1972) saw such autonomy as encouraging creativity, openness and discovery learning, while Rogers (1968) catalogued the fragmented and discontinuous nature of pupil learning that followed from allowing so much discretion to the teacher.

The realities of the situation are complex. It is not a matter of teachers being either completely autonomous or completely regulated in curricular matters. In the first place, legal responsibility for the curriculum does not rest with the teachers but with their employers, the local education authorities. Second, how teachers perceive the preferences of parents has a continuously limiting effect on development. Teachers will not innovate in ways they think might increase parental anxiety about the school, especially since the mid-1970s, when the general contraction in pupil numbers has made it very important for a school to retain as many pupils as it can. Holt (1980) has suggested that perceived parental preference has a similar impact upon innovation at secondary-school level. A third source of constraint upon primary teachers is more directly felt: headteachers exercise considerable control over their subordinates' practice by virtue of their real or perceived ability to influence teachers' career prospects. Teachers will rarely go out on a curricular limb if they think they will hang there forever.

None the less, until very recently indeed, except in respect of religious education, there were no explicit national, and few explicit local, policies on the curriculum that could be used to regulate, constrain or encourage individual teachers' intentions to change the curriculum in their classrooms. The DES (1980a) provided a pragmatic description of the power position:

> Legally, the curriculum is the responsibility of the local authorities; in practice, decisions about its content and about teaching methods, timetabling and the selection of textbooks, are usually left to headteachers and their staff. (pp. 18–19)

In contrast to the other countries, moreover, formal control in England and Wales has been seen as distinctively indirect. Dottrens' (1962) cross-national study suggested that primary school curricula were 'determined by the economic, political and social conditions prevailing in the country concerned', but in this country even the Department of Education and Science, the office of state most directly responsible for ensuring that the conditions of the various Education Acts are adhered to, has exercised an oblique 'influence' rather than 'control'. According to Jenkins and Shipman (1976) it has exercised influence in three ways: through finance, teacher supply and 'official' reports on aspects of the curriculum. All three sources clearly influence the curriculum but, equally clearly, in an indirect way.

POLITICAL CONTROL OVER CURRICULUM DEVELOPMENT

In the recent past commentators such as Becher and Maclure (1978), Kogan (1980), Salter and Tapper (1981) and Lawton (1980, 1983a) have suggested that the accepted convention of teacher autonomy in curriculum matters has been brought into question by the openly interventionist role played by the DES since the mid-1970s. It is possible to exaggerate the novelty and impact of this intervention: in comparison with the early part of this century, when the primary curriculum was controlled by central regulations, the present state of play represents reduced, not increased, centralisation. Nevertheless, within the post-1944 conventions, the destruction of a teacher-controlled agency for curriculum development (the Schools Council), the establishment of a DES unit for national curriculum evaluation (the Assessment of Performance Unit) and the production by the DES of a stream of documents on aspects of the school curriculum appear to be leading to reduced teacher autonomy and increased bureaucratic, and possibly political, control from the centre.

However, the issue of curriculum control is not so simple a matter. The problem is that 'the school curriculum' has different meanings for all those concerned with it. Pupils and parents may think of it as the weekly timetable of subjects; teachers might think of it as the overall scheme of work they plan term by term; and local or central authorities might think of broad aims or areas of knowledge that should be 'covered'. Most contemporary theorists draw attention to the idea that the curriculum incorporates, or should incorporate, knowledge (including values, skills and attitudes) considered to have high value by society. Lawton's (1975) conception stresses this feature, as well as implicitly raising questions about which groups in society are able to do the valuing:

> The school curriculum is essentially a selection from the culture of a society; certain aspects of our way of life, certain kinds of knowledge, certain attitudes and values, are regarded as so important that their transmission to the next generation is not left to chance.

Although it is useful to think of the curriculum as socially valued knowledge, we need to recognise that it is expressed in two forms. There is the *curriculum in policy*, usually developed by identifiable groups inside and outside the school, such as HM Inspectorate, local-authority working groups, or examining bodies. This tends to provide general aims and broad areas of content, and to a lesser degree teaching approaches and evaluation. And then there is the *curriculum in practice*, which is the implementation of teaching strategies in the classroom by teachers, even if they have not articulated them to other people, or indeed to themselves. This is the curriculum as 'today's lessons', and the closest of the two to the curriculum as experienced by the pupils. Similar distinctions have been made by Taylor, Reid, Holley and Exon (1974) and White (1980). The gap between the two forms is commonly believed to be very great, with considerable discontinuity between the practice of individual teachers and the policies of schools, in the shape of syllabuses or schemes. The curriculum in the classroom is not the curriculum in the cupboard.

Thus 'curriculum control' can refer to policy, or to practice, or to both; there is no necessary connection between them. This is especially true, if as Taylor (1970) suggests, the curriculum in practice often proceeds in an unplanned way, routinely and unreflectingly accumulating what Joseph (1984a) has designated 'clutter'. The DES has asserted, or reasserted, its responsibility for curriculum policy, but the policy itself may not have penetrated the classroom.

The sense in which the term 'political' is being used here needs comment. The exercise of control outlined above is political (though not party political) because it is about exercising power. Power is exercised over curriculum development not so much by coercing teachers to change through Acts of Parliament (though Acts such as the Education Acts 1980 and 1981 will affect the curriculum to some extent), but by controlling definitions of the desirable. Controlling ideas of how the curriculum should change, controlling the transmission of images of 'good practice', is a more commonplace, but probably more effective, way of bringing about normal and undramatic changes in existing practice. The metaphor that is sometimes used is an agenda, a list of items that need to be considered and acted upon. Power resides not only in making teachers act upon the agenda items, but in the prior activity of getting items on the agenda in the first place, and thereby allocating priority to them over other, excluded, items.

One illustration will suffice at this stage. Concern for *standards*, especially standards reached by 'able' children in primary schools, has re-entered the curriculum development agenda since the mid-1970s. The groups which got it on the agenda include the DES and HMI, as well as the authors of the Black Papers (Cox and Boyson 1975, 1977; Cox and Dyson 1969a, 1969b, 1970), who traced an alleged decline in standards to an alleged dominance of primary school curricula by alleged progressives. A more recent study by Barker Lunn (1982) suggests that this concern has been transmitted to junior teachers, who are reverting to grouping by attainment or by ability in order to try to meet the needs of more able pupils.

Lawton's model of control

The 'policy–practice' distinction is, of course, too simple, as a model offered by Lawton (1983a) illustrates. Adapted to primary schools, it shows four levels of responsibility in the education system: *national* (e.g. the DES), *regional* (local authorities), *institutional* (the school) and *individual* (the teacher in the classroom). At each level there is pressure from interest groups, such as teacher unions, parents and subject/professional associations, all of which hope to influence the curriculum to some extent. It is a model in which power over the curriculum at school and individual level is relatively con-strained and therefore well suited to a democratic society. The model envisages room for schools and teachers to take into account local and parental expectations.

The model also identifies three dimensions of the curriculum: *content* (including aims), *pedagogy* (methods of teaching) and *evaluation*. Lawton points out that control over each dimension can vary by the level in the system. For example, a primary school may have a mathematics scheme developed by a local-authority working group (content controlled at the regional level), with teaching methods left to the individual teacher's discretion (pedagogy controlled at the individual level) and assessment by means of a set of tests and techniques agreed upon by the whole staff (evaluation controlled at the school level).

Lawton's analysis is particularly useful because it demonstrates the complexity of the situation facing a government wishing to control the curriculum in a direct way. Even so it probably understates the complexity in two ways. First, all curriculum subjects are not equally controllable: subjects such as mathematics or language, where there are widely available schemes, often adopted by a local authority, provide for less teacher auto-nomy than subjects like creative writing or 'topic'. A second factor is that teachers are human beings and vary in the extent to which they are receptive to national or local policies, as well as in their ability or inclination to translate such policies into their practice. Likewise, schools as organisations vary in their openness to local and parental pressures: the curriculum in Haringey may be out of the question in Harrogate. Because of these differences in personal and institutional qualities and ideologies, practice differs from precept. The proof of the curricular pudding is in the eating, not in the recipe.

None the less, for a government, the ultimate purpose of controlling policy is to influence practice, because policy attempts to define what practice should become. It offers images of 'good practice'. The extension of central control over policy and into practice has been started by means of a series of circulars from the DES, starting with Circular 14/77 and culminating, so far, in Circular 8/83. These have required local authorities to report upon the extent to which practice in their schools conforms to central policy. Circular 8/83 actually specifies the particular document, *The School Curriculum* (DES 1981a), to which conformity is expected, and thus takes for granted professional acceptance of the policies incorporated in it. More recently elements in the rate support grant have been earmarked for centrally identified curricular initiatives at primary level, so the system-based barriers to direct control over practice identified in Lawton's model seem to be being dented. Whether one interprets such evidence as unacceptable encroachment by the central on the local authority, or as a reassertion by the government of its responsibility to ensure some degree of national consistency, the consequences for primary school teachers are the same. There is now a clear constraint upon them because there is strong central direction, often mediated through the local authority, about the priorities to be adopted in curriculum development.

FOUR SOURCES OF CONTROL OVER CURRICULUM DEVELOPMENT

From the mid-1970s, therefore, primary school teachers were having transmitted to them messages about the direction in which the curriculum should be developed. The substance and sources of these messages are examined in the rest of this chapter, and some implications for teacher professionalism are briefly raised. It is useful to consider the sources of these messages under four headings:

(a) the construction of a national curricular framework by the DES and associated moves to get it accepted by teachers;
(b) the rise of the movement for accountability and pressure for more explicit forms of evaluation;
(c) the discrediting of progressive ideology and practice;
(d) disillusionment with national curriculum development programmes.

All four sources were political in the sense that they tended to define the curriculum development agenda for teachers. However, the first two involved consciously pre-pared attempts to influence professional thinking which can be traced to the DES. The latter two were less clearly identifiable with particular groups or agencies, and emerged in the general climate of ideas being built up in educational research and analysis.

A national framework: DES/HMI policy for the primary curriculum

One of the significant features of the politics of the curriculum since the mid-1970s in England has been the attempt to influence the school curriculum through the con-struction of a national curricular framework in a series of documents and reports, often distributed free to all schools by the DES. Most of the documents involved were not described as policy statements, but presented either 'for discussion' or as surveys of practice. Only one, *The School Curriculum* (DES 1981a), was presented as a curricular policy or, more ambiguously, as 'guidance'. It opens as follows:

> The school curriculum is at the heart of education. In this paper, which comes at the end of several years of public discussion and government consultation with its education partners, the Secretaries of State for Education and Science . . . set out their views on the way for-ward and the action they believe is now needed on the part of Education Departments, local education authorities, teachers and schools in relation to the school curriculum for the 5–16 age range.

And in a section of the document entitled 'The Recommended Approach' the authors explain that:

> the Secretaries of State have decided to set out in some detail the approach to the school curriculum which they consider should now be followed in the years ahead.

This document cannot be read as an isolated statement unrelated to the stream of other documents on the curriculum issued in the preceding and subsequent years. Another document by the DES (DES 1981b) provided a list of its publications on the curriculum 'for ease of reference and to avoid possible confusion' as follows:

September 1978   Primary Education in England (A Survey by HMI)

November 1979   Local Authority arrangements for the school
                 curriculum (Report on the Circular 14/77 review)

December 1979   Aspects of secondary education in England (A survey
                 by HMI)

January 1980   A framework for the school curriculum
                 (Proposals for consultation by the Secretaries of
                 State for Education and Science and for Wales)

January 1980   A view of the curriculum (HMI Matters for
                 Discussion)

March 1981   The school curriculum (guidance by the Secretaries of
                 State)

The authors ask us to resist the 'temptation to interpret these publications as neatly interlocking pieces of some centrally devised jigsaw with a grand overall design', but the temptation is extremely alluring. The following need to be added to the above list:

March 1977   *Curriculum 11–16* (Working Papers by HMI) (DES 1977)

March 1981   *Curriculum 11–16*: A review of progress (joint study by HMI and
                 five LEAs) (DES 1981b)

March 1982   *Education 5–9*: An illustrative survey by HMI (DES 1982a)

December 1983   *9–13 Middle Schools*: An illustrative survey by HMI (DES 1983a)

December 1983   *Curriculum 11–16*: Towards a statement of entitlement (DES
                 1983b)

October 1984   *The Organisation and Content of the 5–16 Curriculum* (DES 1984)

When this has been done it is difficult to believe that all the documents have an entirely arbitrary relationship to each other. There are differences of emphasis, especially in respect of the secondary curriculum, which may be, as Lawton (1983b) has suggested, the consequences of conflicting ideological groupings within the DES itself. Differences in respect of the primary curriculum have been critically examined by Richards (1982) and are relatively small surface details. In respect of the major positions about the primary school curriculum, they have so much in common that they may be seen as a concerted production if not of an interlocking jigsaw, at least of a well defined frame, within which a common curricular pattern can be stitched. For primary schools, the basic structure was built up in a report called *Primary Education in England* (DES 1978a).

Primary Education in England (A survey by HMI)

This document, commonly referred to as the Primary Survey, was a report of an empirical survey of curriculum practice in a representative sample of classrooms containing seven-, nine- and eleven-year-olds. Although some relatively objective tests were used in the survey (for example tests of reading and mathematics attainment), the majority of the findings and recommendations relied on the subjective, professional judgements of the inspectors.

Three main concerns about the primary curriculum emerge, and they may be thought of as the three S's, that is, concern for standards, sequence and scope. The inspectors portrayed the standards of work set for the pupils identified by the teachers as their 'able' children as generally too low, with a relatively poor match between work set and the pupils' perceived capacities. The more effective use of teachers' expertise was seen as a means of remedying the mismatch. They also argued that there was no area of the curriculum that would not benefit from a set of school-wide guidelines in which children's learning followed a clearly articulated progression; a curricular sequence of concepts and skills would help to avoid the repetition and fragmentation identified in all areas, but most clearly in the social subjects. A similar concern for continuity and progression between schools, as well as within them, was also urged. A third concern was that the curriculum should not be unduly narrow in scope; it should cover the main subjects, or subject areas, and not concentrate on a narrow and restricted set of 'basic' skills. Although they did not wish to encourage any greater diversity, the inspectors claimed that a broad approach to the curriculum, both within and across subjects, would lead to higher attainment, even in basic skills.

Without direct evidence it is difficult to judge the impact of the Primary Survey on teachers' curriculum practice. But the recommendations of the survey were promoted among the teaching profession in a series of national and regional conferences, in which its status quickly approximated to that of a new orthodoxy. In addition, a number of articles, written by the Chief Inspector for primary education and summarising the survey's findings, appeared in journals and books aimed at the classroom teacher rather than at academics (Thomas 1980a, 1980b). Whatever its general impact, it was the only DES document referred to and used by the schools whose curriculum development initiatives form the basis of this book. It is a fair guess that of all the documents listed above, it has been the most influential upon the thinking and practice of primary school teachers.

Assumptions and ideologies

When *Primary Education in England* is considered in the context of the other documents, especially the culminating one, *The School Curriculum*, six main assumptions about the primary school curriculum emerge. They are:

1. The aims of the curriculum should be common to all pupils, even allowing for individual differences.
2. The scope of the curriculum should be broad, and should not be restricted to a narrow core of basic skills.
3. The curriculum should incorporate a recognisable sequence of concepts and skills, to ensure continuity and progression in pupil learning.
4. The curriculum should cater more adequately for able children, whose needs could be met through more effective use of teacher expertise.

5. The curriculum should reflect fundamental social values such as equality of opportunity, and should help pupils to appreciate cultural diversity.
6. The curriculum should provide for pupils' personal, social and moral development, through specific elements such as health education, and in more general areas.

The ideological position underlying these documents is an interesting one. Skilbeck (1976a) identified three educational ideologies: classical humanism, progressivism and reconstructionism. Briefly, classical humanism places great value on cultural heritage, worthwhile forms of knowledge and high standards, often seen as achievable or appropriate for a small elite. It is often thought of as the basis for a 'knowledge-centred' approach to curriculum planning. Progressivism places great value on the child's needs, interests and perceptions of the world in his or her own terms, all of which should be developed as far as possible unaffected by adult cultural forms. First-hand experience, individual differences, pupils choosing what to do, and discovery of knowledge by the pupils have greatest priority. It is often thought of as the basis for a 'child-centred' approach to curriculum planning. Reconstructionism places great value on improving society as a whole through education, by improving the quality of life for individuals in it. A central feature of the reconstructionist curriculum is a core of common elements that provide a basis both for a shared cultural identity and for critical appraisal of society by its members. It is often seen as the basis for a 'society-centred' approach to curriculum planning.

The DES/HMI papers clearly contain elements of classical humanism (both the Primary Survey and *Curriculum 11–16* make reference to able pupils' needs and to the value of worthwhile knowledge for its own sake) and of reconstructionism (for example the stress on a common curriculum and on the curricular implications of the multicultural society), but they appear to lack substantial appreciation of the values of progressivism. Even the document on the curriculum on first schools, *Education 5–9*, stresses the importance of teacher expertise, school-wide schemes and sequence and continuity. Although the value of first-hand experience is acknowledged, the whole thrust of the document (in so far as 'thrust' is an appropriate epithet for so indecisive a report) is away from pupil choice and spontaneity and diversity in learning, and towards specialist knowledge and predictable progression.

This uneasy and possibly incompatible ideological combination, which leaves progressive values largely out of account, may fit reasonably well into curriculum planning at secondary level, assuming that schools and pupils can be convinced that the option system at 13+ should be attenuated: at primary level, however, it signals a clear change of direction in official policy about the curriculum from that embodied in the Plowden Report (1967), a document closely identified with child-centred approaches.

Although this is not the place for a thorough-going critique, two other major problems with the framework may be mentioned. First, there is an inherent contradiction in arguing for common approaches to the curriculum and at the same time frequently and unproblematically using children's 'ability' as a criterion for selecting aims and content. The latter practice will tend to lead to a differentiated curriculum rather than a common one, and this particular slip is showing in *The School Curriculum*:

> this involves, certainly for the more able, and in a simpler form for many others, an introduction to the concepts of history such as chronology, and cause and effect . . .

A second problem is the vague and unhelpful notion of skills as somehow general across the curriculum rather than subject-distinctive. The skills are referred to as general qualities — using resources, observing, classifying, listening, appreciating interrelations, etc. — as though 'observing' a landscape was the same skill as observing a scientific experiment, or 'listening' to another pupil's point of view was the same as listening to a poem being read. This kind of criticism was available to the DES from Dearden's (1980) critique of 'advanced' skills recommended in the Primary Survey, but seems to have been discounted.

An agenda for curriculum development

Despite such reservations about the overall logic of the framework's assumptions, the initiative taken by the central authorities has provided a fairly clear agenda for curriculum change in the primary schools over the next decade. The high-priority items are:

(a)   how to alter or redress the curriculum balance so that all pupils are introduced to science and technology;
(b)   how to ensure a predictable sequence of concepts and skills in all subjects;
(c)   how to match the curriculum to the abilities of the more able pupils;
(d)   how to incorporate a multicultural perspective into the curriculum, especially in monocultural schools;
(e)   how to develop learning applied to relevant contexts and problems;
(f)   how to ensure continuity and progression within and between schools.

Richards (1982) has characterised the initiative as the Inspectorate's taking 'a public lead on curriculum matters based on developing and clarifying a professional consensus'. It might be more accurate to describe the Inspectorate as *asserting* the existence of a professional consensus on the curriculum by glossing over problematic issues raised by their own policy. In particular, the unargued dismissal of much of the contribution of progressive thinking, especially in respect of the significance of the aesthetic areas of the curriculum, pupil choice, developmental stages and humane teacher–pupil relations in schools, needs to be challenged.

The Organisation and Content of the 5–16 Curriculum

The latest of the central initiatives designed to define the curriculum is the publication by the DES in October 1984 of *The Organisation and Content of the 5–16 Curriculum*, a general statement on the curriculum, designated, rather curiously, as 'A Note from the DES', and issued free to all schools. It will be followed by separate statements on individual subject areas. The explicit intention of the note is to raise questions and invite comments on the content of the curriculum outlined and characterised throughout as 'Government policy'.

Despite its title, the stress in the note is upon the secondary curriculum, with twenty-three paragraphs on the secondary, and three on the primary, phase, and an appendix giving examples of curricular patterns in five schools, all of which are secondary. Perhaps this is the result of the note's attempt to address the problem of balance between a common core and options at 13+, an attempt critically questioned by White (1984), but the consequence seems to be a treatment of the primary curriculum that is both bland and cursory. The content, which is expressed as a set of general aims, is organised under eight headings which celebrate pragmatism at the expense of both epistemology and logic. The eight are:

(a) competence in language and mathematics;
(b) science;
(c) history/geography/RE;
(d) aesthetic activities;
(e) problem-solving through craft, design and technology;
(f) physical and health education;
(g) introduction to computers;
(h) insights into the adult world, including how people earn their living.

Although there are difficulties in importing meaning to curricular phrases expressed in this general way, the significance of the note is not the framework itself so much as the two ideas of curriculum planning between which the framework is sandwiched (paras. 4–7 and 9–10). These two ideas focus attention on the way the framework might be used by school staff. They are:

(i) *whole school curriculum planning,* with teachers using the framework to build 'breadth', 'balance' and 'coherence' into the curriculum, whilst still permitting 'differentiation' to allow for difference in pupil ability;
(ii) *the use of 'subjects' as the basis for curriculum planning,* even though in some schools, and for some pupils, subjects may not be the basis on which the timetable is structured.

It is thus extremely easy to read this document as a call for what in this book has been termed 'specialism and collaboration', for school-based curriculum development using specialist expertise and teacher participation in decision-making.

There is no need for paranoia about the construction of a national policy for the curriculum in itself. In some ways, it could provide the basis for protecting the curriculum in a particular school against pressure from unenlightened governors for a narrowly parochial 'community' curriculum, or for protecting all schools from national politicians urging a 'back to basics' approach. It is not how a policy is formulated and promoted that matters as much as how teachers judge its appropriateness for their school in practice. After all, documents issued free to schools by the DES to influence teachers' thinking may simply remain on the headteacher's bookshelf, and not penetrate the working consciousness of the profession. It is how a policy is received, reacted to and reconstructed by teachers as professionals in real schools that counts. Even Circular 8/83, which assumes passive professional acceptance of the policy in *The School Curriculum*, invites individual schools to respond in their own terms.

The movement for accountability and more explicit evaluation

The elaborate construction of the curricular framework was accompanied by a widespread and clamorous pressure for schools to be accountable to the public for, among other things, the curriculum on offer in them. The pressure was increased by difficulties in maintaining expenditure on education and tended to be conceived in simple terms of requiring teachers to show that they were giving the public value for money, through accepting evaluation of pupil performance or teacher effectiveness. Sockett (1976) and White (1980) have explored the concept of teacher accountability, and practical implications have been examined by two research studies, the Cambridge Accountability Project, summarised by Elliott (1981), and the East Sussex Accountability Project, analysed in Becher, Eraut and Knight (1981). From the point of view of curriculum development, two features are particularly relevant: 'giving an account' and 'leading to improvement'.

For primary school teachers, accountability came to mean in the first place that they should give an account of the rationale, operation and effectiveness of the school and the curriculum to representatives of the public interest, mainly on governing bodies. This was due to the report of an advisory committee of the DES, the Taylor Committee (Taylor Report 1977). Taylor made a range of recommendations designed to improve the effectiveness and representativeness of governing bodies, and to enhance the quality of information about the school that flowed both to the governors and to parents. A positive and progressive report, reliant on a dominant image of partnership, it could have led to much needed and authentic co-operation between the teaching profession and a public more informed about the possibilities and problems of improving curriculum practice in schools for which they were jointly responsible.

Giving an account to a client public, however, is only one face of accountability: the other has superimposed on it the image of control, as Taylor made clear in a radical proposal that governing bodies should be given responsibility for:

> setting the aims of schools, considering the means by which they are pursued, for keeping progress under review, and for enabling such progress to occur.

However, control over practice as well as policy was seen by the teachers as not negotiable. The National Union of Teachers (1978), responding to Taylor in a section (2.1–2.7) on 'professional autonomy', argued that only teachers could make decisions about the curriculum because they alone had the 'experience and detailed knowledge of the children' that would enable them 'to evaluate, discriminate and modify curricula'. They added the point (section 4.2) that teachers could not be accountable if they were not fully responsible for curriculum practice.

Taylor made the error of failing to distinguish between policy and practice, between general aims and day-to-day interpretation of them in the classroom. The former may reasonably be seen as the responsibility, if not the legal duty, of governors. Responsibility for the latter, including detailed interpretation of the curriculum in the classroom, and its evaluation, could not be given to anyone other than teachers, if they were to continue to aspire to full professional status. It looks as though the DES sided with the teachers in this respect, possibly because Taylor would have encouraged great local variation and control at precisely the time that the DES was pressing for national consistency and more central control, and the Education Act 1980 did not incorporate the kind of curricular control advocated by Taylor.

Accountability does not merely mean 'telling it like it is', but implies 'telling it like it should be'; accountability should lead to curricular improvement or it remains a process of mere accountancy. Elliott (1981) has indicated the political dimension in this respect:

there appear to be two main views of school accountability representing different ideas about how schooling might be improved. One view is that improvement comes with greater public control over decisions about school organisation, teaching methods and the curriculum. The other view is that schooling is more readily improved when the school retains control over decisions, but becomes more responsive to those whose interests are affected by those decisions.

Most commentators make reference to the accountability experience in the USA, partly because curricular improvement was an implicit criterion for evaluation there, and because control by the local community and by the state administration was a more clearly accepted tradition. The work of House et al (House 1974; 1975; House, Rivers and Stufflebeam 1974) is often quoted to illustrate the deleterious effects on the curriculum of a simple 'value for money' model of accountability. House was invited by a Michigan teachers' organisation to produce an independent report on Michigan's accountability system, which had included state-wide detailed behavioural objectives and a testing system that linked a school's score to its funding — a kind of hi-tech payment by results. He concluded that:

> In implementing the accountability system many activities have been inconsistent with the model's intent — and even counterproductive. The common goals have not been clarified; the objectives were developed by relatively few people and do not represent either a consensus of minimal objectives; . . . the most serious flaws are in the assessment component; it is too narrow in scope to serve as a state needs assessment.

In short, the effect of the public control accountability system had been to narrow down the curriculum, not to improve its quality and effectiveness.

In England similar anxieties have been expressed about the potential impact upon curriculum practice of the DES Assessment of Performance Unit, which was set up in 1974 'to promote the development of methods of assessing and monitoring the achievement of children at school, and to seek to identify the incidence of under-achievement'. In practice, it has become a unit monitoring attainment restricted to three curriculum areas — language, mathematics and science — at primary-school level. According to Gipps and Goldstein (1983), it has had variable impact upon local-authority testing schemes, but it is in the following possibility that the threat to the curriculum may lie. A possible development of the APU's bank of test items is the production of norm-referenced tests derived from the bank by the National Foundation for Educational Research, which could be used by local authorities for more frequent 'blanket' testing to monitor pupil, school, or even teacher, performance. It is still too early to judge this issue, and Gipps and Goldstein show that, although there might be a narrowing down of the curriculum as teachers teach to the tests, in some areas there has been a broadening of the curriculum *within* subjects, presumably because the scope of APU test items is wider than the scope of some school schemes. Despite this, it is clear from Gipps and Goldstein's analysis that the emphasis on the *monitoring* function has diverted effort from the task of identifying ways of *improving* the curricular performance of 'under-attaining' schools. At least one Chief Education Officer, Naismith (1983), has given the impression that his authority might use such monitoring devices to identify 'bad' teachers, and the fear must remain that if teachers come under pressure to teach to the tests the curriculum will revert to the kind of narrowing down that was experienced under selection procedures. In this respect, as in some others, the real threat to the curriculum may lie not at the national (APU) level, but at the local one.

The discrediting of progressivism

Children and Their Primary Schools (Plowden Report 1967) quickly established itself as the fullest attempt to identify and encourage the 'quickening trend' in English primary schools towards progressive, or child-centred, practice. Although the report was concerned with social policy towards education in a broad sense, its treatment of the curriculum came to be regarded as a 'semi-official ideology' of the day, in Davies and Bernstein's (1969) words. 'It was what you went on courses to learn about, what you were promoted for', according to Dearden (1978). It is difficult to summarise the report's position on the curriculum without recourse to what now sound like slogans: the stress on discovery learning, on respect for children as individuals, on the importance of play, on flexibility and spontaneity in curriculum practice, on its insistence that 'knowledge does not fall neatly into separate compartments', and on a materials-rich environment for children to explore. Above all, the ways in which children's interests and enthusiasms should be developed and exploited for the learning process were celebrated. Quoting a report from a group of HMIs, Plowden noted:

> the newer methods start with the direct impact of the environment on the child and the child's individual response to it. The results are unpredictable but worthwhile. The teacher has to be prepared to follow up the personal interest of the children who, either singly, or in groups, follow divergent paths of discovery. Books of reference, maps, enquiries of local officials, museums, archives, elderly residents in the area, are all called upon to give the information needed to complete the picture that the child is seeking to construct. When this enthusiasm is unleashed in a class, the timetable may even be dispensed with, as the resulting occupations may easily cover mathematics, geology, astronomy, history, navigation, religious instruction, literature, art and craft. (para. 544)

In short, Plowden had attempted to open up teachers' curricular horizons by offering them a vision of learning that placed great value on children's reconstruction of the world in their own terms, and thus relatively little value on predictably planned sequences in identifiable subject-derived curriculum areas. Plowden, of course, was as much a centrally generated policy as anything facing primary teachers today; as Jones (1983) said, it was an 'officially sponsored dream'. But it was a dream.

The dream did not endure. The values promoted in Plowden were eroded by attacks from educationalists and political analysts, and from empirical research into the effectiveness and extent of progressive practice. The report's limited and uncertain treatment of curricular aims had been criticised by Peters (1969), and its emphasis on 'interests' as a basis for selecting content for the curriculum was seen as inadequate by Dearden (1976, 1978). Blyth (1968) reproved the Plowden Committee for their unimaginative treatment of social processes in primary schools, which had ignored the potential for developing a 'curriculum emphasising the arts as a basis for an autonomous culture . . . which is more necessary than ever, especially since primary education may have the special responsibility of nourishing children's creative imagination when social pressures are in general inimical to it . . .'.

To these specific criticisms was added the widely noted inconsistency of an argument promoting an approach based on children's interests and integration with a number of chapters treating subjects separately and somewhat conventionally. Thus, despite the welcome given to its broader social policies addressing problems of educational disadvantage, Plowden's treatment of the curriculum was seen as at best theoretically inadequate and at worst a missed opportunity to articulate a consistent, reasoned and distinctive justification for progressive approaches.

The political analysis was much rougher, and came from both the hard right and left of the spectrum. The former was represented by Cox and Dyson (1969a, 1969b, 1970) and Cox and Boyson (1975, 1977) in the Black Papers, which portrayed progressive practice contributing to lowered standards in basic skills and cultural attainment, reduced respect for authority, and declining commitment to the values associated with an academic curriculum. The level of the debate in these papers ranged from the plausible to the pathetic but, as Jones (1983) has argued in a recent appraisal of them, they managed to identify, exploit and transmit issues of genuine concern to the public, and most crucially to parents, by successfully defining what the educational debate was to be about, namely, standards, discipline, parental choice and cultural decline consequent upon the adoption by teachers of progressive ideologies and methods:

> The Black Papers were less the cogent presentations of research than a series of interventions in popular debate. From this point of view the accuracy of their research is less important than their political and ideological acuteness; their selection of targets, presentation of aims, identification of allies and choice of methods; their ability to play upon the heartstrings of those disillusioned with educational reform; and their sense of the strengths and vulnerability of their opponents. Their overall concern was with the ability of state education to produce the qualities needed by a cohesive society with an effective and cultured leadership.

The tune played upon the heartstrings of the disillusioned was amplified to deafening level by the scandal at a London primary school, William Tyndale, in which all the worst fears voiced by the Black Paper authors were portrayed as reality. Different versions, by Ellis et al (1976) and Auld (1976), of the scandal exist, but the important issue politically is that the school came to be a symbol of progressivism taken too far and, since disgruntled parents had voted with their feet, a symbol preventing progressivism from being taken too seriously any more.

The attack from the hard left took a more intellectual form, couched in intense and partly unintelligible neo-Marxist analyses of progressivism, the most celebrated of which was Sharp and Green's (1974) study of a progressive infant school. They suggested that correspondence between social and educational inequalities held as strongly in the progressive school as elsewhere under capitalism, with working-class pupils being subject to the same kinds of hierarchical ordering, and therefore educational disadvantage, as those obtaining in more traditionally authoritarian schools. Characterising progressivism as 'romantic radical conservatism', Sharp and Green suggested that 'the educational ideology of child-centred progressivism fails to comprehend the realities of a stratified society where facilities, prestige and rewards are unequally distributed'. Their conclusions echoed Martin's (1971) message that progressivism would disadvantage working-class pupils, and resonated with Bernstein's (1973) argument that the 'invisible pedagogy' was an extension of the socialisation preferences of the 'new' middle class. Underlying the dense jargon of these studies was a strain of common sense: classrooms organised around principles of independent learning, active pursuit of individual interests, and reconstruction of knowledge through children's planning and linguistic skills would favour children whose early family experiences had prepared them for such activities. Such child-rearing styles were disproportionately concentrated in the middle class, as Newson and Newson (1976,

1977) had shown. Children's interests are distributed in society no less unequally than power and wealth.

Finally, empirical studies of the effectiveness and extent of progressive practice provided a consistently unfavourable picture. Bennett's (1976) well-known study had claimed to show that 'informal' teaching styles were inferior to formal ones, at least in respect of pupil attainment in basic curriculum areas. The publicity associated with the launch of Bennett's book was matched by the lack of publicity given to criticism of its methodology and presentation by Gray and Satterly (1976, 1981) and to Bennett's own revision of his basic classification, acknowledged in Aitkin, Bennett and Hesketh (1981). However, the general picture of the inferiority of progressive methods was repainted by HMI (DES 1978a), who showed teachers using 'exploratory' methods as less effective in matching work to pupils' capacities. The end of the decade saw Galton and Simon (1980a, 1980b) reporting that teaching styles incorporating substantial amounts of class instruction were associated with higher pupil attainment in mathematics and English, and with more high-level cognitive functioning among pupils.

Perhaps more damagingly, evidence from a range of research studies suggested that curriculum practice had not been extensively influenced by Plowden. Bennett and Jordan (1975), Bealing (1972), Boydell (1975, 1980), Galton and Simon (1980a) and Barker Lunn (1982) had all shown that full-blooded progressive methods were a minority pursuit. Even in art and topic, according to Galton and Willcocks (1983), only some 30 per cent of teachers used Plowden-style co-operative forms of pupil grouping, even for part of the time. Counting progressives is no more enlightening than counting reds under the beds, since their influence rather than their number is what matters (in both cases). However, the series of research findings offered a compelling picture of a profession that had not generally implemented Plowden's policies, and according to the recent studies was reducing what little there had been. Reinforcing this picture was an occasional detail from progressives themselves, such as Wragg (1978), in which progressive practice was shown, unintentionally, as operable by only the most talented and industrious of teachers.

Disillusionment with curriculum reform

The 1970s also saw attempts to evaluate the impact of large-scale curriculum development projects such as those funded by the Schools Council and the Nuffield Foundation. Many of these had tended to work to a theory of curriculum change now referred to as the centre–periphery model or the research development and diffusion model, after Schon (1971) and Havelock (1982) respectively. In this model at its simplest, active production of curricular approaches and materials is the role of a central research team, and passive reception of them is the role given to teachers. The defects of the model have been usefully analysed by Macdonald and Walker (1976), but most early approaches to curriculum development were characterised by lack of time and resources given over to the dissemination stage, in comparison with the development stage. And where project materials were adopted by schools they tended to be used in ways which suited the teachers, but which often distorted the developers' intentions or the project's principles.

The evidence about projects' impact upon the primary school curriculum qualified the general impression of ineffectiveness. A survey by Steadman, Parson and Salter (1978) found projects of two types: those well known and used by schools (known by 40 to 80 per cent of headteachers, and used by between 15 and 50 per cent of schools) and those not well known or used. Some projects had impressive records. Breakthrough to Literacy was known by 79 per cent of heads and used in 46 per cent of schools; Nuffield Mathematics was known well by 51 per cent of heads and used in 39 per cent of schools; Science 5–13 was well known by 33 per cent of heads and a further 43 per cent knew something of it.

Other projects were spectacularly unsuccessful. Man: a Course of Study, perhaps the most sophisticated and impressively presented of all the projects, was not known at all by eight out of ten teachers; History, Geography and Social Science 8–13 was unknown to seven out of ten heads and nine out of ten teachers. It was in use in 3 per cent of schools, a record it shared with Project Environment. In addition, Steadman, Parson and Salter's survey showed that a wide range of information provided for the profession as a basis for choice about curriculum development was virtually unknown. A broadly similar picture emerged from Northern Ireland, where Sutherland (1981) argued that reform was hampered by project assumptions about teachers' time and resources:

> The chief problems . . . were the time consuming nature of project involvement . . . shortage of money, difficulty in mastering content of new projects, and absence of anyone to consult who had first hand knowledge of the project.

That is to say, normal primary-school conditions reduced the impact of the projects.

The differential success of the projects is not easily explicable, partly because projects have had different lengths of time for transmission to teachers. The successful ones were nearly all systematically disseminated to teachers, and resourced for that purpose; they tended to be in basic curriculum areas such as maths, language and science, rather than in marginal areas such as social studies. But despite some effective projects, the general picture was of large-scale projects, especially secondary-school projects (which were the overwhelming majority), having little effect on curriculum practice.

The sense of disillusionment with large-scale projects echoed earlier disappointment about curriculum reform in the United States of America, and by the end of the 1970s the Schools Council was looking for alternative strategies in a series of programmes designed to identify and support smaller local and school-based initiatives. It would be wrong to explain the switch as the consequence of a rational appraisal of the empirical evidence about project impact: it has to be seen in the general context of accountability and the mood of financial stringency. In such a climate it was difficult to press for funding of projects that could be presented as having made little impression on classroom practice.

At the same time the Schools Council itself had been subject to scrutiny from a directly political perspective and, as Salter and Tapper (1981) showed, its main problem was political, rather than curricular, impotence. In the 1970s it was subject to severe and sometimes secret criticism by politicians and civil servants. It was unable to counter such criticism effectively, according to Salter and Tapper, because it failed to obtain legitimacy among teachers, and it failed to clarify to itself a clear ideology on curricular issues, especially in respect of positive project promotion. A main reason for this was its marginal 'uncemented' position in the educational system as a whole. The secret criticism, the Yellow Book, had characterised the Schools Council as having 'scarcely begun to tackle the problems of the curriculum as a whole' and as having a performance that was 'generally mediocre'. Inability to mount an effective defence against this kind of attack, and to counter the charge of resisting change in order to safeguard teacher autonomy, led to a decline in the standing of the Schools Council, and in 1977–78 its constitution was reviewed, with changes being introduced that weakened teacher power and put financial control in the hands of the DES and LEAs. In 1982 the Council's work was further attenuated by the Secretary of State for Education and Science, Sir Keith Joseph, who proposed the Council's abolition and replacement by two small, separate advisory bodies, one for curriculum and one for examinations. Membership of these bodies is by nomination by the Secretary of State.

To practising teachers interested in improving the curriculum in their schools these matters may seem distant and irrelevant politicking, but it is important to separate the political decline of the Schools Council and the actual and potential influence upon the curriculum of centrally produced materials and approaches. As has been shown above, several projects have exercised considerable influence upon the curriculum at primary-school level, and eight out of ten of the school-based curriculum developments upon which this book is based used materials, ideas and approaches from centrally developed projects. It is important to stress the word 'used'; they were not simply bought as a total package. The school staff used them as a basis for their own thinking and discussion, taking from them what they found helpful, adapting what they thought necessary, and rejecting what they thought inappropriate. It is this idea of actively responding to externally developed materials that characterises a proper professional stance to curriculum development agencies. It would be a great pity if, because of the political decline of one central agency for development projects, teachers attributed curriculum decline to them all.

SCHOOL-BASED CURRICULUM DEVELOPMENT AS POLITICAL ACTION

Four strands have been identified in the political background to curriculum development in primary schools. Centrally generated documents have created a policy framework emphasising commonness of approach, sequence and continuity, and specialist expertise directed at able children. At local level, the framework has influenced curriculum guidelines and the search for information about the extent of conformity to central policy. Secondly, the movement for accountability has tended to be corrupted into narrow monitoring of pupil, and possibly teacher, performance, instead of developing procedures for appraising sources of curriculum improvement. Principles distinctively associated with English progressivism have been brought into disrepute, and a teacher-controlled agency for curriculum reform has been replaced by a committee comprising government nominees. In addition, schools have been experiencing the combined effects of pupil contraction and expenditure reductions. Taken together the four strands could have become the noose that strangled all enthusiasm for curriculum renewal among primary school teachers.

This has not happened, although there seems little doubt that levels of teacher morale in primary schools have not been sustained. However, one response by the profession has been the resurgence of 'school-based' curriculum development — the idea that the best place for developing the curriculum is in the school, not in some specialised agency outside it (whether the civil service, an educational quango or a teacher training institution), and that the best people to initiate such development are working groups of teachers based in the school rather than specialist educationalists outside it.

There are three reasons for this response. The first is a 'professional' one, in the sense that school-based curriculum development seems to offer, despite a general context that could justify negative and dispiriting responses, at least the promise of a constructive channel for the extension of teachers' skills and energies, as well as anticipating promotion for some of them. The second reason is 'political' in the sense that school-based approaches to curriculum renewal implicitly assert a professional expertise residing mainly in the skills of the school staff, and so it appears to offer teachers the chance to play a dominant, though not necessarily exclusive, role in defining the curriculum policy and practice at school level. There are some problems with this view, not the least of which, as Hargreaves (1982) suggested, is the fact that it seems to be being promoted from the central authorities, not from the grassroots of the profession. A third reason is suggested by research by Wicksteed and Hill (1979) and is essentially a 'pragmatic' one. Primary school teachers welcome the existence of a general curriculum framework, and see it as desirable. Wicksteed and Hill's 600 teachers saw no threat, and considerable political and professional advantage, in having a generally agreed common core of the curriculum specified in the kind of broad terms that left the detailed reconstruction of the curriculum in practice up to their professional judgement.

> Teachers do not want complete freedom to decide the curriculum of their individual classes, but they do not want the whole of the curriculum dictated to them . . . Teachers do accept that many parties have a legitimate interest in curriculum priorities and need to be consulted. Decisions cannot be left to the teaching force alone, but what is essential is that teachers should be free to tailor . . . general priorities to particular school and classroom contexts.

If these teachers were typical, there has been no great surge of radical challenge in the profession to the centrally produced agenda for change, but there has been an attempt to demarcate curriculum control. The underlying political stance of school-based approaches is that curriculum practice in the school is to be the profession's prerogative.

Other chapters in this book examine the implications of exercising such a prerogative, but the merging of the 'professional' with the 'political' in curricular matters has become clear, as Kogan (1980) suggested:

> Some social expectations (for the curriculum) will be enunciated as part of some national consensus by the Secretary of State and by HMIs. Other inputs will be those of local parental and other client expectations. But that does not mean that the school's curriculum is simply a resultant of external forces. Teachers have their own accumulated knowledge of what the curriculum is and should be. They also have the particular role of interpreting social expectations as part of the curriculum. Where they feel that social expectations are wrong, then politics comes into play. That is to say, they should say they are wrong and that they are not going to pursue objectives that they feel to be false or shallow or the result of parental anxiety or panic.

Thus primary teachers engaging in school-based curriculum development are of course engaging in professional activities: in so far as they claim to be defining the curriculum in their schools, they are engaging in political activity also.

2

School-based Curriculum Development in Theory and Practice

'School-based curriculum development' is a clumsy term, used to refer to activities which, because they take place in the unique contexts of individual schools, are necessarily diverse. This chapter attempts to place some structure on the idea of school-based curriculum development by linking material from four relevant areas. First, *theoretical concepts* are outlined; second, these concepts are qualified by reference to the *practice* of curriculum development in primary schools; third, *contextual factors* influencing the nature of such development are examined; and finally, the *values* underlying school-based curriculum development in primary schools are briefly elaborated.

CONCEPTS OF SCHOOL-BASED CURRICULUM DEVELOPMENT

One of the problems faced by anyone attempting to understand school-based curriculum development as an idea is that it is used very much as a catch-all concept. For example, as illustrated by Mitson (1980), it means something as substantial as promoting independent learning styles across the whole curriculum to two whole year groups of secondary school pupils, together with appropriate staff training and resources development; or it may be a small-scale revision of a language programme in a primary school, such as that described by Timms and Lees (1981).

The DES (1978b) has stressed the significance of school-based approaches, but two writers in particular have helped to sharpen the formulation of ideas about them. Eggleston's (1980) introduction to six case studies provides a useful starting-point:

> It is essentially a process in which the detailed strategies for a curriculum appropriate to the needs of the individual children in a specific school, or even in the specific unit of a school, are developed by cooperative discussion, planning, trial and evaluation.

Although it is unclear whether Eggleston was describing school-based curriculum development or prescribing a particular way of doing it, four features of his definition are worth picking out:

1. It is *particularistic*. The curriculum-development activity is focused upon the diagnosed, or perceived, needs of the specific school or part of it.
2. It is *process-oriented*. In terms of 'strategies for the curriculum' intended, the process by which these are developed is important in itself.
3. It is *participatory*. The appropriate style for developing the curriculum is co-operative, that is, staff working together to produce plans for change.
4. It is *preliminary*. The curriculum developed is to be seen as experimental, in the sense that it is open to evaluation and appraisal after its implementation.

One of the interesting things about this definition is the stress, not on the curriculum as such, but on the *roles* that teachers have to play in the process of its development, and the attitudes that are required to underpin it.

This characteristic is also central to the analysis offered by another writer, Skilbeck (1976b). He identified three models of school-based curriculum development — the *rational-deductive*, the *rational-interactive* and the *intuitive* — and located them within differing politico-educational frameworks. The first operates in centrally directed educational systems, where the task of the school is to 'interpret central directives' and the role of the teacher is as a mere functionary in a bureaucratised educational service. The second emerges in mixed systems, such as those in England and Wales, which stress the active role of teachers in adapting the curriculum at school level within rather broad general outlines of national policy. Teachers working within this kind of framework have a more complex role than in the rational-deductive model and have more demands made upon them; they 'have to act as course assessors, to help construct syllabuses, to select learning materials and to devise learning systems'. The third model stresses the individual teacher's decision-making and creativity, and leads to great diversity between teachers and between schools, and to inconsistency between 'national policy and individual school programmes'.

Although school-based curriculum development may share elements from all three, the rational-interactive model represents the style and values most appropriate to contemporary English schools, especially because of the stress put upon the range of roles expected of teachers, and the assumption that teachers have to negotiate the fine details of their roles (rather than simply accept pre-defined ones) by working in partnership with each other. Thus in this formulation also, school-based curriculum development is as much about changing roles and relationships among a school staff as it is about changing schemes of work or methods of teaching and learning.

A second paper by Skilbeck (1982) offered a substantial analysis of the concept, rationale and aims of school-based curriculum development, and suggested a model for school use, with a commentary on the difficulties in implementing it. He identified a number of characteristics, including the idea of the curriculum as a set of:

> experiences of value developed by the teacher and learner together from a close and sympathetic appraisal of the learner's needs and characteristics as a learner.

But, although Skilbeck identified the need for freedom for the teachers to define relevant learning experiences, he also noted the requirement for appropriate support systems, including national or regional curricular guidelines. This is an important point, not least to counteract the danger of a simplistic polarising of 'school-based' and 'non-school-based' approaches to curriculum development. A major goal of school-based curriculum development in Skilbeck's terms is the continuous adaptation by teachers of externally defined curricula into forms of educative experiences unique to the teacher and learner.

> We need a system for curriculum development that combines the advantages of national policy making, national centres for the production of materials and for research and development, with the flexibility, adaptability, and professionally satisfying features of local initiatives and creativity. (p. 20)

Thus school-based curriculum development is predicated upon the concept, admittedly idealised, of teachers who creatively reconstruct the curriculum within a recognised framework of local and national expectations: it is not predicated upon passive acceptance of external definitions of the curriculum, or the myth of the 'autonomous' school, existing independently of its political and economic context. Given the political development, outlined in Chapter 1, of a national framework for the curriculum, the relevance of Skilbeck's model for teachers in England and Wales has increased considerably.

Skilbeck's analysis enables us to add two further characteristics of school-based curriculum development to the four identified earlier. These concern the relationship between the school's curriculum and national or local guidelines, and the view taken of the role of the teacher. We can summarise these by saying that school-based curriculum development is:

1. *Framework adaptive*. Despite its particularistic focus, it need not run counter to national or local curriculum guidelines, but may on the contrary ride on them, if staff adapt them to suit their specific situation.
2. *Role extensive*. It assumes acceptance by teachers of a wider role than that restricted to classroom performance and it consequently assumes change, or flexibility, in their existing roles.

The teacher as educationalist

The teacher role in curriculum development, discussed in the theoretical positions encapsulated above, is to do with what Keddie (1971) called the 'teacher-as-educationist' context. In her study of secondary school teachers, Keddie noted two different aspects of their activities: their role beliefs and practices in the context of their classrooms when instructing pupils (the 'teacher-as-teacher' context); and their beliefs and practices elaborated in extra-classroom situations, when discussing educational ideas and principles with colleagues, and with outsiders such as advisers and parents (the 'educationist' context). Keddie's somewhat jaundiced view of the disparity of beliefs between the two contexts need not concern us here, but the distinction itself is very fruitful for analysing teachers' roles in school-based curriculum development. For most of their time, teachers in the Warwick inquiry were, as *curriculum developers*, operating in the educationalist[1] context, that is to say in situations where they were required to discuss educational policies and practices with their colleagues and other adults. This is a fairly novel role for teachers in primary schools, where traditionally it has been reserved for the headteacher, if anyone. More commonly it has been allocated to the local-authority advisers or other educationalists in courses located, and often focused, far from the contexts of the schools themselves.

Eggleston and Skilbeck have provided a frame within which a fairly well-defined picture of school-based curriculum development can be held. It is dominated by *process* — by teachers collaborating in working groups as professionals to interpret general curricular assumptions into a specific curriculum practice suitable for their particular context. This process requires teachers to develop a role for themselves as educationalists in the sense that they will have to familiarise themselves with national and local curriculum documents, justify and articulate curricular objectives, implement and sustain innovation, and evaluate and account for it. Thus the distinctive arena for school-based curriculum development is the staffroom rather than the classroom, and the distinctive discourse is concerned not only with the surface details of curriculum practice, but also with the assumptions underlying it.

CURRICULUM DEVELOPMENT IN PRACTICE: GRADUALISM AND SPECIALISM

The theoretical analyses discussed above are necessarily generalised, and need to be qualified somewhat in the light of the practice in the Warwick inquiry schools. Brief outlines of the programmes have already been provided, which suggest two characteristics that are perhaps distinctive to primary school curriculum development. They can be considered under two headings, namely *gradualism* and *specialism*. To dichotomise rather too simply, gradualism qualifies the idea of 'development', while specialism qualifies the idea of 'curriculum'.

Gradualism

By gradualism I mean three related features of the notion of 'development' which stress the limited expectations that may be held for it. These three limitations may be thought of as the *problematic*, the *unpredictable* and the *incremental* qualities of curriculum development in primary schools.

The problematic nature of curriculum development derives from the fact that there is a conceptual difference between development and change. The latter is neutral and implies merely that practice has altered, not that it has been improved. 'Development', 'renewal' and probably 'innovation' imply not merely change, but change for the better. What counts as a change for the better in education is problematic. An analogy with the

---

[1] I prefer this more conventional, less inelegant, term to Keddie's original.

practice of medicine may be helpful. If a doctor diagnoses, say, constipation in a patient and prescribes a change of diet as a remedy, there is not much professional or lay disagreement about what would constitute a change for the better in the patient's condition. Not being constipated is generally regarded as an improvement on being so. But the school curriculum is a more difficult area for diagnosis, with less sure a basis for agreement about what constitutes improvement. A curriculum where there has been, so to speak, little movement for a number of years is not necessarily in a worse condition than one in which there has been a great deal of it.

One of the points that follows from this is that, although the term 'curriculum development' is widely used throughout the literature and in this book, in practice it cannot be shown in advance, and often it is not known even in retrospect, whether changes are actually developments. At best it is commonly a matter of belief, intuition and professional judgement of those involved. Indeed, to return to Eggleston's emphasis on the *process* of development, it was quite striking to note how frequently the teachers in the Warwick inquiry reported that the major benefit, for them, of school-based development activities had been the experience of being involved in the process rather than, or in addition to, any changes in actual curriculum practice. It was as though they were hedging their bets on the curricular outcome of the initiatives.

Second, there is *lack of predictability* in outcome. Given the experimental approach characterised by Eggleston as 'discussion, planning, trial and evaluation', there is the built-in risk that the evaluation might show no tangible development in the desired direction. Indeed such changes as emerge might be in unpredicted or unconnected directions. This seems to have been the case in the Oxfordshire primary school reported in a case study for the Open University prepared by Clift (1982). He reported a self-evaluation exercise by the school staff, lasting over a year, and involving at least seven in-school staff meetings, to prepare a review of the school's policy, provision and practices across a range of activities, including the curriculum. It appears to have been characterised by serious, professional involvement by the staff, and to have been efficiently and yet flexibly organised. It covered, among many other matters, problems of curricular aims and how they should be described, curricular practice, including the grouping of pupils and catering for individual differences, and the provision of curricular guidelines, and was carried out by effective teacher collaboration. The case study author reported in the postscript (p. 37) that the changes that followed this activity were:

(a)   a new duplicator;
(b)   a loss of a member of staff without replacement;
(c)   a new staff toilet.

It is perhaps very much to be hoped that, for these teachers, the process of their endeavours was valued at least as highly as the products. But it does illustrate in an extreme way the uncertainty of school-based development — its almost chancy nature and the unpredictability of its outcomes. As Shipman (1973), writing about larger-scale curriculum development activities, noted:

> Curriculum projects may be important as initiating, stimulating and accelerating change, but not necessarily in the anticipated direction.

A third characteristic of the notion of development in the curriculum is *incrementalism*: that what is involved is not a fundamental change, but an extension of existing practices. The foundations of the school's curriculum are not being dug up and re-laid: the structure of the curriculum is being renovated a little, that is all. This kind of development cannot promise or deliver a dramatically different curriculum. It is not designed to do that, nor is it resourced adequately for it. The kind of sweeping changes in curricular aims and practices currently being promoted for the 14–19-year-olds, for example, could not easily be developed in the school-based mode precisely because they are predicated upon external intervention fundamentally to redefine curricular aims (and upon substantial external funding) at least in the innovation period. School-based curriculum development is a more modestly conceived activity, designed to build upon existing mainstream curricular practice, and predicated upon the assumption of a curricular framework about which there is already consensus, or which can be taken for granted. It is incremental, not radical, change in the curriculum, with slow, small-scale, almost routine, benefits, accruing over time from a school staff gradually building upon its collective strengths and, where possible, remedying weaknesses. There should be little of the heady rhetoric associated with large-scale national projects of the 1960s and early 1970s, not just because such rhetoric tends to lack credibility in the routine of school life, but because school-based approaches are designed to improve the normal curriculum, not graft abnormal practices on to it.

Discussions with teachers in the Warwick inquiry illustrated this incremental quality in an interesting way, showing the mundane and highly pragmatic nature of what was involved. In School 1, a staff group met to review their curricular policy in social studies, and attempted to revise an existing scheme by constructing it around some basic concepts and skills, drawn partly from some Schools Council curriculum materials and partly from their experience with the previous scheme. No grand claims were made, or were felt necessary to be made, about either the changes that might follow or the process itself.

> Many frameworks were tried in private and rejected; it was felt important to demonstrate that the content . . . could be organised conceptually. To test this we developed a matrix, setting four broad conceptual areas of Environmental Studies (i.e. the previous scheme) across four conceptual themes from 'Home and Family' (a Schools Council project). When we did this, we simply jotted down in the matrix what we thought would work, given what had worked before, and the overall conceptual scheme we were developing. And then we met and looked at what we'd written down and tried to sort it out from there.

In another school, the art specialist had been attempting to influence work in other teachers' classes, and she told me:

> There is the scheme of work, which everybody has, and it gives teachers quite a lot of help I think — you know it lists Topics by each year, and the appropriate media, and says what materials there are and how you can use them. But really what happens quite often is that they simply come and ask me, in the staffroom. For example, a couple of weeks ago Janice just came and said she thought she would try her class using pastels, which she hadn't done before and was a bit worried about. It's there in the scheme and I supposed that's why she thought about doing it, but really she did it because she could come to me and I showed her — actually I went in with her and helped the children when they were trying it out. They just need some help with the actual technique or it becomes a terrible smudge on the paper . . .

What strikes one about these statements is their very ordinariness, their tentativeness and the absence of extravagance in what is being claimed. They are the voices of routine improvement not radical, or even substantial, change, expressing the gradual, incremental quality of school-based curriculum development at primary-school level. They embody the view of HMI (DES 1978a) that:

> a slow but steady build up from the points of strength of individual teachers is probably the only way forward. (8.65)

Specialism

Specialism refers to the exploitation of expertise in a subject or, more accurately, in a curriculum area. This exploitation took a variety of forms in practice but three can be distinguished: specialist teaching, subject teaching and subject diffusion.

Specialist teaching

This occurred in two cases (I and J), with teachers used to teach a number of classes and having no class responsibility themselves. The two cases provide ambivalent evidence, limited though it is, for the idea of specialist teaching as a basis for in-school development. Both teachers taught their subject to all the older (years 3 and 4) children in the school, but none the less needed to influence the quality of work with the younger children, who were taught by class teachers. They exercised responsibility for raising the quality of work done throughout the school, though they also acknowledged a reduced impact upon the younger classes. They appear to have experienced little of the conflict and strain that other postholders felt, as reported in Chapter 4. This was probably because teaching one subject and not having class responsibilities dramatically reduced the range of the other demands made upon specialists.

On the other hand, as Chapter 3 suggests, the two teachers used as specialists tended to have involved their colleagues less in the process of curriculum development than did other postholders. Furthermore, the specialist teachers did not involve colleagues in evaluation of their programmes. This suggests, accepting that these are two cases only, that specialist teaching, whatever its merits in classroom practice of the specialist, may, in terms of initiatives of a school-wide kind, tend to produce leadership of a more isolated, less collective style than would otherwise be the case.

Subject teaching

This occurred when teachers with specialist subject knowledge taught one or two other classes on a regular basis, while retaining a generalist class-teaching role with their own class. This occurred in two cases (B and F). A related version of subject teaching was when a teacher irregularly, and for limited specific purposes, taught alongside colleagues, or swapped classes, in order to teach a specialist topic or skill or to demonstrate a skill and show the quality of work that could be expected. This happened in three other cases (E, G and H).

Subject diffusion

This occurred in all the programmes, when teachers with expertise were consulted by others who needed advice, or when they took a lead in curriculum planning and review groups. It was the main mechanism for spreading specialist knowledge from the post-holder to the other staff. It was what the Inspectorate meant when they talked of postholders' having an 'influence' on the work throughout a primary school. With organisational arrangements reflecting the class-teacher principle, even where some subject teaching occurred, this diffusion model was the dominant style of in-school development.

One of the heads explained the approach in the following terms:

> We had specialist teaching here some years ago, and given our staffing we could still use it much more than we do. But we've more or less abandoned it, except for French and our Remedial Specialist . . . There are two reasons. The main one is that the children here need a lot of structure and the class teacher provides that best of all . . . So the second reason follows once you've decided that. It is to *use* teachers who were specialists to lead curriculum review groups, and we've been doing that here for the last couple of years now . . . it doesn't always come off, but it's staff development as well as curriculum development.

The stress on the use of teacher specialism in the curriculum development programmes is largely explicable in terms of the political analysis in Chapter 1. All the programmes, except for cases B and J, were focused on issues raised in the Primary Survey, which stressed the need to provide for greater progression and continuity, to cater for able children, to fill the gap in science, to extend advanced reading skills, and so on. Although it may not be a permanent characteristic of primary school curriculum development, it probably provides quite strong evidence of the impact of the survey, an impact followed up in two later surveys by HMI (DES 1982a, 1983a) in which 'specialisation' and its contribution to curriculum development in first and middle schools were further examined.

THE CONTEXT OF SCHOOL-BASED CURRICULUM DEVELOPMENT

There is an ecology of curriculum development. Just as certain kinds of plant and animal life flourish in favourable conditions of soil, light, temperature and the balance of relationships in their overall environment, so the context of primary schools inhibits or encourages the growth of the kind of curriculum development discussed above. Factors in this context can be considered as *external* to the school or *internal* to it, although the distinction is not clear cut. External factors are those derived from the educational system itself, from its administration, finance, demography and from teacher career opportunities. Internal factors include the role relationships of teachers and the ways in which authority is exercised by the headteacher.

External influences

Staffing and resource allocations

The objective raw indices of PTRs in primary schools have shown a progressive small improvement over the past decade, with the national primary mean PTR moving from 25.0:1 in 1973 to 21.8:1 (including middle deemed primary) in 1983 (CIPFA 1973–83). The rate has slowed down in the last three years, but the trend is still towards improvement. Moreover, the proportion of classes with over 30 pupils has also reduced, according to data released by Joseph (1984b). Both kinds of 'improvements' are partly created by falling rolls, which require some relatively small classes to be tolerated. There is considerable evidence that small improvements in PTR and/or class size are not associated with raised standards of attainment, and it is probable that the marginal changes in PTR and class size do not, of themselves, positively or adversely affect a school's potential for curriculum renewal.

In a period of contraction, the range of skills and expertise within a staff group and the way they are deployed may be a more critical matter for curriculum development than PTR. The contraction in the school population may affect the potential of an individual school in two ways. It may push a school into competition — however unwillingly — for pupil numbers, or rather for parental esteem, with a neighbouring school with which it would previously have been seeking co-operation. In this context curriculum innovation which might be considered risky, is unlikely. More important, however, overall staff expertise may be affected, because the impact of falling rolls will lead to loss of flexibility in the ways that staff can be used, and sometimes to arbitrary loss of specialism. Even if staffing is reduced in line with pupil numbers, a school's ability to deploy teachers in ways that can effectively exploit their skills and expertise will become limited and, most crucially perhaps, the opportunities to free teachers for necessary curriculum development activities in school time will be lost.

It is for this reason that some local authorities have developed what they refer to as 'curriculum-led' staffing policies. Although there is a suspicion that such policies could be used primarily to decide that small schools are not viable, an interesting consequence of them is that the local authority has to make clear what its conception of an adequate primary school curriculum is, for curriculum-led staffing policies in effect move from a ratio as an index of staffing needs to a curricular range. For example, one local authority produced a statement of staffing policy which emphasised

> the minimum number of classes that each type of primary school ought to be able to form if a satisfactory curriculum is to be available to pupils.

It went further towards defining the curriculum by which its staffing policy should be led:

> If an adequate middle school curriculum is to be provided . . . then the staffing must provide — in addition to the requisite number of class teachers — some who are capable of specialising in science, craft, foreign language and music.

Thus, in theory at least, staffing allocations, and curriculum-led staffing policies, can be seen as supporting school-based curriculum development, precisely because, having broadly defined the curriculum provision thought to be appropriate, they highlight the need to identify, develop and exploit staff expertise in order to maintain and renew the local authority's conception of the primary school curriculum. This still obtains as a principle, even where teacher-redeployment strategies adopt criteria other than curricular specialism. At the present time it is unclear whether decisions about which teachers should be redeployed are based on curricular demands, degree of seniority or local political pragmatism: probably all three are involved to differing degrees. There is no logical reason why redeployment of staff should in itself reduce curriculum development possibilities, assuming that the nettle of curriculum-led staffing priorities can be grasped. Put at its most basic this would mean that a teacher with essential specialist curricular expertise would not be redeployed simply because he or she might be the youngest, or the most vulnerable, or the least likely to cause a fuss, or a part-timer. Equally, it might mean that a teacher with expertise in a shortage area might work in two schools rather than, as is normal, only one.

In the recent past the real value of capitation resources allocated to schools has fallen quite substantially, and in some local authorities the reductions were regarded by HMI (DES 1981c, 1982b) as endangering educational standards. Although it is a truism to say that such reductions adversely affect the potential of a school staff to improve their curricular provision, the effects will vary greatly according to the nature of the particular curriculum development programme. There is a great difference in impact of resource expenditure upon a programme requiring for its introduction in a school the purchase of new sets of materials and equipment (as might be the case in developing from scratch a science programme) and one requiring different applications of existing materials and approaches (as might be the case in developing and implementing a revised policy on aspects of language). It has been argued earlier that school-based approaches in primary schools tended to be developments of existing practices, and resource reductions may go some way towards explaining that feature. If so, it suggests that such reductions will influence the nature of school-based development, rather than stifle its growth entirely.

Teachers' perceptions of contraction

The objective experience of contraction may not necessarily be the most powerful constraint upon development; the ways in which such contraction is perceived subjectively by teachers may be a far more important determinant. Put crudely, curriculum development depends much more upon the ability of a staff to harness its collective energy and enthusiasm than upon marginal reductions in staffing, or even real reductions in resources. It is upon teacher morale that the progress of innovation hangs, and morale itself has been damaged by contraction. In part, the impact of contraction has been cumulatively routine, with teachers coming in each morning to uncleaned rooms, dusty desks and other evidence of reduced expenditure, which has nothing directly to do with the curriculum, but which effectively eats away at teacher enthusiasm. But the dramatic impact is upon the teachers' perceptions of reduced career and promotion opportunities, which are real enough and may help to discourage innovation amongst career-minded teachers.

This is, however, very much a two-edged sword. Under an expanding system, teachers were sucked up into senior posts by a kind of capillary action and, having obtained their promotion, would demonstrate their merit afterwards (or not). They would be given their special-responsibility allowances and then earn them. In a contracting system such promotion as there is will have to be earned in advance. As a local-authority adviser put it:

> Previously we promoted Mrs X in order that she would develop science in a school; now we may be able to reward her *if* she has developed it. And this has to apply to Scale 1 teachers as well — they will have to learn to lead other teachers in an area of the curriculum before they get a responsibility post.

Of course the degree of certainty of promotion differed in the two situations. However, the point about shrinking career opportunities is that they too will be perceived differently; some teachers will doubtless be confirmed in their view that there is no point to curriculum development if it is not certain to be rewarded, whilst for others it will at least be a surrogate for, and at best a precursor to, promotion. It would be unrealistic to ignore such a factor in examining the context of primary school curriculum development, and it may be for that reason that a number of recent commentaries have included the notion that it should help to raise morale and channel the professional energies of teachers who would previously have been promoted more easily.

There is, however, a small irony in the situation. Whatever the general disadvantages of reduced promotion opportunities, from the point of view of school-based development there is one advantage. For development of this kind to be originated, implemented and above all maintained requires a relatively permanent, or at least stable, staff group. Frequent and widespread teacher mobility is not conducive to school-based approaches to curriculum development.

Thus the impact of the external factors, even in a contracting system, upon a school's ability to develop its curriculum is not overwhelmingly and inevitably adverse. Perhaps the most optimistic element is that primary pupil rolls are expected to stabilise in the mid-1980s and arbitrary loss of specialist skills within a staff group will occur less often. A further issue in the next decade, currently being canvassed in some local authorities and nationally, is the idea that INSET (in-service education of teachers) could become part of the contractual obligation of teachers. If this were to be successfully negotiated it would give considerable impetus to school-based curriculum development, especially if, as is also being considered, it is allied to earmarked resources and a re-aligned career structure for teachers.

Internal influences

Much of the discussion in the literature about school-based curriculum development is implicitly about secondary schools, so the internal issues raised are problems of relationships between subject departments, of developments 'across the curriculum' and of managing large institutions. For primary schools the internal factors pressing upon change are different. Two have been clearly identified: *zones of authority* and *devolution of curricular decision-making*.

Zones of authority: the classroom and the school

'Zones of authority' were a focus of a study of primary schools by Taylor, Reid, Holley and Exon (1974), who reported and analysed the views of primary school teachers on the 'operational' curriculum, i.e. the curriculum in practice in a school. They identified two separate zones of authority: the classroom and the school. In terms of perceived influence, the classroom was by far the stronger zone and, if generalisable, their findings suggest clear obstacles to the development of school-wide policies on the curriculum, for if teachers see their classrooms as the major arena for their control over the curriculum, any attempt to develop it from a different basis by locating the development in the arena of the whole school is likely to start from a position of relative weakness. Individual teachers may opt out, regard it as interference, or simply alter any school-wide policy in the privacy of their own classrooms, legitimising their behaviour by invoking autonomy. The issue is peculiarly strong in primary schools, which are hier-archically ungraded, and where a teacher leading a curriculum development activity is in a position of equality with his or her colleagues, even if he or she has superior expertise in a particular field. The contrast between the formal and perceived power position of the secondary school head of department, seen as senior and officially recognised as such, and that of the primary school scale postholder is very great.

Devolution of decision-making and the authority of the head

Recognised authority, in respect of the primary school curriculum, is nearly always perceived as residing in the office of headteacher. There is a legal basis for this, but in an age when a broad liberal curriculum in mathematics, English, science, art, music, craft, physical education and social and moral understanding is expected to be offered to all children, the notion of the headteacher as an authority in all these fields is no longer credible, if it ever was. There is therefore a mismatch between authority and respons-ibility for the curriculum in primary schools, with teachers who are responsible for developing aspects of the curriculum in which they are the 'experts' having little in the way of formal authority ascribed to them, and the headteachers, who have the authority, lacking the expertise. Lack of formal status is compounded for postholders by lack of informal recognition from their colleagues, according to HMI (DES 1978a), who found few primary schools in which the postholders had a school-wide influence in their subject.

> It is disappointing to find that the great majority of teachers with posts of special respons-ibility have little influence at present on the work of other teachers. (para. 8.45)

There are some practical implications of this comment for the primary school post-holder's workload, but the major issue concerns the attitudes of primary school staff toward curricular authority. Some shift towards a kind of collaborative decision-making about curriculum matters has been proposed by a number of commentators on primary schools, including Coulson (1978) and Razzell (1979), although the latter appears, as Harling (1980) shows, to understate the obstacles to such an approach being adopted generally. The problem may not be so much the attitudes of headteachers as those of other teachers. When headteachers delegated responsibility and authority to their deputies, according to Coulson and Cox (1975), the problem was that other teachers did not accept the transfer of authority as legitimate.

This brief review of the internal factors has been deliberately uncritical of them in order to report in summary form the prevailing view of the internal culture of primary schools. This internal culture is seen as structuring both teacher relationships in primary schools and teacher perceptions of curricular authority in classrooms and schools so as to provide a major constraint on postholder-led curriculum initiatives development. A critical re-analysis of the relevant studies is provided in Chapter 10, which suggests that in some respects teacher relationships and teacher attitudes, although still a problem, are beginning to change.

However, the view that attitudes and teacher relationships are critical to the success of school-based curriculum development, and probably more critical than the external resource and policy factors, was supported not simply by studies of English primary schools, but also by a report in which an international perspective on the school context was provided. The findings of this report are discussed below.

OECD's The Creativity of the School'

The cross-national study on the 'creativity' of schools carried out for OECD (OECD/ CERI 1978) defined creativity much as school-based curriculum development has been defined in this chapter:

> A school's creativity is an awareness within the school of the problems it faces, a capacity to devise and adopt solutions whether initiated from outside or generated internally, and a willingness to evaluate their effectiveness. (p. 15)

A major interest of the study was the factors influencing school creativity, and two of these, which reflect the external/internal dichotomy above, were:

(a)   administrative relationships between the school and outside institutions;
(b)   organisation and relationships within the school.

The report offered three findings of particular relevance. It commented first on staffing/resources, second on school relationships, and third on teacher autonomy.

The problems of stimulating innovation in systems where promotion was impossible or difficult were examined in the report. It raised doubts on economic grounds about the efficiency of substantially and contractually reducing teaching duties so that curriculum innovation could be sustained, although it accepted the usefulness of limited reduction for a particular specified purpose. Perhaps most interestingly it doubted the utility of limited reductions in class size as a way of enhancing the creativity of the school. It concluded:

> Rather than seeking a general, across-the-board increase in teaching resources, schools should be encouraged selectively to redeploy existing resources to support creative innovation and in particular to provide incentives to key teachers to initiate or implement desirable changes. (p. 51)

Second, the report looked at the relationship between creativity and the internal organisation of the school. It identified four types of school organisation: authoritarian/bureaucratic, consultative, collegial, and full participatory. The collegial type is an organisation where decision-making is in the hands of the professional teaching staff, and the head acts as an executive. In consultative organisations, the power of decision-making remains with the head, but power is delegated and procedures for consulting teachers, students and parents are set up. These two organisational types were less likely to inhibit effective creativity than the other two.

The explanation for the greater effectiveness of these types is probably connected with the report's view that focusing upon the individual teacher was not the best way to induce change:

> the individual teacher working alone in his classroom is an inappropriate unit. Rather, the small group of teachers with their group of students should be the basic unit of organisation. This is necessary both for interpersonal stimulation and essential mutual support. Such groups, which need not be stable over a long period, would be united by a common task but could be organised in many different ways . . . (p. 53)

Of particular interest is the study's commentary (pp. 148–9) on the problems associated with professional development in a collegial school, which include the need to recognise the distinction between the *practice* of collective decision-making and the legal position of the head.

A third point reflected uncertainty about teacher autonomy if collective decision-making was a prerequisite for creativity:

> In the literature on the creative school, there is a degree of ambivalence as to the autonomy of the teacher. It is often applauded as a necessary precondition of creativity, but the autonomy of the individual teacher is, in fact, under pressure in current developments. It is obviously important that the teacher should enjoy freedom from close supervision if he is to be encouraged to be creative. On the other hand, the creativity of the school as an organisation assumes a degree of collaboration that to some extent reduces the individual autonomy of the teacher. Since evidence on teacher satisfaction indicated that teachers value their autonomy very highly, there is the danger of a loss of satisfaction which needs careful consideration. (p. 149)

Thus the conclusions of this comparative study were similar to those provided by the national context, and support the idea that the internal arrangements in a school — the climate of relationships between teachers, and their attitudes to authority and autonomy — are more critical to the success of school-based curriculum development than, within limits, the external factors of staffing levels, administration and resource allocation.

VALUE ASSUMPTIONS OF SCHOOL-BASED CURRICULUM DEVELOPMENT

It is now possible to summarise the preceding argument by identifying three main features of school-based curriculum development in primary schools. First, it involves teachers in a more *collaborative role* with other teachers, working together to reconstruct, through informed discussion and critical appraisal, general curricular guidance into specific school-wide policy and practice. The process turns teachers into educationalists. Second, it involves teachers drawing upon the *specialist expertise* of curriculum postholders in order to improve existing practice and policy in a small-scale, gradualist fashion, with an openness to evaluation. Third, *internal relationships* as perceived by teachers, especially relationships resting upon authority in respect of the curriculum and classroom autonomy, are critical to the kind of developments being encouraged.

When summarised in the above way, school-based curriculum development can be seen to embody something more than advice about how change *can* occur — about mechanisms of change. It embodies a set of professional and moral values — what kinds of change *should* occur, and how they should be brought about.

This point has been explored in a particularly sharp way by Henderson and Perry (1981), who argue that curriculum development involves what is referred to as 'organisation development'. By this they mean three things. First, the curriculum cannot be treated on its own, as a separate entity unrelated to the school as a whole, which is an integrated social system. Developing the curriculum means developing the school, especially the staff. Second, a static, mechanistic organisation is inappropriate for a changing society, which requires organisational structures and relationships that are dynamic, responsive and organic. Third, development occurs through a 'process of education and re-education', in which all those involved, not just the senior staff, are themselves continually learning.

> The concept . . . should not imply the responsibility for initiating and organising staff development belongs *solely* to the head and senior staff, that they alone are capable of determining what is best for staff. If the head and his senior lieutenants decide upon school needs and the kind of professional development necessary to meet them, this becomes another type of 'top-downwards' model . . . It is not appropriate to an organic social system, where development depends upon shared responsibility for mutually agreed goals, based on sensitive understanding of the needs of the system as a whole. (p. 25)

Although Henderson's and Perry's discussion is mainly concerned with the appropriateness of different organisational structures for effecting change in schools, it does highlight the moral dimensions of curriculum development — the idea that some ways of introducing change are better from a moral point of view, as well as from considerations of their effectiveness for bringing about change. For school-based curriculum development in primary schools, two such value assumptions need to be articulated, even if briefly. They refer to two characteristics identified in the practice of the inquiry schools: *collaboration* and *subject expertise*.

One useful way into the question of value assumptions is to ask what benefits would accrue to a school in which staff collaboration and subject expertise were key characteristics in the processes by which the curriculum was developed. There might be five such benefits — three concerned with staff collaboration and two with subject expertise — which are offered here as a kind of moral criterion reference list.

1. *Staff collaboration.*
    (a)   Curriculum policy and practice would be arrived at through collective discussion and decision-making.
    (b)   Initiative and responsibility for developing the curriculum would be devolved to relevant staff groups.

(c)   Staff groups would be led and serviced by the postholder acting as 'educationalist'.

2. *Subject expertise.*

(a)   Greater continuity and consistency in the subject throughout the school would be practised.

(b)   Class teachers would have enhanced respect for the postholder's expertise in his or her subject and increase their own confidence and competence in it.

When the benefits claimed for it are stated in this way, two value positions underlying school-based curriculum development can be confronted by teachers who engage in it. The first position is fairly easily expressed. It is morally desirable that a curriculum policy and the school-wide practice that flows from it — the curriculum as experienced in the classroom by children — should be based as firmly as possible in specialised expertise. Consistency in curriculum practice is only valuable in so far as it is consistently right, not wrong. Similarly, increasing teachers' confidence in a subject, and increasing their respect for a postholder's expertise, are worth while only if such confidence and respect are justified.

The second value position is that decisions developed collaboratively, and taken collectively, are arrived at by a morally better process than those arrived at by other means. (It does not, I suppose, follow that they are necessarily better decisions in themselves.) The position is derived from respect to be attached to teachers as people and professionals; decisions designed to affect the personal and professional life of teachers in school should be developed only through a process in which their responsibility and commitment are recognised and explicitly acknowledged. To avoid the process, inherently difficult as it will be, would be to treat teachers with something bordering on contempt.

There is, as Hargreaves (1982) has hinted, the danger that a rhetoric of grass-roots democracy and participation might provide a distraction from the conventional exercise of undelegated authority both inside and outside the school. This is a constant danger in a profession that has been schooled to defer to authority as well as to exercise it. However, it will be lessened if the teachers involved in school-based approaches to the curriculum acknowledge and confront the values upon which it operates.

If these values are to become palpable and authentic in the life of primary schools, curriculum postholders will play a central part. It is from them that expertise will have to come: they will literally, as well as formally, have a special responsibility for their subject. They will have to be, or become, the resident 'expert', responsive to other teachers' needs. Likewise, collective decision-making needs to be efficiently led, serviced and informed by them. Thus school-based curriculum development raises fundamental questions of value for all the staff in a school — questions of the value to be placed on specialist expertise and group decision-making in the school, and the inherent challenge that both pose to conventional claims of classroom autonomy. The implications for the 'management' of curriculum development in primary schools are discussed in Chapter 6, but for curriculum postholders they offer an interesting, challenging and possibly daunting extension to their professional life. This extension is explored in the following two chapters.

3

The Role of the Curriculum Postholder

NEW EXPECTATIONS FOR THE CURRICULUM POSTHOLDER

Until fairly recently, if a primary school teacher were given a post of responsibility, and the associated increase in salary, it would probably have been considered a reward for general competence, or at least for durability, in the classroom. Although such a post might have had specified duties attached to it, they were not often the main reason for allocating it to a particular teacher. The story of the teacher given a Scale 3 post with responsibility for the school lavatories is probably apocryphal, although the existence of a Scale 3 post with responsibility for stuffed toys was recently reported to me. Be that as it may, many teachers received special allowances for responsibilities in which they had no special expertise, and occasionally no interest. This was not necessarily a bad thing, for the common understanding amongst primary teachers was that the designation of the duties for which a special post was held was a nominal one: the salary allowance was in fact allocated to the person rather than to the position. In recent years changes both in the criteria for allocating posts of special responsibility and, more importantly, in what is expected of postholders have been proposed.

A sceptical interpretation of the way the system previously functioned is to see it as one of the ways headteachers could control their staff; they were able to retain and reward teachers of whose work they approved and, in a period of educational expansion, to encourage others to look for their promotion elsewhere. A less sceptical view is that the system of allowances for specified areas of responsibility, designed for the departmental structures of secondary schools, was inappropriate for primary schools, and headteachers were merely adapting it in the interest of their schools, as they perceived it.

The latter position was hinted at in Blyth's (1965) authoritative study of primary education in England and Wales. He commented upon the undifferentiated nature of the formal relations in the typical primary school, with only the head and possibly the deputy head separated out in terms of the functions they performed:

> Among the remaining members of staff, the formal structure is much more indeterminate than in a secondary school . . . Some concession is usually made to the totally unmusical among teachers, and to the absolute non-starters in physical education; but for the rest, the teachers are simply Teachers. (p. 163)

Blyth provided a detailed analysis of roles in primary schools, identifying aspects such as 'instructor', 'parent-substitute', 'organiser', 'welfare worker' and others, but nowhere did he identify a distinctive role for the holder of a post of responsibility for a curriculum area, almost certainly because in the early and mid-1960s none existed. Only in a passing reference was the potential noted:

> Graded posts are ill-adapted to a class teacher system, apart from functions such as that of librarian, though sometimes a member of staff can advise a whole school on one subject area. (p. 164)

Children and their Primary Schools (Plowden Report 1967) had a little more to say about postholders, whom it referred to as 'consultant' teachers, but conceived of as subordinates, in curriculum terms, to the headteacher and local-authority advisers. Thus (para. 934), heads might 'invite the help of' assistant teachers in preparing schemes, in giving advice to their colleagues, and in the selection of books, materials and equipment. Consultants might also take over another teacher's class for part of a week 'in order to raise the quality of the work' (para. 937) or in order to ensure coverage of particular curriculum areas. They might also be freed for some part of the week (para. 938) to exercise satisfactorily a responsibility for 'guiding' other teachers. These few elliptically expressed suggestions were the main reference to the role of the postholders that Plowden made, other than to state as one of its recommendations that the 'planning of schemes of work should increasingly be undertaken by assistant teachers'. Indeed even in its general discussion of graded posts (paras. 936–7) it gave consideration to age-group responsibilities rather than to curricular ones. In effect, Plowden did not identify a substantial role for curriculum postholders, other than as, so to speak, curriculum acolytes to their headteachers.

The early DES pamphlet about middle schools, *Towards the Middle School* (DES 1970), was written, as the title suggests, before middle schools had been established in any extensive way. It included consideration of the curriculum, internal organisation and staff deployment in middle schools and offered a rather detailed prescription for the activities of curriculum postholders. It suggested that a school's schemes of work should contain objectives, 'starting points', resources and evaluation, and that they should be devised by referring to the teachers with appropriate expertise. Where teachers were not used as specialists, postholders were to act as 'consultants' in their subject. This role included a diverse set of activities, such as leading a team of teachers and establishing links in the subject with other schools. In the theoretical example of a timetable for a primary (8–12) school in the Appendix to the pamphlet, one of the organisational priorities made explicit was that there should be 'opportunities for consultants to advise other members of staff, as well as teach their own classes'. In addition it would be helpful if there were 'some periods when both the consultant and the class teacher work with the class. This enables the consultant to profit from the class teacher's knowledge of the children and increases the amount of individual help available in what might well be unstreamed classes.'

The views of both the Plowden Committee and the DES about the significance of postholders were characterised by considerable tentativeness. Her Majesty's Inspectors were much more unambiguous. In their 1978 survey, *Primary Education in England* (DES 1978a), they claimed to have evidence providing positive associations between the achievement of higher standards in primary school classes and the effective implementation of a particular role by the curriculum postholders. They described the relevant aspects of this role in a number of sections in the survey, which are illustrated in the following summary:

1. It should include planning programmes of work in consultation with the head, advising other teachers about the programme and encouraging a consistent approach in the school. In addition to planning a programme, the postholder should be involved in the 'supervision' of it. (4.5–4.6)
2. There was a better 'match' of work to children's abilities in schools where the postholder had strong influence[1] throughout the school and not just in her own class. Although this was true for all age and ability groups, it was especially noticeable with the work set for more able children. (7.36)
3. The postholder's level of knowledge and expertise was important, if she was to give a strong lead in planning, carrying out a programme of work, and influencing others. (7.37)
4. The status of the postholders was a significant issue: their standing in the school needed to be improved in general. This standing, 'which is a product of the ways in which teachers with special posts regard themselves and also of the attitudes that other teachers have towards them', was explicitly seen as a matter of social relationships in the school as well as position on the salary scale. (8.45)
5. In addition to planning and implementing the scheme of work and advising other teachers, the postholder should develop acceptable means of assessing the scheme's effectiveness, and this might 'involve visiting other classes in the school to see work in progress'. (8.46 and 8.58)
6. The postholder's role required time to be allocated for performing the range of duties involved, some of which (keeping up-to-date in the relevant subject, for example) assumed time outside school hours, while others need to be carried out while the school was in session. (8.47)

The inspectors summarised their view of the role as follows:

Teachers in posts of special responsibility need to keep up-to-date in their knowledge of their subject; to be familiar with its main concepts, with the sub-divisions of the subject material, and how they relate to one another. They have to know enough of available teaching materials and teaching approaches to make and advise upon, choices that suit local circumstances. And they should be aware of the ways in which children learn and of any sequences of learning that need to be taken into account. Additionally, these teachers

---

[1] The relevant tables, 12a, 12b and 12c in the Annex to Chapter 7, do not explain how 'strong influence' was operationally defined, and it has to be assumed that it was arrived at from inspectors' judgements, as in other aspects of the survey. The tables do not show distinctions between subjects in this respect, which is a pity, since it would be particularly interesting to compare the evidence on subjects taught mainly by specialists, such as music, and on those taught mainly by class teachers.

should learn how to lead groups of teachers and to help others teach material which is appropriate to the abilities of the children. They should learn how to establish a programme of work in cooperation with other members of staff and how to judge whether it is being operated successfully. They should also learn how to make the best use of the strengths of teachers of all ages and help them to develop so that they may take on more responsibility . . . (8.64)

This expanded and elaborated specification of the postholder's role was presented with the authority of HM Inspectorate. A year after publication of this survey, it appeared to receive the imprimatur of the National Union of Teachers, whose survey about middle schools (National Union of Teachers 1979), whatever its ambivalence about the schools themselves, contained illustrative, though not necessarily representative, organisational arrangements for an 8 12 school. It listed the responsibilities of the subject co-ordinators, now called 'subject area consultants', in a way that reflected the recent changes in their role definition (p. 10):

a)   to advise on the curriculum and prepare schemes, if necessary, within their particular field of expertise (including books and materials),
b)   to contribute to general curriculum development in the school,
c)   to advise colleagues on any problem of content, background knowledge, sources or method involving their particular field of expertise,
d)   in collaboration with year group leaders to guide probationary teachers, and
e)   whenever appropriate to liaise with colleagues in the first and high schools.

Although this list was perhaps excessively coy about the postholder's role in visiting colleagues' classes to see work in progress, it implicitly seemed to be accepting the wide-ranging definition that had been developed by the Inspectorate.

In what was explicitly described as a 'follow-up' to the Primary Survey, Thomas (1980) discussed the role of the teacher as postholder:

The earlier paragraphs of this article illustrate once again how much primary school teachers need to know when planning and executing each part of the curriculum. If they are to keep up with recent advances in aspects of the curriculum, in understanding how children learn, and familiarise themselves with the resources currently available for teaching, then they must commit themselves to a considerable amount of reading as well as attendance at courses and, it is to be hoped, the observation of other teachers at work.

There was support for this expanded idea of the postholder's role in the two major reports concerning specialist areas of the curriculum, *A Language for Life* (Bullock Report 1974) and *Mathematics Counts* (Cockcroft Report 1982). The former was rather more concerned with making a case for a language or English 'co-ordinator' in primary schools than with specifying in any precise detail what her or his functions would be. After making the general claim (13.22), Bullock stated:

The task would be a demanding one, and a consideration of what it would involve makes it all the more surprising that such an important role is filled in so few schools. In the first place the teacher would act as consultant to his colleagues on matters of reading and language. It would fall to him to assess the results of screening and to discuss with his colleagues the diagnostic procedures and special help required by individual children. It is important to emphasise however that his concern extends beyond the language and reading needs of the slow learner, and should equally involve those of the able child. He would obviously need to be well informed of current developments and new materials and this would include a knowledge of children's literature . . . (he would also) play an important part in any re-grouping arrangements. (13.23)

If Bullock was rather vague in its specification, Cockcroft was quite explicit, perhaps as a result of having had the Inspectorate's Primary Survey available to it. After recording some unease about the mathematical background of general class teachers in primary schools, the report allocated a separate section (354–8) to the role of the mathematics co-ordinator:

> The effectiveness of the mathematics teaching in a primary school can be considerably enhanced if one teacher is given responsibility for the planning, co-ordination and oversight of work in mathematics throughout the school. We shall refer to such a teacher as the 'mathematics co-ordinator'.

> In our view it should be part of the duties of the mathematics co-ordinator to:

> prepare a scheme of work for the school in consultation with the head teacher and staff and, where possible, with schools from which the children come and to which they go (we discuss this further in paragraph 363);

> provide guidance and support to other members of staff in implementing the scheme of work, both by means of meetings and by working alongside individual teachers;

> organise and be responsible for procuring, within the funds made available, the necessary teaching resources for mathematics, maintain an up-to-date inventory and ensure that members of staff are aware of how to use the resources which are available;

> monitor work in mathematics throughout the school, including methods of assessment and record keeping;

> assist with the diagnosis of children's learning difficulties and with their remediation;

> arrange school-based in-service training for members of staff as appropriate;

> maintain liaison with schools from which children come and to which they go, and also with LEA advisory staff.

Cockcroft added that it would have been easy to extend the list by considering the need to keep up to date with current developments in mathematical education, and to help probationer teachers and colleagues lacking confidence in mathematics.

The attachment of special significance to the postholder for the quality of the curriculum through the school was confirmed in two 'illustrative' surveys by the Inspectorate (DES 1982a, 1983a) of work in first and middle schools. Both surveys stressed the difference that could be made to standards in the schools if postholders saw their role as more than merely providing resources for other members of staff. This meant the development of the curriculum through postholder-led collaborative effort, as the survey on first schools showed:

> Few teachers are expert in all parts of the curriculum . . . The necessary help, support and advice may in part be given by heads and local advisers. It may also be provided by other teachers on the staff who have a special interest, enthusiasm and responsibility for a part of the curriculum and who act as consultants. Such teachers may give support in a variety of ways: by producing guidelines and schemes of work; by leading discussions and organising study groups; by disseminating work done on in-service courses; by working alongside class teachers; by assembling and organising resources; and occasionally by teaching classes other than their own.

> In half of the survey schools a member of staff had responsibility for the work of the children in language, but in many instances this responsibility did not extend much beyond a concern with the provision of materials and resources.

In 30 of the schools, teachers, sometimes deputy heads, had overall curriculum responsibility for mathematics. In a few of these schools they were leading work groups on the production of guidelines, organising school-based courses for the staff and overseeing the work in mathematics in the school as a whole. In a few instances work of good quality could be directly attributed to the influences of the teacher 'consultant'; for example, regular staff discussions had been held, support and help had been given to other teachers on choice of work, planning lessons and assessing children's learning. Too often, however, the role of the teacher with responsibility in this important part of the curriculum was limited to the production of guidelines or checklists or even, as with the equally important area of language, solely to the provision and organisation of teaching materials. (paras. 3.19–3.21)

Thus in the past fifteen years or so, some of the major educational documents have transmitted a gradually clarifying image of the responsibility and significance of the curriculum postholder in primary schools. In the first place what has been expected of the postholder has been brought into sharper focus: the duties of the job have been specified in greater detail. Teachers who want to know the range and nature of the responsibilities attached to a curriculum post can now find out what is typically expected of them by the Inspectorate, by national committees and even to some extent by their union. A second change is that the significance of the post has been highlighted: the curriculum postholder, whose responsibilities were previously not only vaguely defined, but also not considered particularly important, has now emerged as a major figure in the national effort to protect and renew the primary school curriculum. The postholder's role has moved from a position of marginality in the curriculum to one of centrality. A minor and relatively insignificant role prescription mainly concerned with helping headteachers to write schemes of work has been transformed into the substantial expectation that the postholder will provide the main, and possibly the only, impetus for maintaining and raising standards in the primary school.

It is possible to summarise the activities now expected of curriculum postholders by constructing a broad twofold classification of them, with five subdivisions:

1. *Curriculum skills*, that is those skills and qualities involved in knowledge about the curriculum area for which the postholder has responsibility.
   - (a) Knowledge of subjects. The postholder must keep up to date in her or his subject, and must know its conceptual structure and methods, etc.
   - (b) Professional skills. The postholder must draw up a programme of work, manage its implementation, maintain it and assess its effectiveness.
   - (c) Professional judgement. The postholder must know about, and discriminate between, various materials and approaches in her or his subject, must relate them to children's developmental stages, manage the school's resources, and achieve a match between the curriculum and the pupils' abilities.
2. *Interpersonal skills*, that is those skills and qualities arising from the postholder's relationships with colleagues and other adults.
   - (a) Social skills. The postholder must work with colleagues, leading discussion groups, teaching alongside colleagues, helping develop their confidence in his or her subject, advising probationers, etc.
   - (b) External representation. The postholder must represent his or her subject to outsiders (other teachers, advisers, governors, parents, etc.).

The categories are not offered as discrete ones; a postholder engaged in developing a new scheme of work in science, which involves leading workshops for staff, will obviously be using both curriculum and interpersonal skills. The classification is offered merely as a method of ordering analytically the range and nature of the demands upon postholders that have emerged in the literature.

Explanations for the new role

This shift to an emphasis upon a more specialised role for the postholder can be interpreted in a variety of ways. At the most general level, that of changes in the society as a whole, it may be seen as a symptom of the pattern of change exhibited in most social institutions and identified by Bernstein (1973b), following Durkheim, as a shift from more 'closed' relationships to more 'open' ones, as society has moved from 'mechanical' to more 'organic' forms of control. In societies whose regulatory principles are organic, more specialised roles emerge and greater division of labour develops. Although such relationships have been institutionalised in secondary schools for a substantial time, the new emphasis upon them in primary education may be seen as the first evidence that that most mechanically controlled of educational institutions, the English primary school, is at last becoming influenced in its organisational features by the wider social changes, especially the pressure towards specialisation, that have characterised other institutions.

Other levels of explanation are less abstract and metaphysical. It may be seen as a response to the alleged failure of centralised curriculum development projects in the 1960s and 1970s to make much of an impact upon the quality and effectiveness of the primary and middle school curriculum in practice. In the context of this perceived failure, the response of the schools has had to be to look to the development of their own staffing skills and expertise for curriculum renewal, especially in schools providing an extension of primary practice, as happens in 8–12 schools.

Another view, more overtly political and possibly more cynical, recognised by Hargreaves (1980), is to see the change as a response to educational contraction, not merely of pupil numbers and resource allocation, but also of staff morale and career opportunities. In this perspective, encouraging a shift to school-based approaches to curriculum development, with postholders taking on a major and distinctive role, would be attractive to central and local authorities and politicians, because of its cheapness and its potential for channelling the professional energy and commitment of able teachers who would previously have been rewarded by promotion. In Hargreaves' words it offered 'a possible solution to the problems of maintaining teacher morale and an impetus for curriculum innovation in a contracting educational system'.

These views are not mutually contradictory: to some extent they complement one another. It is difficult to believe that the general pressure for more specialisation is merely an ad hoc response to contraction and would not have been generated anyway in technologically advanced societies. At the same time, however, it is hard to resist the interpretation that the new role for postholders has been invented as, to some extent, a surrogate for promotion. Whatever the most powerful influence, the emergence of the curriculum postholder as a significant feature of primary education in the 1980s has made it all the more important to know more about how postholders actually perform the new role allocated to them and what their achievements in it are.

ROLE PERFORMANCE OF THE CURRICULUM POSTHOLDERS

The case studies in the Warwick inquiry were produced by recording, and discussing with the postholders themselves, what kind of activities postholders became involved in as school-based curriculum developers. The activities varied considerably, and to understand the role more fully some general description of them is necessary.

As a starting point, it is worth providing two 'job specifications' for curriculum postholders in two of the inquiry schools. The first was drawn up at School 1 as it became reorganised from a junior into a middle school, and thus there was some pressure for the staff, and certainly for the headteacher, to make expectations of teaching roles in the new school explicit. It was a general specification, in that it applied to all curriculum areas and subjects.

Specification of the curriculum postholders' role at one school
Teachers with special responsibility for curriculum areas will not generally act as specialist teachers. However they should be prepared to:
  i.   head up working parties to draw up schemes of work and guidelines;
  ii.   organise workshop sessions for staff when necessary;
  iii. keep up to date by reading, attending courses and then reporting back to staff;
  iv. act in an advisory capacity to the rest of the staff;
  v.   work alongside a member of staff needing help;
  vi. be involved in ordering books and equipment;
  vii. keep an overall picture of how the work is progressing within the school.

The head had added notes about v. and vii. to the effect that these aspects of the role were not easy to make arrangements for when the postholders were full-time class teachers.

The second example was for a specific subject (science) in a combined (5–12) school, and was the specification drawn up by the head when it became possible for him to advertise a vacancy for a Scale 2 post with responsibility for science (and games).

Specification of the science postholder's role at one school
  i.   to be responsible for integrated science and its development through the first and middle school;
  ii.   to develop a guide and encourage teachers in the teaching of science;
  iii. to be responsible for science equipment, and to check it regularly and advise on replacements;
  iv. to attend in-service training and subject meetings;
  v.   to talk to parents, governors, advisers and inspectors;
  vi. to assess the effectiveness of science teaching and curriculum at regular intervals.

The first thing to notice about these specifications is the way in which they reflected the five dimensions identified earlier; they were national expectations 'writ small', i.e., interpreted at school level. They too expected postholders to exercise both *curriculum skills* and *interpersonal skills*. Second, although there is some variation in the way in which the job was specified, the level of specification in both was adequately set in the sense that it provided a simple indication of the kind of activities envisaged, without going into excessively daunting detail. The same cannot be said of the following role specification offered in one local authority's in-service course for teachers holding responsibility posts for physical education:

Physical Education in Primary Schools
Job Description for Curriculum Leader

1. To devise a continuous and progressive scheme of work.
2. To ensure continuity and progression from year to year, and by liaison with feeder and next stage schools, continuity throughout schooling.
3. To assess whether the programme is being implemented successfully.
4. To assess quality of work, and whether there is a good match, i.e. work appropriate to children's needs and abilities.
5. To help in lesson planning and organisation.
6. To advise colleagues as necessary on teaching method.
7. To take demonstration lessons when necessary.
8. To work with other teachers in teaching situations.
9. To give advice and help with apparatus handling.
10. To provide sources of reference.
11. To promote school based in-service training.
12. To be responsible for procuring, within the funds available, the necessary resources for teaching the subject.
13. To be responsible for checking the equipment regularly, and reporting when it needs attention.
14. To make staff aware of safety factors related to apparatus use.
15. To attend meetings related to physical education and be prepared to share the work of committees as appropriate.
16. To organise or delegate the organisation of annual events, e.g. sports day.
17. Ensure that all staff are aware of procedures to be followed if a child is injured or is ill during a PE lesson.
18. Any other reasonable duties which heads might from time to time require.

As one of the teachers attending the course said, 'And when you've done all that, just change the water into wine'.

In practice, of course, teachers, like everyone else, do not necessarily do all that is expected of them. In order to describe what the postholders had actually done in their role as curriculum developers, a content analysis was carried out on the ten case studies. This was done by listing the skills practised by the postholders when they were engaged in the school-based development and assembling them in the categories and sub-dimensions identified in the literature. In this way it was possible to produce a tabular summary of these skills, and to show which skills were involved in each development. This has been done in Table 3.1.

The complexity of the postholder's role

Table 3.1 is a simple catalogue of skills, but even so, three points emerge about the performance of the postholder's role.

First, engaging in the process of school-based curriculum development required a considerable *range of complex skills*. It was not a simple or unidimensional activity. If

Table 3.1   *Range of skills expected of the curriculum postholders in ten school-based curriculum developments*

Skills involved in school-based curriculum development	Case study									
	A	B	C	D	E	F	G	H	I	J
1. Curriculum skills										
(a) *Subject knowledge*										
(i) updating subject knowledge	√	√		√		√	√	√		√
(ii) identifying conceptual structure of subject(s)	√		√			√	√	√		
(iii) identifying skills in subject(s)	√		√	√		√	√	√	√	√
(b) *Professional skills*										
(i) reviewing existing practice	√	√	√	√	√	√	√	√	√	√
(ii) constructing scheme/programme	√	√	√	√	√	√	√	√	√	√
(iii) implementing scheme/programme		√	√	√	√	√	√	√	√	√
(iv) assessing scheme/programme	√	√	√	√	√	√		√		
(c) *Professional judgement*										
(i) deciding between available resources	√	√	√	√	√	√	√	√	√	√
(ii) deciding about methods	√	√	√	√	√	√	√	√	√	√
(iii) identifying links between subjects	√	√	√		√	√	√	√		
(iv) ordering, maintaining resources	√	√			√	√	√	√	√	√
(v) relating subject to its form in other schools	√		√	√		√		√		
2. Inter-personal skills										
(a) *Working with colleagues*										
(i) leading workshops/discussions	√	√	√	√	√	√	√	√		
(ii) translating material into comprehensible form	√	√	√	√	√	√	√	√		
(iii) liaising with head and/or senior staff	√	√	√	√	√	√	√	√	√	√
(iv) advising colleagues informally	√	√	√	√	√	√	√	√	√	√
(v) teaching alongside colleagues		√			√	√	√	√	√	
(vi) visiting colleagues' classes to see work in progress		√	√						√	
(vii) maintaining colleagues' morale, reducing anxiety, etc.		√			√		√	√		
(viii) dealing with professional disagreement	√	√	√	√		√				
(b) *External representation*										
(i) consulting advisers, university staff, etc.	√	√		√	√	√				√
(ii) consulting teachers in other schools	√			√		√				√

the five sub-dimensions of skills are taken as rough categories of skills, it can be seen that skills in all five were exercised by five of the ten postholders, and in four by the remaining five. The table, therefore, even at its face value, illustrates the range of the role demands that were met by postholders.

Second, any one of the skills listed may itself be very *demanding of time and effort*. To take the example of the skill 'identifying the conceptual structure of subjects' is to see something of its potential challenge to a postholder. For most postholders, exercising this skill took the form of identifying *a* conceptual structure, or constructing one, rather than referring to the substantial work in some subjects done by scholars in the field, in relation both to the subject and to children's cognitive development in it. This limited process was extremely demanding, even when, as was true of the social studies and science cases, it was built around an external curriculum development project in which the conceptual structure was incorporated into published curriculum materials.

Likewise, within the dimension 'working with colleagues' the list does scant justice to the nature of the demands the postholders were expected to meet. Leading workshops or handling discussion sessions might, in addition to the management of the sessions themselves, require considerable preparation. An important skill, much admired where it was practised well, as in Case study D in Chapter 8, was the ability to render educational ideas, theories and language (or simply jargon) into a more everyday form. This skill took the form of preparing summaries of research, identifying and illustrating main concepts in a field of study, preparing discussion papers, and preparing materials in a visual form for oral presentation.

Third, skills 2(a)(iv)–(viii), in addition to demanding considerable charm and character, also required sensitivity and tact, and a number of headteachers made the point that such *personal qualities* in the postholder were prerequisites for the successful implementation of the development. Even an apparently simple task such as giving advice to a colleague informally in the staffroom had to be done without seeming to patronise. If this could be difficult within a school, the potential for problems was increased in the matter of external representation, especially in discussions with teachers from other schools.

At the level of the school, therefore, when postholders attempted to meet the recent demands made upon them for renewal of the curriculum, they were faced with a task of considerable complexity — a characteristic that has been understated in the literature. On the whole, the educational documents have assumed that what was required was merely to make the case for a distinctive role for the postholder, or to list the kind of duties that the postholder should fulfil. In doing so, they have been perhaps a little ingenuous, and may have led to an underestimation both of the complexity of school-based curriculum development and of the qualities needed for effective exercise of the postholder's role in it. If this is so, it is to be regretted, because teachers entering upon school-based development without an appreciation of its complexity are likely to experience unexpected difficulties and, in the long term, disillusionment with the process of development itself.

Other role responsibilities

This point is further highlighted when the overall school context in which postholders were operating is considered, for postholders were not, of course, responsible only for curriculum development in their schools. Table 3.2, which should be read in conjunction with Table 3.1, shows the other main responsibilities held by curriculum postholders in the case-study schools, as well as the levels of the posts.

It can be seen that, with the exception of two teachers used as specialists, (I and J), one of whom was a part-timer, and the headteacher (E), these postholders had extensive responsibilities for other specific areas of school life. Seven had responsibility for class teaching, four were year co-ordinators, and three had responsibility for a second subject in the curriculum. Perhaps the widest range of responsibility was held by the deputy head (B) who shared a class with another teacher and was responsible for combined studies in the fourth year and for remedial work throughout the school, in

Table 3.2 *Other major responsibilities of ten curriculum postholders with scale level held*

	Case study									
	A	*B*	*C*	*D*	*E*	*F*	*G*	*H*	*I*	*J*
Responsibility										
Class teaching	√	√	√	√		√	√	√		
Year co-ordination		√	√	√			√			
A second subject		√				√		√		
Management		√		√	√					
Level	2	d.h.	3	3	h.	2	3	3	3	2 (0.5)

addition to the managerial aspects of her position as deputy head. Also having a very demanding range of responsibilities was the Scale 3 postholder (D), whose duties included language throughout the school, teaching her first-year class, co-ordinating the work of the three first-year classes, and liaison with the feeding first schools.

Thus meeting the expectations that they should exercise a role as curriculum developers in the school was only one of several legitimate demands made upon curriculum postholders. It was argued earlier that merely to fulfil the curriculum-development role satisfactorily was a complex and demanding responsibility; to be required to do so whilst meeting other role requirements, some of them more substantial and perhaps, like class teaching, more immediate, raised for the postholder questions of priority as well as questions of feasibility. The problems of differing role demands will be explored in the next chapter, but for curriculum postholders successfully to meet all the demands made upon them, they must be possessed of a remarkable range of skills and professional expertise. 'Good' primary school teaching has rarely been systematically investigated, because of the problems of definition, but where the problem has been sidestepped, or solved already, as in the case described by Wragg (1978), the characteristics appear to be high work rate and great versatility in professional skills.

ROLE ACHIEVEMENT OF CURRICULUM POSTHOLDER

The final question to ask about the postholders as school-based curriculum developers is 'What did they achieve?'. There were substantial expectations of them, and they exercised a wide range of curriculum and personal skills, but the ultimate test is whether any worthwhile changes resulted from their efforts. The distinction has already been made (in Chapter 2) between curriculum change and curriculum development, and it is a distinction that bears upon judgements about the achievements of curriculum postholders. There is little doubt that the postholders brought about changes in their schools: changed or new schemes of work were produced, changes in groupings of staff and pupils were introduced, new curricular experiences were offered to pupils, and staff discussed new approaches to their teaching. The central issue, however, is whether these changes were improvements and, if so, in what sense.

There is one obvious sense in which the changes can be considered as improvements: the staff involved in them considered them to be so. Even when allowance has been made for the inclination of those who have put a lot of work into a project to believe it has been worth it, the professional judgements of the teachers involved in the particular developments were positive. Of course they had reservations, and there was no school in which improvements to the processes could not be envisaged. But overall, the teachers thought that the postholders' activities had led to genuine development in the school's curriculum.

However, important though this view is, it does not take us very far, because the teachers' agreement that the changes were worth while is a very generalised one. It does not provide any specific criteria for evaluating the programmes. One way forward was suggested in Chapter 2, where five benefits of school-based development were proposed, focused on the key values of staff collaboration and subject expertise. It is useful to apply these proposed benefits to the case studies.

A preliminary point must be made. The postholders were in many ways breaking new ground; they were developing procedures, relationships and ways of working for which few guidelines and even fewer ground rules existed. For this reason any general conclusions about their achievements must be tentative ones, qualified by the novelty and uncertainty of the context. Thus it would be more realistic to talk about what the postholders were beginning to achieve, what new processes were *emerging*, what approaches were *being* established, rather than to see any achievement as somehow complete and already solid. For the fundamental problem with school-based curriculum development, as with other styles of curriculum development, is maintaining it after its initial impetus has slowed down. It is not being claimed, therefore, that substantial and solid changes were fully realised by postholders, only that they were pioneering changes which could become more firmly established if they continued and if information gained from them were used in developments in other schools.

Subject expertise

Continuity and consistency in a subject through the school

There appear to have been major moves in the direction of establishing consistency and coherence in the schools' curricula, by the provision of explicit statements of the concepts and skills to be covered in particular subjects or subject areas. Typically the processes comprised:

(a)   a review and appraisal of existing schemes and practices in the school;
(b)   a revision of the existing scheme, usually by a small sub-group of staff;
(c)   adoption of the revised scheme by the whole staff group;
(d)   implementation of the revised scheme;
(e)   evaluation/monitoring of the revised scheme in practice.

Two characteristics of these revised schemes may be seen as considerable improvements on previous practice. First, they tended to stress 'concepts and skills' rather than a list of content to be covered, with the aim that the pupils would be helped to learn the basic structure and methods of the subject, rather than the more superficial and particularised content of earlier syllabuses. Second, the schemes put the concepts and skills into a sequence that incorporated the principle that pupils' learning should be developmental: new work should build upon earlier work.

A clear sequence in the curriculum framework enabled teachers to be aware of the place of the work they were doing in the overall pattern and of its contribution to the continuity of the curricular experience provided for the pupils. Thus if staff discussion of revised schemes of work did little else, it brought teachers face to face with the school-wide implications of a subject, and compelled them to consider the work in their own classes in a school-wide context.

This latter consequence can be seen especially clearly in the case studies presented in Chapters 7, 8 and 9, and most impressively perhaps in the staff discussion of the Chapter 9 case study. There the focus of the staff's concerns was not predominantly on their own classroom teaching of science — What equipment shall I use? Which experiments work best? and so on — but on the problematic nature of the *school* policy towards science embodied in the revised scheme. Thus discussion was dominated by school-wide issues such as: how far child-centred forms of writing up experiments and observations should be encouraged; the extent to which the school policy should be about scientific *methods* of observation, recording and experiment, and the extent to which an agreed set of topics should be covered; the possible effect on other curriculum areas of developing a broad-based approach to science; and the extent to which the organisation of the teaching of science would transmit a false gender image of the subject to the pupils.

This movement towards greater consistency and continuity through the school was attributed by headteachers to the influence of HMI's *Primary Education in England*, though in two cases the heads saw that survey's recommendations as legitimising existing practices in school. The curriculum theorist will already have detected, however submerged his influence, the ideas of Bruner (1963), about the need to build a curriculum around a subject's basic conceptual structure, and to incorporate within it a spiral sequence that enables children to experience the concepts in increasingly complex forms. Bruner argued that designing the curriculum in this way would be economic in the sense that pupils would come to understand the fundamentals of a subject and would be able to incorporate new data into the basic conceptual structure they had acquired. If the renewal of the curriculum in these primary schools is along Brunerian lines, however unconsciously or second-hand, it is difficult to see it as anything but an improvement on some previous approaches.

Enhanced staff confidence in the subject, and respect for the postholder's expertise

One of the aims of freeing the postholder to work with other teachers, either as a 'consultant' leading in-service activities in the school or working alongside them in their classrooms, is that the class teachers' confidence in the postholder's subject should be increased. By getting 'expert' advice, or by seeing work done by children being taught by the postholder, the teachers' own expectations and confidence in the subject can, albeit slowly, be raised.

In all the case studies this tended to happen as, so to speak, a spin-off from the main curriculum development. In seeing how the language postholder (in Chapter 8) analysed the language problems of the children in her own class, the other teachers picked up approaches for their own classes; in seeing how the art/craft postholder had taught craft skills to their classes, two teachers in School 6 had increased their belief in their own ability to teach such skills; by using a purpose-built pack on electricity made for her by the science postholder, an infant teacher had been able to develop a little confidence and competence in experimental science which otherwise she would have lacked; and so on. In these small and apparently routine ways, teachers' confidence was being built up by the postholders. There was nothing dramatic about the change in confidence levels — indeed the way it was done was almost incidental to other, more apparently mainstream, purposes — but it was present in all the cases.

A related consequence of this kind of activity is enhanced respect for the postholders' expertise. Postholders were able to keep up to date in aspects of their subject, for example, by attendance at out-of-school courses. It followed from this that they were able to give a lead to other teachers when it was needed. In this respect it is noticeable that all the postholders were consulted informally about their subject (skill 2(a)(iv) in Table 3.1), which suggests that they had established themselves as subject experts not only formally, through their official position of responsibility, but also informally in the real life of the school through their personal relationships.

A second factor in the development of respect for subject expertise flowed from the highly successful relationships that the postholders made with outside experts, mainly local-authority advisers and university staff. Over all five skills in the dimension 'professional judgement', including important decisions about methods and materials, there was confident and constructive exercise of a leadership role by the postholders. This was partly because it was fairly familiar territory (the skills were ones that most postholders had to perform as the foundation of their responsibility) but it was also the dimension where external support for the particular development had been most clearly in evidence, and had been negotiated by the postholders' consulting the external experts. It represents the area where collaboration between those developing the curriculum within the school and those outside it had been most effective.

In the case of the language programme (Chapter 8), for example, this collaboration had arisen from the postholder's following the Open University's Post-Experience Reading Diploma and being invited by the university to try out new materials in her school. She thus became better informed in general about approaches to language and reading (and better qualified) than most of her colleagues, and also understood more fully the underlying assumptions of the approach in the trial materials. Likewise the social studies postholder (Chapter 7) had spent a considerable time on in-service courses informing himself about the available materials and resources in the field, and thus was in a better position than his colleagues to offer informed judgements when it came to decisions about the selection of materials and approaches by the school for its new programme.

Staff collaboration

Collective decision-making

Decision-making about the curriculum contrasted with that in schools investigated by Brown (1971), who found headteachers in her innovatory primary schools making the decision to adopt innovation on their own, and without resort to staff meetings or other group activities. In the Warwick inquiry schools, schemes of work were produced by small sub-groups of staff, who reported back to the whole staff at appropriate occasions, and always at the stage of the final draft.

It is, of course, always difficult for an observer to know with certainty that a decision-making meeting is as it appears to be, and that there is no disguised control by the headteacher. Perhaps, however, the two cases that most clearly illustrate that effective decision-making about the curriculum had passed into the hands of the staff group are the developments in Schools 1 and 7, which happen to be concerned with revision of the schemes in similar subject areas — social and environmental studies. In both these schools the original schemes had been written by the head. Their revision was carried out in staff groups working independently of him. Both heads characterised this as a 'step forward', as though the school organisation was going through a developmental stage. Moreover, Chapter 9 provides an account of the staff meeting called to evaluate how a new science scheme was working. In this meeting there was explicit criticism of the timetable arrangements that prevented women teachers from teaching physical science to their classes, and of the use of the postholder for subject teaching with the fourth-year pupils. Since these were arrangements devised by the headteacher, it is at least arguable that the staff views were not being suppressed in deference to the head's presence. Given the opportunity to participate in decision-making, most teachers in these schools took it intelligently and responsibly.

One reservation should be mentioned about the use of the terms 'participation' and 'collective decision-making'. Although it is true that these staff groups tended to report back to whole staff meetings, or be open to all members of staff, it would be more precise to say that school decision-making was by the active participants in the curriculum development programmes, rather than by the whole collectivity of the staff, some of whom did not participate at all, or at best attended a staff meeting and passively accepted what was proposed. Participatory decision-making therefore might be a more accurate description of the achievement in these schools, since none had found a solution to the passive resistance to curriculum development exhibited by a minority of teachers.

Devolution of responsibility

The collective style of decision-making in these schools did not occur automatically or inevitably. The headteachers reported that they had planned for it to occur, by gradually encouraging groups of staff to work together on curriculum reviews in the school and then to report back to the whole staff group. Collective decision-making about curriculum policy assumed prior devolution of responsibility for the development of such policy to sub-groups.

Typically, the sub-group contained teachers from each year group in order to provide for effective representation of the interests and needs of every year group, and to enable more effective dissemination at the implementation stage. Such a staff group is more likely to produce a scheme which is tailor-made to the school's existing practices, and which builds upon existing strengths (that is, a real development of the work in the school) than is an individual postholder, however expert.

Again, this was not a spontaneous process. Teachers were encouraged by head-teachers to learn how to work in such groups. The head of one school said:

> For the last two years we've had curriculum review groups of one kind and another in the school so staff are used to working together in this way. I attend most of them, but I don't need to take a very active role in them now. I attend to show that I think it's important rather than to take part, because the group has to decide things.

It may be that the fluency and openness of the working group in this school (whose meetings are illustrated in Chapter 8) owed much to the staff's previous experience of meeting and discussing curriculum issues. They had become accustomed to giving accounts to one another, were unafraid of admitting mistakes in front of one another, and were arriving at judgements on curriculum practice in an authentically collaborative way.

The postholder as educationalist

Devolution to small working groups has an attractively democratic ring about it, but the management of such groups was complex and time-consuming. Such groups do not cohere naturally, and postholders co-ordinating them found it necessary to work hard in order to 'service' them. For example, in School 2 a group of five staff met once a week to review and devise a substantial language policy for the school. In between these meetings the postholder produced 'minutes' of the previous discussion and a draft paper for the next meeting. She introduced the draft, led the discussion and amended it as the meeting progressed. This process, with interruptions for seasonal activities and a period of illness, covered about two terms. But the process also meant that few substantial amendments were made at the full staff meeting because of the time-consuming but effective staff consultation that had occurred during the working sessions. Even so, and perhaps ominously, in the whole staff meeting, according to the head, 'the point was strongly made that drawing up the policy was easy compared to implementing it'. Thus the production of new schemes of work in the schools was testimony not only to the achievement of devolved responsibility, but also to the sheer hard work of the postholder.

However, the skills of a hard-working secretary were not the only ones employed by a postholder in leading a working group. She also had to deploy her subject expertise. She had to put into written form the staff's objectives for a revised scheme of work, and to provide and elaborate upon justifications for the approaches taken. She had to apprehend aspects of educational research and theory and 'translate' such material for her colleagues. She had to lead staff discussions with advisers, and with staff from other schools. In all these activities the postholder was extending her role from teacher to educationalist.

Even the apparently limited development of three mornings' work on the enrichment programme (Case study E) required of its leader that he inform himself of recent research by discussions with a local university lecturer, translate what he learned into a comprehensible form for other teachers, develop some objectives for the programme, negotiate participation by advisers and manage some simple evaluation techniques.

Thus the achievement of the postholders was not merely that they had enabled new schemes of work to be created, revised policies to be implemented and innovations to be evaluated, but that they had done so by exercising a role in which the principles upon which change had been predicated were made explicit through accounts to their professional peers. Obviously the extent to which this occurred varied, and postholders experienced difficulties with the role. But the extension of their role in this way led to the development of their own professional abilities as well as of the curriculum itself.

Conclusion

In essence, therefore, there has been detected a shift in curricular practice and values in the primary schools which participated in the study. This shift is characterised by respect for the dictates of the nature of the subject areas and expertise in them, and commitment to a more collaborative approach to the process of curriculum renewal. This shift may be tentatively seen as the beginning of a change in primary school ideology, in the sense that the values underlying the practice are different from those that supported primary school practice in the late 1960s and early 1970s. The substance of these values, outlined in Chapter 2, will be explored in the final chapter of this book, but for the moment one implication needs reiteration. They had, or will have if developed further, consequences for the authority relationship between the head and the postholder, and for the authority relationship between the postholder and the class teacher. In both relationships authority will have to shift to the postholder, because she or he will be expected to act as the ultimate arbiter of what should count as knowledge in her or his area. This is bound to raise problems concerning traditional assumptions of curricular authority and organisation in the school, for on the one hand the headteacher has always been seen as the authority in curricular matters, exercising it on behalf of the governors and local authority, and on the other hand, traditional conceptions of class teachers — that they are 'autonomous' in their own classrooms — are also brought into question in schools where greater respect is given to the specialised knowledge of the postholder, and where collaborative processes produce curriculum policies that have implications for practice throughout the school. Located in the middle of this network of problematic relationships is the postholder's role, and some problems consequent upon its location were experienced by teachers in the Warwick inquiry. These, and some other role conflicts of the postholders, are examined in the next chapter.

4

Conflict and Strain in the Postholder's Role

CONFLICT AND CURRICULUM DEVELOPMENT IN SCHOOL

> The one thing I won't do is to go into other classes to see how it's (the new policy) working . . . I started to do it at the beginning, you know, in the time I was given to see what was happening throughout the school, but I didn't get much further than asking Donna who's got a first year class just like me. I could tell straightaway, even in the staff room not in her classroom I mean, that, well, she didn't really want me in. It's a bit silly because we're in and out of each other's classes quite a lot but if I was going in like, well, officially to see how she was putting the policy into practice — well it would be too inspectorial, as if I was checking up on her . . . and anyway think what it would be like in the staffroom — resentment and bad feeling. I don't think it would be worth it and I told the head so. I'd rather leave it to them to make the first move, ask my advice or something and then perhaps I could go and talk about how it's going.

This is how one of the postholders described the strain imposed on her relationship with one of her close colleagues when she tried to monitor the implementation of a school-wide policy they had developed together. It illustrates an aspect of school-based curriculum development only infrequently alluded to, namely that conflict and strain are generated by it. In the Warwick inquiry seven of the postholders reported encountering some conflict or strain arising from their role as curriculum developers. By 'conflict' I mean 'disagreement over professional issues' and by 'strain', 'unease about professional relationships with colleagues'. Another way of putting it is that 'conflict' refers to actual disagreement whereas 'strain' refers to potential disagreement. There is no implication that teachers engaged in curriculum development activities were constantly quarrelling or arguing with each other: on the contrary, something of the extent and quality of staff collaboration has already been illustrated in the preceding chapter. What the case studies revealed was that the process of curriculum development itself often exposed facets of those subterranean differences of value and of professional judgement that normally remained undisturbed beneath the surface of routine relationships in school. Although these differences occasionally erupted into the open, they more normally took the form of an underground rumble of ambiguity.

Another illustration may be helpful. In School 1, a group of four teachers planned and agreed upon a team teaching arrangement called combined studies. In the first year of its operation they met regularly but informally to monitor how the scheme was progressing and to plan new units of work in detail. One of the problems that emerged concerned the relative inflexibility of the curricular sequence they had planned, which meant that the individual teachers could not control the pacing of their pupils' learning according to their perceived individual needs, but had to go along with the common team pacing. The four teachers seem to have experienced what has commonly been said of team teaching arrangements, namely that although designed to create some flexibility, they sometimes turn out to be less flexible than the educational needs of the pupils' demand. The four did not agree about how far this problem had been resolved, and at an early stage in the year it had been a matter of great concern and some frustration for them.

> You know that you've got three sessions with them — and half way through the second session you think, 'Oh I'll have to get them moving on quickly so that they've got things finished in time.' Whereas you really would like to consolidate the skills they've started. For example I did lino-cuts with them and really there are a lot of developments of lino-cutting that it's good for them to work on but I only had time to teach them the techniques, give them some practice and then let them produce and display a simple lino-cut design.

Likewise, one of the teachers felt that in order to progress through the agreed topics he was not able to give enough time initially to what he regarded as a very important study skill: note-making. He believed very strongly that note-making from documentary sources, from class lessons and from audio-visual sources such as radio and TV programmes was a study skill fundamental to the approach of learning built into the scheme of work. The teacher also stressed that for the relatively few children slow at learning, it was important to have more than the allotted time on it. For this reason, in the first term particularly, this teacher reported his sense of frustration, and to some extent disillusionment, with the curriculum development programme. The postholder said of the situation:

> He got very fed up, he was really down about it, and we used to say 'Look it'll be alright, we'll find time for it' and we'd listen to what he was saying and we knew he cared about it. We discussed his frustrations about it (note-making and the problems of the slower pupils) and we tried to take them on board.

This kind of conflict and strain amongst teachers was reported by Evans and Groarke (1975) in a substantial language development programme in a junior and infant school, involving the authors, eight teachers from the school and three from other schools. They experienced two forms of conflict: opposition to the programme itself and disagreement about the priorities within it. About the former the authors say, with a frankness rare in the literature on school-based curriculum development:

> There was dissatisfaction and this showed itself in a variety of ways. Sometimes we felt a cold disillusionment and one teacher confessed she felt all her previous teaching had been a waste of time. Other teachers reacted strongly against the exercise itself, handling the uncertainty with a show of scepticism and amused malice. (p. 127)

According to Evans and Groarke, their development also produced disagreement of a professional nature — about curriculum priorities:

members of staff felt that discussion of language development was pushing out other priorities, and staff often felt slighted by the scant attention paid to other cherished curriculum objectives they were working towards with children. (p. 134)

Another study where conflict is explicitly discussed is by Hargreaves (1980), in what is essentially a report of the suppression of staff disagreement about educational values, with the head and deputy head of a middle school (8–12) effectively dominating a staff workshop/discussion, with the consequence that educational alternatives to their own position could not be explored.

That conflicts of one kind or another are experienced by teachers engaged in school-based curriculum development is not entirely surprising. Its inherent difficulties had been suggested by Skilbeck (1972):

the task is complex and difficult for all concerned. It requires a range of cognitive skills, strong motivation, postponement of immediate satisfaction, constructive interaction in planning groups, and emotional maturity.

It would be unrealistic, and potentially counter-productive, to pretend that school-based curriculum development is easier, smoother or more trouble-free than it may turn out to be. For this reason, if for no other, a fuller analysis of such conflict needs to be offered, and the one that follows is based upon the seven cases in which conflict and/or strain for the curriculum postholder emerged.

THREE SOURCES OF UNCERTAINTY IN THE CURRICULUM DEVELOPMENT ROLE

In general, conflict was derived from the fact that the role of the 'teacher as educationalist' is fairly novel in primary schools, and so by definition is not clearly specified. It was therefore experienced as a role suffused with uncertainty, not because postholders themselves were necessarily uncertain, but because the activity itself was an ambiguous enterprise; it was often difficult to be sure, while it was being carried out, that the effort involved would be worth while. Furthermore, responsibilities are not clearly demarcated in primary schools, so although the postholder might have successfully initiated a new curriculum policy, individual class teachers were the ultimate arbiters of the curriculum practice in their own classes. So the postholders in the research schools were, as curriculum developers, very much 'making' their role rather than 'taking' it, improvising a role for themselves rather than stepping into a fully scripted one; achieving a role rather than having one ascribed to them. Since they were feeling their way, negotiating the rules and roles as the developments proceeded, differences and disagreements were encountered, and occasionally some professional nerve-endings were set on edge. Three sources of such uncertainty were identifiable:

(a)   ambiguity in relationships with class teachers;
(b)   conflicting priorities;
(c)   strain in the 'teacher as educationalist' role.

Relationships with class teachers

Perhaps the most distinct source of ambiguity in the postholders' role as curriculum developers was the mismatch between their formal status and their actual power, as perceived by themselves and by their colleagues. Curriculum postholders were given the responsibility for developing their subject throughout the school, for implementing developments and for monitoring progress. However, alongside such formal responsibilities, there existed a set of informal perceptions and relationships — how the postholders' responsibilities were perceived by their colleagues — which did not necessarily fit with the official specification. Her Majesty's Inspectors (DES 1978a) appear to have conflated these distinctive aspects of the postholder's status in their proposition (para. 8.45) that the status should be improved. In the Inspectors' view the standing of postholders:

> . . . is a product of the ways in which teachers with special posts regard themselves and also of the attitudes that other teachers have towards them.

This appears to be too simple a view of a very complex network of formal and informal statuses, for the relationships within it embodied a particularly pervasive strain. In every case the postholders talked of their anxiety about appearing to 'dictate' to the class teachers, or 'impose' the curriculum on them. One postholder made the situation quite explicit. She had developed a school-wide scheme in environmental studies and after staff discussion it had been accepted as the school's official scheme. The new scheme had been a development of existing work.

> We didn't sweep away everything that we'd been doing. We took what we thought was working well and extended it, and built it into an overall scheme so that there was more progression in it.

Nevertheless, in the postholder's words, there had been considerable 'hostility' to the scheme from many class teachers on the grounds that it reduced their autonomy. They had claimed that the scheme contained 'too much to get through', and that if you were always a first-year teacher you would always be doing the 'same old topics' year in, year out. The interesting thing is that neither of these objections was particularly valid: the scheme and the postholder encouraged teachers to be selective, and to develop their own versions of topics to be covered, so long as they did not cover work or topics designed for other year groups. (The headteacher had a somewhat different perspective on the issue. He regarded 'hostility' as an inappropriate term for the response of some of the teachers. He described it as 'some resistance initially' to the new scheme, but reported it as short-lived and limited.)

We have seen something rather similar in the description of the team teaching programme earlier, and it emerges also in the staff evaluation of the science scheme which is discussed in Chapter 9. What was happening in these and the other cases was a clash, or a revealed tension between 'institutional' interests (i.e. the development and implementation of a school-wide policy to secure overall progression in the pupils' work) and 'individual' interests (i.e. the perceived freedom of teachers to control and implement the curriculum in their own classes). There were clear echoes here of the 'zones of authority' issue highlighted by Taylor and his colleagues (1974) and referred to more fully in Chapters 2 and 10.

It is not being suggested that there was a constant curricular guerrilla warfare between the postholders and the class teachers as people. Instead, what did emerge from the case studies was the tension between these roles, a tension compounded by the fact that postholders were usually class teachers as well. Thus, paradoxically, from the point of view of curriculum development, the concept of the class teacher's 'autonomy' in curricular matters was to some extent shared by the postholders themselves, despite the fact that the consequence of their curriculum development activities was to bring such a concept into question.

Language and participation: styles of ambiguity

Two aspects of school-based curriculum development reflect this tension in a particularly clear and interesting light. The first concerns the language of the curriculum documents in the schools, and the second concerns the participatory style of the curriculum decision-making, described more fully in Chapter 3. In both, the essential ambiguity in the roles of postholder and class teacher was made palpable.

In respect of the language in which school curriculum documents were couched — the terminology of curriculum change, so to speak — there was a resolute tentativeness, apparently designed to avoid at all costs the impression that policies would be imposed if they were not implemented. This comes through in the vocabulary adopted, in that syllabuses are not syllabuses but 'guidelines' or 'frameworks' or 'policies', and curriculum content is not content but 'concepts' or 'conceptual areas'. Moreover, the documents themselves were written in a style notable for its delicacy. For example, a review of curriculum practice in a school would have to suggest the need for change, and at the same time refute the implied criticism of class teachers' existing practices. A report written specifically for the research by the postholder whose work is described more fully in Chapter 7 is a good example of such sensitivity:

> If adhered to, the original Environmental Studies Scheme would have ensured progression of content and avoided repetition, but generally speaking staff devised their own themes. The result was (to state the extreme case): i) lack of progression, ii) repetition of content, iii) imbalance of work, iv) skills developed unsystematically, v) no effective record keeping, vi) difficulty in providing resources and materials, given the unpredictability of coverage.
>
> Nevertheless, it was generally thought that in spite of these problems the school staff taught Environmental Studies using a topic approach rather well. There was variety of approach, techniques and methods, the children were well motivated, and the work produced was generally worthwhile and attractively presented. This was attributed chiefly to the fact that the staff had freedom to develop the topic from the beginning and make their own decisions about content, methods, aims, objectives progression, etc. As a result (it was believed) the teacher communicated an enthusiasm for learning through the topic.

In short, the autonomy of the class teacher was seen as a contradictory source, both of problems and of pride. The postholder's language retains its curricular cake, having first consumed it.

Similarly, with the detail of the revised policies themselves, there was a clear reticence about appearing to direct class teachers. Where there were indications of work appropriate for children to cover, the policies offered them as 'suggestions'. In one case, where the policy had been agreed upon and accepted by the whole school staff, the preamble made explicit its respect for the class teacher's professional autonomy, even though providing a statement of agreed intentions and practices:

> The policy has been divided into sections covering the aims and ideals of each skill and providing suggested reading for the teacher. Much of what is included here is designed as an aid to the individual teacher, rather than a list of inflexible rules. As well as this the policy exists to lend some cohesion and continuity to our approach.

A feature of the policy's format was that interspersed among the sections were lists of curricular experiences to be practised with the children, headed 'Suggestions for Development'. Indeed the policy made a point of stressing those few issues that could not be regarded as 'discretionary' for class teachers. In this, therefore, as in most other policy documents, the language made explicit the uncertainty of the postholders' relationship with the class teachers: the former were not directing the latter to teach given content, but were responsible for offering a framework within which it could appear that both individual autonomy and institutional consistency would be safeguarded.

The collaborative and participatory style of the curriculum decision-making was illustrated in the preceding chapter. This style — usually involving a working group of staff whose deliberations were disseminated through whole staff meetings — may also be interpreted as evidence supporting the essentially ambiguous relationship between postholders and class teachers. The style can be seen as a response by postholders to their relative lack of power in order to ensure the implementation of changes in the classes throughout the school, for a revised scheme produced by active staff participation in discussion and workshop sessions would embody ideas likely to be acceptable to class teachers. It also followed that class teachers could not logically or legitimately complain that they were being dictated to, since they either had participated in the production of the scheme or had agreed to its final version. In either case, it ensured that the postholders would not have to have recourse to power they did not possess, in order to implement or sustain the innovation. Thus, although the widespread practice adopted by postholders, of encouraging a participatory style in the production of new schemes or programmes, may be justified by a rhetoric stressing its superiority as a strictly educational process, it can also be seen as a symptom of the ambiguity in the power position.

Monitoring progress throughout the school

A further problem of relationships and status arose when innovation was monitored, even if very indirectly, by the postholder. She was not a superior to some of her colleagues, and in her relationships with most of them she saw herself, and was seen, as an equal. And yet the postholder was expected to visit classrooms to see work in progress, and in three of the seven relevant case studies she had timetabled time available for this purpose. The quotation at the opening of this chapter typifies the ambiguity, in that the postholder was anxious that her relationships with her colleagues should not be adversely affected by her performing a role that could be interpreted as 'inspecting' their work.

The case studies where problems associated with monitoring progress were absent, or not referred to, in a limited sense provided evidence supporting the general analysis of ambiguity. In the school where the headteacher was the initiator of change, such ambiguities did not emerge, probably because the headteacher's role and status are defined more clearly as superior to other teachers'. The other two cases were the only ones where the postholders were used as specialist teachers. In one case, music in School 8, the innovation did not actively involve other teachers, and there was therefore no basis for ambiguity in her relationships with other teachers. In the case of the art/craft specialist in School 7, it may be that the postholder's status as 'specialist' provided her with a stronger base from which to monitor work in progress.

The postholder concerned certainly saw it in these terms. As she said when asked to comment on her role as specialist:

> Well one thing that's very important is that the pupils see me as 'the Art teacher' and they get sent to me with their work if it's very good . . . of course I am responsible for Art in the school but really it's more how they see me — the teachers as well as the pupils. I've got two periods on Friday morning to, you know, go and see the class teachers and their Art work but it's not the official time that matters it's well if the teacher needs some help with say needlework, they automatically come to me about it — they accept that I'm supposed to help them. It's rather like the pupils, really, as I said, seeing me as 'the Art teacher'.

If she was right, it looks as though there was a better match between her formal and informal status than in some other schools, and that this followed from her specialist teacher role. It is something of a paradox that she also adduced the 'good personal relationships' in the school as one further basis for her being able to monitor work in progress, since these were precisely the reasons given by the postholder at the opening of this chapter for not engaging in such activity.

Passive resistance to change

In the last resort, in these primary schools, the postholders were brought up against the realities of their relative lack of power when faced with teachers who responded to initiatives for innovation by the tactic of passive resistance. A minority of teachers in the schools were uncommitted either to the particular programme or to curriculum development activities in general. One head explained to me that:

> There is a hard core in this school, and in most schools I've known, who are just 9–5 teachers. They don't want to change what they do. In a curriculum development programme it's the teachers who don't need to change who take part in it, and the ones who do need to change, who never attend. It's like the parents of children really — the ones you need to see on open evenings don't come and the ones whose children are doing OK always turn up.

Heads and postholders agreed that as things stood there was little that could be done to bring about change in the classroom practice of teachers uncommitted to it, or disinclined to become involved. Even allocation of formal staff meetings for discussion and decision-making could not ensure participation by the uncommitted, let alone guarantee change in their classroom practice. Faced with passive resistance to innovation, the postholder was impotent.

Conflicting priorities

Promoting curriculum change within the school was not an exclusive or even the main responsibility of the postholders in the schools in which the inquiry was carried out. All but the two postholders used as specialist teachers had a number of other major responsibilities to fulfil, as has been illustrated in Table 3.2. This characteristic spread of obligations might be designated 'role diversity', which is a term sociologists use to describe a position in which there is too much for its occupier to do. This diversity was a source of conflict for postholders because it raised questions of priority in the allocation of their time and energy. There is, for all primary school teachers, a limit to how much time and energy can be allocated to one activity, if several others make equally legitimate claims over the same period. There was a sense, therefore, in which, for at least some of their time, curriculum development had to be seen as a relatively marginal role by postholders.

It is not being proposed that curriculum development activities were seen as marginal by the postholders or other staff, in the sense that they regarded them as unimportant. However, the importance of the activity has to be put into the context of the overall role demands made upon teachers as staff members, not just as postholders with responsibility for designated areas of the curriculum. These other demands make equally strong, and in some senses stronger, claims upon the postholders' time and energy. This can be illustrated by referring to the other most widely held responsibility: class teaching.

On the face of it, class teaching should make only routine demands of time and organisation upon experienced teachers, although this is not to underestimate the workload involved. However, at the time of the inquiry, there was evidence that class teaching was itself creating more demands upon teachers. Falling rolls in the schools had led to the introduction of some classes of mixed age composition. Class teachers were also under pressure nationally to give more consideration to ways they could cater for the needs of the more able pupils in their classes, and for those of pupils with other special needs. And in schools where a teacher left, the post was filled, if at all, by a teacher on temporary contract. The consequences were unfavourable to development.

In one of the schools this kind of pressure had limited the nature of the postholder's commitment to curriculum development:

> It's not that I'm not interested in it (curriculum development) — of course I am — but my class have had two temporary teachers last year — it's nobody's fault, it couldn't really be helped, it's just the case that you know they had the two of them who've been cut, and now they've got me and I think I've got to build up, well er to give most of my effort this year to giving them stability, and getting them to know the standards I expect . . . and really I think that's more important, right now, for these kids than having another go at the curriculum policy . . . Perhaps I should do both but I've got a personal life of my own as well you know . . . and the time it takes to do it properly, I just think I've got to concentrate on the class this year.

Four postholders had responsibility for co-ordinating work across a year group. What this involved in the different schools, or indeed in different years within a school, varied, but the general responsibility could be a substantial one because of its 'pastoral' aspect.

In one of the schools it included the responsibility of getting to know the children in the year group individually, maintaining general disciplinary levels, and organising the use of equipment, resources and facilities within the year group. In relatively small schools, of course, a year group co-ordinator will be one of only two teachers working with the year group, but in three-form entry schools and above the demands will be substantial.

In one of the smaller schools in the inquiry, a two-form entry school, the demands of year co-ordination were particularly pressing and had led to a slower pace of curriculum development than would otherwise have occurred, according to the headteacher. The postholder for art/craft in the school had been attempting to introduce a substantial component of craft, design and technology (CDT) into the classroom practice of teachers throughout the school. He had the advice and support of the recently appointed deputy head, who had developed CDT in his previous school, where the quality of the work had attracted some national and regional attention. There was therefore in the inquiry school both the interest and expertise to develop CDT, and appropriate policy documents had been created. But enabling the development to take root in the class-room practice of the teachers had been restricted by other demands, especially the need to provide support and consistency across the year groups, for one of which the postholder was co-ordinator. The head explained:

> It's been very difficult (to move faster). We've had staff cuts that have reduced flexibility, so that the postholder can't work alongside the class teachers and that's the crucial thing. And then we've got three teachers on temporary contracts, so I've had to ensure that the experienced permanent staff take a major role in the year groups, to make sure that there's good general work, that the temporary teachers get to know the ropes, and that the normal work is consolidated. There's a limit to the amount of curriculum development you can do in the present situation — our rolls are stable, it's not from falling rolls, it is that we've lost staff and new staff aren't permanent. In this situation, innovation isn't necessarily the most important priority, and may not even be a good thing.

To demonstrate the other main claims upon the postholders' commitment is not in itself to demonstrate the perceived marginality of curriculum development for them, but it does suggest on the face of it that if postholders are satisfactorily to fulfil the range of regular and routine demands made upon them by the various school roles they occupy, curriculum development activities cannot make a predominant claim upon their time, or can only do so intermittently. It also suggests that if an unusual burst of energy is necessary to plan, launch and evaluate a new programme, the less dramatic but no less important commitment to *sustaining* the innovation may be what is adversely affected by the other legitimate role demands.

There was support for this interpretation from a follow-up discussion held with the head and postholder in the development reported in Chapter 9. In the school concerned a new approach to science had been planned, implemented and evaluated, with the consequence that a number of areas where the development could be consolidated and improved had been highlighted. For example, the postholder saw the need to produce, index and store sample collections of pupils' work in science, and to give class teachers concrete illustrations of the kind and quality of work they should expect from pupils at given stages in the scheme. Class teachers had also asked for the production of more resource packs to support the development and some consideration of appropriate language work. Talking of these demands upon the postholder, the head commented:

He needs time to think a bit more about it, to reflect about the stage it's reached. He needs a term free of his other jobs to consolidate what's been achieved. Perhaps some time at the university, and visiting some other schools; some time to work with the other teachers in the school and then some time to produce materials and resources. He can't do what is necessary without time — he works all the hours God gives him already, and he's also in charge of boys' games as well as his own class. He won't be able to do what needs doing now, or at least he won't be able to do it as well as he could do, if he has to do all his normal teaching and other things as well.

This kind of problem may be inevitable in primary schools, for the teacher's role is already extremely diverse even before the demands for school-based curriculum development are met. The postholder at Abbotsmead Junior School, Susan Timms, expressed the position neatly, in Donoughue et al (1981):

> . . . I would like to say a little more about another aspect of the time factor . . . like most schools we have Harvest, Christmas, drama and musical evenings, sports days, swimming galas, school reports and consultation evenings, to name a few. In school we have displays to feature children's written work, art and craft, Christmas parties, Halloween, Bonfire night, sports matches with other schools, clubs for chess, nature, drama, dance, gymnastics, a school choir and instrumental groups. While I fully appreciate the need for an up-to-date curriculum, no one would suggest that it be at the expense of the above activities. So, while in one sense curriculum progress seems to be slow, anyone contemplating in-school curriculum development must be aware and considerate of the competition which already exists for the time of the teacher.

The educationalist context

Keddie (1971) saw the educationalist context as an ideological arena in which teachers confronted value issues in a school through the discussion of educational ideas:

> The educationist context may be called into being by the presence of an outsider to whom explanations of the department's activities must be given, or by a forthcoming school meeting which necessitates discussion of policy of how things ought to be in a school. (p. 135)

The dominant feature of the context is a requirement for teachers to give an account of their educational policies and practices. In the Warwick inquiry this feature — a matter, quite literally, of accountability — encompassed a wider range of activities than appears to have been the case in Keddie's school. It included activities such as drafting aims and objectives for a new scheme of work and introducing its rationale to a staff group (Case studies A, C, F and H), justifying an approach to curriculum planning through defining the conceptual structure of a subject (Case studies A and H), organising, preparing and presenting material for a staff INSET programme (Case study D), discussing curricular policies with local-authority advisers and/or secondary school staff meetings (Case studies A and F), displaying pupils' work as examples of the quality and standard to be expected by other staff (Case studies F, G and I) and teachers' familiarising themselves and their colleagues with aspects of educational research and theory (Case studies D and E).

This kind of activity was relatively novel for most postholders; indeed the head-teachers of six of them saw the curriculum development programme as one way in which the postholders could gain experience of leading a group of staff for the first time. The head in Case study D, for example, said:

> The need to provide opportunities for staff development is understood and considered important within the school and the invitation (to the postholder to develop a staff INSET programme) was seen as a chance for her to extend and develop her already strong interest in language work. It was also an opportunity for her to practise and develop a leadership role in influencing the thinking and practices of her colleagues.

The role was also a source of strain even where it was most clearly seen by the staff group as having been exercised effectively. It is possible to analyse this kind of strain by looking at both the contexts in which the teacher acted as educationalist and the nature of the acts themselves. The contexts were all ones in which the postholder was highly *visible* to her colleagues; the nature of the acts themselves required the postholder to give *accounts* of curriculum policies and practice; and it is under these two headings that role problems are described and illustrated below.

Role visibility

One feature that particularly distinguishes the 'teacher as educationalist' role from that of the 'teacher as teacher' is that the former tends to be carried out in front of colleagues and other professionals, whereas the latter tends to be performed in front of pupils. As 'educationalist' the postholder is highly visible to professional peers; as 'teacher' she or he is mostly invisible. There are some qualifications to this distinction, for example where teaching is carried out as part of a team or when postholders do some private reading and research to update themselves in their subject. But in general it was true of the postholders in this inquiry that a characteristic of their role as curriculum developers was its high degree of 'visibility', that is, its tendency to be carried out at crucial times in front of colleagues and other adults, or under their scrutiny.

In Case study E, it took the very limited form of giving staff involved examples of how an option for pupils should be described, whereas in Case study I it was a more 'public' business of displaying work done by pupils in the postholder's class for other colleagues to see. On the face of it, displaying work done by pupils is a routine part of every teacher's activity; display is used in corridors, foyer and classrooms both to illustrate the nature of the school work to visitors and to transmit to pupils a sense of the value placed upon their work by the teachers. However, samples of pupils' work carried out under the tuition of the postholder had to serve a further, different function in five of the case studies. In them, the quality of work done by pupils taught by the postholders was offered as *exemplary*, as setting standards for other teachers and pupils to emulate. In short, it became a requirement placed upon the postholders publicly to demonstrate professional excellence in their curriculum area to their colleagues.

In Case study G, display took on almost a 'demonstration lesson' form. The postholder had been asked by a class teacher to help her with screen-printing techniques in her class. Although he had given some advice outside the classroom to the teacher, she was still unsure about the practical work and skills involved. The postholder's class was taken by the head for two sessions so that he could work alongside both teachers in the year group and demonstrate the skills with their own children. After this the teachers were able to develop the work in following lessons and one in particular expressed greater confidence about her own skills. The postholder used this example to illustrate the importance for 'non-specialists' of having a specialist working with them on practical skills even if for an apparently limited amount of time.

> The important thing is to see it in practice with your own pupils — there's no other way in which you can get the feel for what they are capable of — standards if you like. The most useful thing is if I can go in and teach their class, or some of their class, with them and together we can actually see the skills involved, how to demonstrate them, how to help the children when they get into difficulties, and what to expect from them . . . of course it means it's got to work or there's no point to it. No amount of discussion outside the classroom is going to be a substitute if you can't show what you mean in practice.

Another aspect of visibility, and a more common one, was the practice of running discussion groups, or staff workshops, in which the postholder's organisational ability and specialised knowledge were simultaneously under the scrutiny of colleagues.

In the case study discussed more fully in Chapter 8, the significance of the postholder's handling of the staff working group was highlighted by the teachers involved who made the point that the sessions 'didn't just happen'. They had needed to be structured and led by someone who could provide overall direction. One of the staff involved said:

> There would be problems if the discussion sessions had just been started cold. They needed someone who is familiar with the material, and who knows the background to it . . . The last thing I'd want would be where we'd get to the stage where we'd say 'What shall we talk about this week?'.

In the particular case, on the face of it, this role appeared effective and relatively trouble-free, to judge from the comments of the teachers involved. However, discussion sessions in other cases often brought into question the underlying values of the curriculum development project, with which the postholder was, of course, particularly associated. When this happened the postholders' knowledge and expertise were very much put to the test in that they had to provide justification for the project, and this is not an easy matter at the best of times.

Another kind of arena in which postholders were subjected to scrutiny was the kind of meeting in which they had to represent their subject to people other than their colleagues in school, usually teachers in other schools or local-authority advisers. In one of the case study schools the headteacher and the postholder had attended a liaison meeting with the 'academic board' of the nearby secondary school in order to give an account of the overall curriculum development plan. The official minutes of the meeting recorded the wide range of accounts that were required of the head and postholder in the meeting, but they did not bring out its daunting atmosphere. The head said afterwards of it:

> This was a formal and somewhat forbidding experience: while I could not say I detected open hostility (to the curriculum design overall) at least the meeting began in a cool and somewhat critical manner. As it progressed and people were able to voice their worries, the tension eased and Jane (the postholder) and I felt at the end that it had been a very worthwhile exercise.

The illustrations that have been presented above have been selected to show the varieties of *context* in which the postholders were subjected to peer-group scrutiny. But within those contexts, postholders had to provide accounts of the curricular policies they were promoting, and an examination of the nature of the accounts themselves suggests further sources of strain, for the accounts needed to address problems of educational theory and research, themselves far from unproblematic areas.

Giving accounts of the curriculum to professional peers

Teacher accountability has been discussed mainly in terms of teachers' accountability to non-professionals, to governors, parents and other members of the community. For example, Taylor (1977) raised the need for school staff to explain curricular policies in prospectuses and other documents for parents, and to give an account of curricular achievement to governing bodies. The kind of account that flows from such an obligation is a carefully prepared document, privately scrutinised in advance, with a perceived audience of non-professionals. Documents produced for this purpose tend to be, quite properly, essentially *descriptive* accounts. The kind of accounts that postholders provided for their colleagues and other adults were both more complex and qualitatively different. Accounts were commonly oral and unscripted, because they were given in response to questions that were not known in advance, and were directed at a professional audience, sometimes including people perceived to be 'experts', such as local-authority advisers. In addition, even where there were prepared curriculum documents, they were not merely descriptive accounts but were normally *justificatory* ones: they did not simply explain a policy or programme, but attempted to justify it by reference to educational values and principles of one kind or another.

An illustration of the nature of a justificatory account in written form is the following statement from a curriculum policy document in Case H, where the aims and scheme of work in part of the school's environmental studies were elaborated.

HISTORY
Why teach History?
It enables one to see one's own life as part of a steadily unfolding narrative. It provides a sense of perspective. It provides examples for comparison. It arouses sympathy and understanding of people of other times and other countries. It allows one the opportunity to draw conclusions from available evidence.
What can we teach between 8–12?
In a sense there is no limit but as only the most able children will have developed an appreciation of historical time by the age of 12, then we should try to give them a general understanding of (a) the recent past 19th century and onwards, (b) the Middle Ages and (c) the ancient and classical worlds from which our civilisation has sprung.
How can we teach History at this age?
Our aim should be two-fold: (a) to give an opportunity for the children to study an earlier Society in some detail and (b) to give them the opportunity to discover for themselves and to learn to sift and weigh evidence.
    Some history teaching must be didactic. The teacher tells a story and there is no better method for introducing say the Greek Myths: provided that there is opportunity for

discussion, interpretation and possibly dramatisation, then this is a good approach at all ages.

Some teaching will depend upon television and radio programmes. Again it is the quality of the discussion that determines the success with which the material is used. It is not sufficient to regurgitate the facts. The children should be provoked to ask 'Why?' and to keep on asking until they have reached a satisfactory conclusion.

Other topics may depend upon a combination of methods involving a wide use of reference books and audio visual material. Again it is not sufficient to simply repeat the information from the book. Children should use a reference book to find the answer to a particular question. If it is a question that they have raised themselves, then so much the better. The teacher's role is to guide the child to the relevant material and this can be done only if the teacher has a wide knowledge of the sources of the information available. We have a wide selection of charts, slides, transparencies and pictures that can be used by children and teachers. Close observation can often reveal a wealth of information.

There is no better method of developing a sense of history than examining the artefacts that previous generations have left behind. Houses, clothes, weapons, utensils, jewellery, paintings, journals, letters — the list is endless. Some can be brought into school while others necessitate visits but always the emphasis should be on questioning to attempt to fathom the place of this particular article in the historical pattern.

Look with caution on textbooks.

They tend to over-simplify and to repeat hoary myths, long disproved by scholarship. Teach children to be sceptical. In many cases we really do not know exactly what happened, let alone why someone acted as he did.

Characters in history were not necessarily more logical in their actions than we are ourselves. Given the benefit of hindsight, we can develop reasons that the participants may never have considered let alone acted upon. I recall a boy in my class looking at a picture of David Livingstone's wife and advancing his own original theory as to why Livingstone travelled so far into the wilderness. He may have been right at that!

Teach children to challenge evidence. 'How do we know that?' should be a constant question and one that can rarely be answered by saying 'Because it's in the book!'

Use drama and role play. It may not reveal the truth but it can help children to appreciate that Duke William did not know the outcome of invading England or indeed whether Normandy might not have been attacked during his absence.

What topics shall we teach?

Broadly speaking, I should like to feel that by the time a child leaves this school, he or she will have some knowledge of the following:

1. Pre-history.
2. The Ancient World. Egypt, Greece, Rome.
3. The Vikings and Normans.
4. Medieval Society.
5. The Tudor Age.
6. The Industrial and Agricultural Changes of the period 1750–1830.
7. The Victorians.
8. Britain in the 20th century.

In addition, I should like to see an understanding, at least, of the development of technology and some idea of Man's understanding of the Universe.

It is instructive to put aside one's own ideas about history in the curriculum, and about whether or not one agrees with the views being advanced in the policy (as well as one's reaction to sexist humour) and to reflect upon the nature of the account itself, which is presented, as most such accounts must be, relatively briefly, and in jargon-free language. The aims in the first paragraph include both cognitive and affective dimensions; there is in the second paragraph recognition of the psychological constraints of concept development in young children; and in terms of pedagogical styles, paragraphs

3 to 12 advocate the adoption of variety rather than uniformity. The Brunerian idea, that problem-solving will aid discovery learning, is also adumbrated in these paragraphs, as is the notion that children's learning should be disciplined by evidence, preferably of a first-hand kind.

Oral accounts, called for in staff discussions, have the same justificatory style, but tend to be more wide-ranging. For example, in School 5, a staff meeting was called to evaluate the first year's operation of a new science scheme, and the postholder's role in it. The meeting was good-humoured and positively constructive, but there were a number of occasions when some fundamental issues were raised which the postholder was required to confront. These included: the apparent curricular priority given to science at the expense of other subjects (geography, for example); the extent to which an agreed content area as a set of concepts was necessary, if the aim was to develop scientific methods of observation, recording, hypothesising etc.; the extent to which subject teaching of science in the fourth year was hindering integration with topic work, for example; and the issue of transmitting a gender-differentiated image of science. (Chapter 9 gives fuller details.)

The issues were not raised in the formal terms that have been used to summarise them above and did not lead in the particular case to the postholder's being personally or professionally threatened. But because they were genuinely felt problems, and because they were expressed as value issues, the postholder was being required publicly to confront them with, for example, his own account of the advantages of the use of subject teaching. (As a matter of fact it was the head at this stage who drew attention to some of the arguments for specialist teaching.) The point that needs to be stressed is that despite the context — an atmosphere entirely devoid of personal antipathy — the postholder was being required to give an account of, a justification for, educational practices, if the programme were to continue its development. And the account was subjected to, and arose from, professional scrutiny that was as probing as it was public. Perhaps this kind of role context is part of Goodacre's (1984) reason for suggesting that postholders need 'assertiveness training'.

Thus, as curriculum developers, postholders were brought up against the need to enter into forms of educational discourse and rapidly acquire fluency in its use. Perhaps the most difficult area was a directly practical one: the need to specify, organise and explain the major conceptual and skill structures of a subject. To do this at all requires considerable time and knowledge: to do it and feel that it has been done with authority is a formidable undertaking. It is not being suggested for a moment that postholders were required, or should have been required, to undertake a substantial formal 'course' in educational theory before engaging in school-based curriculum development, but once they had engaged in it, they were confronted with the need to adopt ideas and forms of discourse with which, initially at any rate, they were unfamiliar and insecure. Such insecurity was only intensified if familiarity had to be acquired in haste and alongside more routine but exacting demands of everyday teaching.

In part uncertainty in the role derives from the nature of the activity itself. The school curriculum is essentially problematic, and its developers had to live with and tolerate ambiguity for the most part. But the degree of uncertainty was reduced by two postholders, who had been able to gain access to highly specialised advice. In Case D this had happened by the postholder following a post-experience course before the development activity was planned, and in Case E the postholder gained access to an authoritative source, a local lecturer who happened to have specialised in the field concerned. Most postholders, however, had to operate in contexts in which such sources were either not available or not available when needed.

Tolerance of ambiguity: the postholder's virtue

It was argued in Chapter 3 that national policies encouraging postholders to establish a role for themselves as curriculum developers in their schools have underestimated the complexity of the task. This chapter has attempted to illustrate a further point, that conflict and ambiguity in the role have also been underestimated. Some sources of this conflict have been illustrated in order to show how pervasive a feature of school-based curriculum development it was in the inquiry schools.

There is evidence that some aspects of this kind of conflict and ambiguity in the schools in this study are not unique to them. Other studies of the teacher's role in primary schools by Coulson (1978) and by Leese (1978), as well as the analyses already referred to by Lortie (1969) and by Taylor, Reid, Holley and Exon (1974), have exposed the structural problem of the autonomy of the teacher in relation to school-wide policies. Similar sources of ambiguity were reported by Ginsburg and his colleagues (1977), who noted the relative influence of the head, deputy and year heads, as against that of the 'subject adviser', in middle schools, and commented that innovatory schools provided for teachers 'considerable ambiguity and confusion as to the most appropriate way to perform their role'. The wide spread of responsibilities also exists in other schools, as studies by Bornett (1980), Ginsburg et al (1977) and Blyth and Derricott (1977) have shown about middle school teachers and Rodgers et al (1983) have shown amongst postholders in primary schools.

Thus, in an indirect way, the analysis of the postholder's role offered in the chapter is congruent with other studies, even though direct empirical examination of the role of postholders in curriculum development has been made only rarely. Where it has, as in Donoughue et al (1981) and Goodacre and Donoughue (1983), the picture of conflict and uncertainty is supported. It follows that the ambiguities and uncertainties identified are not exclusive to the schools studied, but are probably typical of general teaching roles in primary and middle schools. Indeed, it is highly likely that school-based curriculum development simply focuses in a specific and palpable way conflicts and dilemmas inherent in contemporary teaching generally. The conflicts are, so to speak, particularly sharp symptoms of a general condition.

It would be wrong, however, to leave an impression of curriculum postholders as permanently and unmitigatedly angst-ridden individuals, poised ambivalently between the contradictory demands of curriculum renewal, class teaching and collegial goodwill. Although such conflict has been identified in the postholder's role, the term 'conflict' is itself a term to which sociologists have perhaps too ready recourse. There was potential conflict in school-based curriculum development, and postholders bore the brunt of the ambiguity, dilemma and uncertainty. The ambiguities were not personal or professional defects: they arose from the ambiguity of the curriculum development enterprise itself, and from the uncertain role relationships built into the schools, shored up by both the conventional wisdom and the intellectual isolation of the primary school staffrooms. This is not the same thing, however, as saying that postholders were unable to promote curriculum development because of the role conflict, or that where it was promoted it had little impact. It is to say that the task of school-based development was difficult, stressful, and had little in the way of tangible or immediate measures of success, other than the intrinsic sense of achievement. Despite the difficulties, the case studies revealed the postholders making active attempts, in less than ideal contexts, to renew the curriculum in the schools, mostly in a participatory style. All these attempts were perceived as effective by the headteachers, the postholders and the participant teachers, although in varying degrees. Apparently it was possible for the postholders simultaneously to promote such curriculum renewal and to tolerate the ambiguity and conflict that it brought to the surface.

5

Evaluating School-based Curriculum Development

APPROACHES TO EVALUATION OF THE CURRICULUM

Evaluation is like speaking prose; teachers do it all the time, even though with different degrees of self-conscious effort. When a group of teachers involved in a curriculum innovation meet informally and briefly over coffee at break and chat about 'how it's going', they are practising evaluation as surely, if not as systematically, as if they were administering questionnaires to each other or standardised tests to the pupils. As with classroom teaching, curriculum development is shot through with evaluative activity, simply because evaluation is concerned with the exercise of professional judgement about the curriculum by teachers. Davis (1980) saw it as 'the process of delineating, obtaining and providing information useful for making decisions and judgements' and thus emphasised the idea that curriculum evaluation is a means to a particular end, a method of servicing the exercise of professional judgement. The main point at issue here is what forms evaluation of the curriculum might take.

There is a distinction between measurement and evaluation. Measuring pupils' learning or 'curriculum outcomes' by administering tests may be part of evaluation, but evaluation is a process that comprises many other activities. This is particularly true where evaluation is concerned with process, in this case the process by which teachers work together to improve the quality of the curriculum as experienced by pupils. Parlett (1974) has suggested that evaluation of curriculum innovation should aim to portray a fuller picture than may be acquired by measurement techniques as commonly understood:

> It should set out not to 'test' so much as to 'understand and document' an innovation —
> examining its background, with its organisation, its practices and its problems, in addition to
> its outcomes . . . It should provide for all concerned with the curriculum or programme, as
> well as for outsiders, an informed and accurate description of the operation of the scheme,
> summaries of the various points of view expressed by those associated with it, and a detailed

historical-type account of the innovation over time — its teething troubles, success stories and the improvements devised.

A good example of this approach is provided by Evans and Groarke (1975). They described a stage-by-stage evaluation of their language programme, including consideration of school climate, aims of the programme, appraisal of current practice in the school, testing of pupils' speech performance, and the development and trial of some language materials. It is fairly difficult to separate, in the authors' account, development from evaluation, since they appear to have been very much integrated. However, evaluation included not only the testing of pupils, but also formal and informal staff discussions, reading of selected books, appraisal of classroom practices, exploration of disagreements between staff, the development of a 'portfolio' of the overall programme itself, and an attempt to explain the differential levels of participation in the programme by the teachers. To have restricted evaluation of the programme to the measurement of pupils' speech performance would have been rather like judging a marriage by the number of children conceived in it: a concentration upon products which ignores the (often more interesting) processes, contexts and relationships involved.

It is common, following Scriven (1967), to make a distinction between 'formative' and 'summative' evaluation. Formative evaluation is carried out in the process of teaching, so that evaluation can feed back quickly into the activities of teaching, and thus influence learning for the better. When a teacher watches a pupil learning how to make a coil pot, for example, and sees him pressing too hard on the coil and distorting the final shape, she will show him what he is doing wrong (evaluate his learning) and help him improve his technique in the process *before* he completes the pot. At the risk of appearing in *Private Eye*, we might say that formative evaluation is an ongoing evaluation situation. Summative evaluation is conducted at the end of a learning sequence to indicate how effectively a pupil has learned. It tends to be too late to affect the quality of the particular piece of learning, although in theory it can be used to improve teaching the same skill or knowledge to other pupils, or to influence a subsequent learning task by the same pupil. A mark and written comment on a piece of a child's personal or creative writing is of this kind. Thus the difference between the two is not merely their timing, but also their purpose. Given the process-orientation of school-based change, there is likely to be an emphasis on formative approaches.

Another common distinction concerns style and underlying values; it is between 'illuminative' or 'interpretive' evaluation and 'objective' or 'scientific' evaluation. Illuminative evaluation, according to one of the inventors of the term, Hamilton (1976), is a style relying on an evaluator *working with* a curriculum-development team in order to open out the development to intelligent criticism and appraisal. This style is not restricted to any initial objectives that a development has because, recognising curriculum development as a dynamic and evolving process, it provides a commentary on the development as it is being processed. Therefore it often points out unintended consequences of a development, or contradictions within the theory and practice of a project. Above all it stresses the importance of collecting a plurality of judgements, not a single form of it — of obtaining and recording a variety of (relatively subjective) views of a curriculum development rather than presenting one apparently objective view of it. The best-known illustration of this approach is perhaps the case study by Shipman, Jenkins and Bolam (1974), who evaluated the Keele Integrated Studies Project in this way.

Objective evaluation relies more upon pre-stated objectives and a scientific or technical approach to evaluation, often using pre-existing 'tests' of attainment to obtain measures of the impact of curriculum change. Thus, when a teacher adopts a new mathematics scheme and uses, for example, the appropriate Richmond tests to measure the pupils' progress in mathematics, she or he is, implicitly at least, using an 'objective' evaluation style. Parlett and Hamilton (1972) have likened the objective approach to agricultural experiments to compare two varieties of compost:

> Students — rather like plant crops — are given pre-tests (the seedlings are weighed or measured) and then submitted to different experiences (treatment conditions). Subsequently after a period of time their attainment (growth or yield) is measured to indicate the relative efficiency of the methods (fertilisers) used.

There are problems with both objective approaches and subjective ones. The former tend to be too technically sophisticated for widespread, and too time-consuming for routine, use. Shipman (1983) quotes the fact that the statistical model upon which testing for the national monitoring of attainment by the APU was based was itself the subject of an academic dispute of considerable sophistication, so that the DES had to seek further external advice about its technical suitability. If the experts disagree, says Shipman, how can normal teachers be expected to judge the suitability of apparently objective tests? A further problem is that 'objective' tests are not absolutely objective in the sense that they are culturally impartial, or that they never become outdated, or that they cannot be misused. Such tests, therefore, should inform professional judgement, not become a substitute for it.

Subjective methods also lead to difficulties. They lack technical reliability and validity, and can encourage uncritical and self-congratulatory approval. In addition, a subjective approach often takes the form of staff discussion, and discussion of this kind is open to domination by senior staff, as in the case quoted by Hargreaves (1980). Suppression of truths, rather than their illumination, may follow such an approach. For this reason, subjective approaches to evaluation should always involve a commitment to collect a plurality of views, in order to provide some protection against the emergence of one apparently consensual view that is in reality the view of only the most articulate, the most informed or the most powerful staff members.

Thus evaluation of curriculum development has to be eclectic; it is not a matter of plumping for a single approach to cover all purposes, so much as a matter of selecting approaches that suit a school's purposes. Amongst primary teachers in general there is great faith (perhaps too much, according to Levy and Goldstein (1984)) placed in objective approaches to evaluation, which are, however, infrequently used: the common and routine sharing of opinions and judgements with colleagues, which is very widespread, is not highly respected, and often not even recognised, as an evaluative activity. This is not an entirely sensible, or indeed professional, attitude to evaluation. Evaluation is not essentially either objective or subjective, but is the exercise of professional judgement in the light of *all* the available kinds of evidence, both objective and subjective and everything in between. For example, if a school has adopted a new mathematics scheme, evaluation of its adoption could include consideration of the results of a standardised test of mathematics attainment, judgements about the level of interest and involvement shown by pupils, and an impression gained from the pupils themselves and from parents. In addition, discussion might be held with colleagues in another school using the scheme, and perhaps with a local-authority adviser, in order to get a view from someone knowledgeable but not directly involved.

THE EVALUATION OF SCHOOL-BASED CURRICULUM DEVELOPMENT

In respect of evaluation of school-based curriculum development, the problems outlined above can be seen by considering recommendations from two authoritative sources, one from OECD/CERI (1979), stressing scientific objectivity as the only valuable approach, the other by Shipman (1983), suggesting starting with teachers' intuitive professional judgements and using them in a more systematic way.

The OECD study eschewed the use of teachers' intuition, and advocated scientific measurement techniques, with rigorous controls, as the dominant approach.

> Let us begin by saying what evaluation is *not*. For example, suppose that a change has been made in a school and that at an end of term staff meeting all the teachers agree that they are happy with it. This is not evaluation: it is too subjective . . . In considering evaluation, we should be thinking along two lines; first how can we show objectively that things have moved in the intended direction? And second, how can we demonstrate that these effects are due to school based curriculum development and not to other influences?

After acknowledging the difficulty in achieving this counsel of perfection, the OECD report advocates:

(a)   building in measurable objectives at the beginning of a development;
(b)   the use of control groups of pupils and statistical tests of significance;
(c)   the setting up of 'evaluation teams' independent of the development group;
(d)   the use of attainment tests and attitude scales;
(e)   an evaluation scheme to sample the long-term, as well as the short-term, impact.

Amongst this array of propositions for scientific evaluation as *the* way to appraise school-based development, the report notes that 'it is important that teachers should not get discouraged by the difficulties' involved in carrying out this kind of evaluation.

For busy primary school staff this kind of proposition looks exceedingly impracticable, if only for the reason that evaluation would take more time, energy and expertise than the development of the curriculum itself. The tail would wag the dog. The construction of measurable objectives for, say, consistency in the teaching of language skills is extremely time-consuming; 'technical' research skills are not normally available among the staff, and pupils often cannot, for practical or ethical reasons, be treated as control groups. The school staff is often too small to permit an independent evaluation team, useful though the idea is; and long-term monitoring of impact could only be entered into at the cost of further curriculum development.

Nor is it entirely sensible to dismiss the fact that all the staff are 'happy' with a development. Unalloyed ecstasy is rare enough in the staffroom, especially if it arises from curriculum development. If it is authentic unanimity, it does suggest a startlingly successful innovation. But in any case, the issue is not the happiness of the staff, but the reasons for it: the accounts they are able to provide of how an innovation has worked out, in what ways and for what reasons they judge it to be an improvement on previous practice. To dismiss these accounts, if they have been elaborated in staff meetings and subjected to the professional scrutiny of peers, as teachers being 'happy' with things, is to devalue the exercise of professional judgement. To propose as the only worthwhile alternative a sophisticated, but cumbersome, scientistic methodology is to encourage teachers to opt out of the evaluation enterprise altogether.

The approach recommended by Shipman contrasts with the OECD study. According to him, much of the routine activity engaged in by teachers, both in their classrooms and in their school-wide discussion groups, is in itself evaluative. What is needed, therefore, is to make these activities rather more systematic, and in particular to make the subjective and intuitive judgements of individual teachers subject to the judgements of other professionals — colleagues in school and in other schools, advisers and others. Where appropriate, these judgements should be informed by 'scientific' test results. He offers a medical analogy: a doctor's judgement will be informed by tests of one sort or another — urine samples, temperature measurements — but also by reference to the patient's case history and symptoms reported by the patient, and by a second opinion sought from another doctor.

From the point of view of in-school curriculum development, Shipman's analogy is not perfect, partly because doctors normally work on their own and only exceptionally consult colleagues, whereas a teacher as curriculum developer is normally working as a member of a staff group and only exceptionally on his or her own. Secondly, Shipman's approach seems to be based on an assumption that school staff will move to consensus in most cases, and thus underestimates the potential for conflict. The likelihood of unresolvable differences in professional judgement is much greater in the practice of schooling than in the practice of medicine. Nevertheless, it offers a more practicable approach precisely because it incorporates what teachers already do anyway, and it demystifies evaluation by giving recognition to judgements based on professional experience and collegial accountability. This approach seems more suitable for an activity which is essentially a process in which colleagues co-operatively plan, implement and evaluate their attempts to improve the curriculum in their schools.

The practice of evaluation in ten school-based curricular developments

At this stage it is useful to return to the inquiry schools in order to analyse the practice of evaluation in their curriculum development programmes. Brief narrative summaries of evaluation practice in each case study are offered, followed by an analysis of their strengths and weaknesses in the light of the preceding discussion of approaches to evaluation.

Case study A: Revising a social studies scheme of work

1. *Review* of existing scheme by the postholder and working group of staff. They

identified six problems with the current scheme, which became the criteria for judging the new scheme. These six were:

(a)   lack of progression in content;
(b)   repetition of content;
(c)   imbalance of work between traditional curriculum areas;
(d)   no consideration of the systematic development of skills;
(e)   no effective record-keeping;
(f)   inefficient use of resources.

2. *Appraisal* of the 'conceptual structure' of the working group's proposed new scheme by a whole teaching staff meeting.
3. *Appraisal* of 'minimum content' by a series of meetings by teachers within each year group.
4. *Review and discussion* of possible materials on an in-service course by postholder.
5. *Discussion and comment* on the scheme by staff from the receiving secondary school and the neighbouring primary school.

Case study B

A group of teachers implemented a team teaching programme designed to enable the pupils in a year group to be taught in relatively small groups for part of the week.

1. *A review* of previous practice and resource availability was undertaken by the head and the postholder.
2. The four staff involved developed an almost archetypal *formative evaluation*. In the course of the first year, they met regularly to appraise the working of the new arrangements and to take account of these appraisals in planning the next units of work in detail. In addition, at the end of the year they drew up some conclusions about the arrangements overall and some suggestions for modifications for the following year. The issues raised included:
   (a)   the tendency for the routine demands of materials preparation, day-to-day teaching, etc. to obscure the overall aims and intentions of the team arrangement;
   (b)   the tendency of the common approach to teaching to reduce the flexibility inherent in normal class teaching;
   (c)   the tendency of the common pacing of teaching and learning to reduce the opportunity for teachers to cater for individual needs, especially of those children finding difficulties in the work;
   (d)   the extent to which study skills such as note-making should be incorporated into the programme;
   (e)   the impact of the grouping arrangement on the pupils' sense of belonging to an identifiable class group.

Case study C

A working group of staff had developed a school-wide language policy which had been adopted by the school staff as a whole.

1. *Review* by the head and postholder of existing practice led them to define a need for a school-wide policy in language.
2. *Appraisal of draft proposals from the language co-ordinator* by the working group of teachers, who met to discuss and amend the drafts of one section of the policy proposal at each meeting.
3. *Appraisal by the whole staff meeting of the overall language policy produced by the working group*.
4. *Monitoring of the implementation of the policy* throughout the school by the postholder, and subsequently by the head.

Case study D

A staff group followed an in-school programme examining the language they used in the routine classroom assignments they set for pupils. The group was following what was in one sense almost entirely a self-evaluation programme, in which each teacher appraised her own and her colleagues' language use in selected classroom activities. The programme included:

1. *Appraisal of individual teachers' classroom practice* by the working group.
2. *Completion of evaluation schedules* by members of the working group.
3. *Appraisal of the overall programme and its implications for practice and policy in the school* by the working group.
4. *Commentary on the programme* by a visiting teacher who had led a similar programme in her own school.
5. *Commentary* on the programme by an LEA adviser.

Case study E

A group of staff and LEA advisers planned and implemented an enrichment experience for all pupils in a year group.

1. *Review by* the headteacher of the curriculum provision in the light of the perceived needs of able children. Following this it was decided that an enrichment experience was required.
2. The programme was planned in *consultation* with an external 'expert' from the neighbouring university, who advised against providing a programme restricted to the very able pupils. Criteria were identified for evaluating it.
3. *The head evaluated* the impact of the programme by questionnaire to staff and pupils who participated in it.

Case study F

A scheme for science was revised and implemented throughout the school, and its operation was evaluated at the end of the year in a whole staff meeting.

1. *Appraisal of existing practice* carried out by the headteacher, concluding with the judgement that a more structured approach throughout the school was desirable.
2. *Appraisal of first draft of the scheme of work* by head, deputy, postholder and LEA adviser.
3. *Appraisal of aims and structure of the scheme* by whole staff group.
4. *Appraisal of basic approaches* in the scheme by first-school teachers and separately, by junior/middle-school teachers.
5. *Appraisal of the implementation of the scheme* by whole staff meeting after the first year of operation. This included commentary on the value of materials prepared by the postholder and on problems of continuity, of excessive prescription of content and of integration with other curriculum areas. In addition, the restricted opportunities for the postholder to work alongside other teachers and the implicit gender differentiation of the science programme were posed as problems to be examined. Some specific improvements in resources, TV programmes, etc. for the following year were proposed.

Case study G: Incorporating craft design and technology into work in art/craft through the school

1. *Review* of the existing art/craft work by the postholder and deputy head, who concluded that the traditional work in the school, though of good standard, required development towards CDT.
2. *Postholder revised* scheme of work and submitted it to the first- and second-year teachers and to the third-and fourth-year teachers separately for their comments.

Case study H: Development of a school-wide scheme in environmental studies

1. *Appraisal of existing topic work* undertaken by the postholder at the head's suggestion. She concluded that, despite some good work in individual classes, overall there was a lack of coherence, and little clear progression, especially in respect of historical and geographical skills.
2. *Appraisal of her revised scheme* was carried out by the whole staff. This appraisal included some disquiet about the extent to which teacher autonomy was reduced.
3. *Evaluation of the implementation of the scheme* carried out by the postholder, mainly by judgement of the quality of work produced by the children, especially in observation and recording of first-hand experience, and the extent of their use of reference material.

Case study I: Maintaining development in art/craft throughout the school

The art/craft postholder was used as a specialist teacher, and allocated time in school for working alongside other teachers and *monitoring the quality of the work throughout the school*, including commenting on the quality of work throughout the school, advising colleagues on sequence and progression in skills, and encouraging improvement in display throughout the school.

Case study J: Maintaining a multicultural approach to music

1. *The postholder, with advice from a local-authority adviser, decided* it would be desirable to incorporate steel-band playing into the traditional music activities in the curriculum.
2. *The postholder monitored* the development and maintains it now that it has been accepted into the routine activities of the school. She evaluated it favourably by its impact on the school life generally, by its contribution to the music education of all pupils, and by its cultural value.

ANALYSIS

A composite picture

The variety and complexity of evaluative activities summarised above suggest that evaluation of school-based curriculum development occurred in an extremely ad hoc way, tied down to the particular programme and the particular context. And in one sense this is true: the teachers in these schools were operating mainly without an explicit theory of evaluation, and with a partial model of what forms of evaluation should be applied to their programme. It is possible, however, to provide a composite picture of evaluation as practised in these schools, to illustrate the kind of information provided by evaluation activities at different stages in development. The composite picture has four elements — *review, planning, implementation and adoption* — which can be thought of as relating to stages in the curriculum development process.

1. *Review*. Appraisal of existing practice within the particular curriculum area through-out the school *to provide information* about problems with the existing practice in comparison with recommendations in 'official' documents, etc., and the criteria by which change should be judged.
2. *Planning*. Scrutiny of proposal for change by staff and others *to provide information* on its professional suitability and on perceptions of its appropriateness, resource needs, etc.
3. *Implementation*. Assessment of the innovation in action, including an appropriate range of evaluative techniques, *to provide information* about whether, and with what modifications, it should be adopted into the school curriculum.
4. *Adoption*. Monitoring of the adoption of the curriculum change as it operates in the routine contexts of the school *to provide information* about problems involved in maintaining it.

Two comments about this model should be made. First, although there appears to be a linear sequence in the model, in practice evaluation could become cyclical, with the fourth element — monitoring of an adopted or routinised innovation — becoming over time a version of the first, since it would become concerned with reviewing existing practice. Thus the dominant, though not exclusive, approach is formative.

Secondly, the purpose of the model is to summarise essential features of practice, in order to examine strengths and defects, which are discussed below under two main headings *evaluative imbalance* and *evaluative audiences*. The discussion explores the idea that in practice evaluation of school-based development was lacking in balance and restricted in range.

Evaluative imbalance

What emerged in the evaluation practice of these schools was its tendency to imbalance: to concentrate evaluation on one particular phase of a development rather than spreading it across the development overall. In Case study D, almost the entire evaluative effort was on the first element — a collective examination of the classroom practices of teachers with respect to their own language use in pupil assignments — with a minimal intention to evaluate changes seen as desirable following the review. Thus at the end of the programme, in discussions about whether or not it should be extended to examine the consequent changes in classroom practice, the teachers recognised the need to evaluate further, but gave it relatively low priority:

> I think it's good to finish now, and perhaps next term we should get together say in the fourth or fifth week of term to see what difference it's made to how we teach, but that's all.

In contrast, in Case study C it was the review stage that was carried out very briefly, by the head coming to a decision that a new school policy was necessary:

> In consultation with the subject leader for Language, I decided which method would be best in tackling the problem of developing a language policy. Finite areas were identified, such as creative writing, 'mechanical English' etc., and a group of five staff agreed to act as a working party to discuss weekly each subject in turn.

Perhaps an extreme example was Case study J, where the development in music involved the incorporation of a West Indian musical tradition (steel bands) into a more traditional scheme of work, without any review of existing practice. The initiative arose from the postholder's belief, encouraged by a local-authority adviser, that it would be worth while, given the multicultural nature of the school's intake. The 'review', so to speak, was implicit and private rather than explicit and public.

In Case study F sustained evaluative effort occurred during the implementation stage, with an extended and wide-ranging staff meeting called to evaluate the operation of the science programme. (The case study forms the basis of Chapter 9.) This meeting raised issues for modifying the scheme, and the head and postholder were made aware of the need to monitor the working of the scheme in the following year. However, they were faced with a dilemma over priorities. The staff had made suggestions about what they felt they needed in the way of practical resource packs, more classroom-focused checklists for topics, rationalisation of television programmes, and so on. There was not enough time both to work at making these available and to monitor the programme systematically, especially as this included being freed to work alongside other teachers. Given the stated priorities of the staff, monitoring was given lower priority in practice, however reluctantly.

This kind of imbalance is to some extent inevitable, simply because unique programmes have unique emphases. There could be no ideal evaluative balancing act by which all the development phases had equal amounts of time and energy devoted to them. But two improvements seem to be called for if these programmes were at all typical. One concerns the first stage, the review element, and the other the fourth stage, the adoption element. At the review stage, there is the need to make *explicit* the criteria by which a programme is to be judged. At the adoption stage, priority needs to be given to more effective *monitoring* of a development's progress once it has been adopted.

Explicit criteria for evaluation

Most of the developments had some kind of review of existing practice, even though, as has been illustrated, it varied from the intensive to the cursory. None the less, it was only in two cases, Case studies A and E, that the staff made explicit and public the criteria by which innovation could be evaluated at a later stage. In the former this was done by the staff group producing a list of the problems they perceived in the existing practice; this was a simple but useful kind of checklist or *aide-mémoire* against which the implementation of the innovation could be set. In the latter, four criteria were identified and used in a questionnaire. In two other cases, the existing practice was perceived as lacking 'structure', 'progression' or 'coherence', in a general sense, but the criteria by which enhanced structure would be identified and evaluated in a revised scheme of work were not elaborated. In the other cases where the review was undertaken there was little attempt to identify the criteria by which the development overall could be judged; evaluation at this stage tended to take the form of the head and the postholder making a judgement that was undisciplined by the views of colleagues, and relatively inexplicit in terms of criteria.

There are three convincing reasons why teachers engaged in school-based development should make explicit, at an initial stage in such a development, the criteria for its evaluation. First, they and their colleagues are going to be investing considerable energy and time in the programme and, as Chapters 3 and 4 illustrated, time and energy are at a premium. It is imperative for such teachers to have agreed ways of judging the extent to which they have spent their time effectively. A second reason is that most evaluation of school-based programmes relies upon the collection and sharing of relatively subjective judgements. The initial and explicit identification of criteria helps to 'objectify' such judgements; it provides a set of reference points outside the individual teacher against which subjective judgement may be tested. This is especially important when conflicting judgements emerge, as they inevitably do. A third value of objectified criteria is in relation to 'outsiders' to whom teachers may wish, or be required, to give an account of their development programme. These outsiders may be, and tend increasingly to be, governors, parents, teachers in other schools, local-authority advisers, etc., and identifying criteria will help in communicating a programme's effectiveness to them.

The production of criteria, which might commonly take the form of a relatively simple checklist such as those produced in the Primary Survey need not be time-consuming, but would substantially extend the value of what is currently done by way of a review of practice, by making it part of a more systematic and public evaluation procedure. A variety of sources for the development of externally referenced criteria now exist, and this issue is discussed later in this chapter.

Monitoring progress

At the other end of the development programme, when it has been adopted within the school, there appear to be two main problems with evaluation. The first is that generally it does not appear to be given high priority. Teachers in most of the case study schools simply did not have the time to continue the evaluation of the programme in a systematic or collective manner, having devoted much energy and time at the stages of planning and implementing the change. The second problem was to do with the internal politics of primary schools. In most schools the monitoring of the programme by the postholders was fraught with difficulties associated with their role relationship with class teachers, as we have seen in Chapter 4, and this may explain why monitoring of the adoption of the innovation was carried out in only three schools, and in one of these was taken over by the head, despite time having been allocated to the postholder for this purpose. There is no easy solution here because of the power of the belief in teachers' classroom autonomy amongst primary teachers.

However, there was an ideological mismatch in the programmes. Monitoring meant in practice *individual* appraisal by the postholder. But 'monitoring' could be defined in more collaborative terms than merely the head or the postholder observing the innovation in classrooms: it could also include the collection and sharing of all the teachers' experience of the innovation, in much the same way as evaluation of the implementation stage. The problems in the case study schools may well have derived not so much from teachers' unwillingness to evaluate adopted programmes so much as from the mismatch between value assumptions operating in the processes of the *collective style of development* (i.e. planning and implementation stage) and those of the *individualistic style of the post-development evaluation*. A team of teachers who have been working together to produce and implement a plan for improving the curriculum through their school may take unkindly to an evaluation process which appears to remove responsibility for monitoring the programme from the collectivity and to allocate it to the individual, whether postholder or headteacher. It implies inspection by superiors of subordinates and runs counter to the values of collaboration upon which the development of the programmes was predicated.

Evaluative audiences

A second issue arising from the evaluation practices in the schools is what may be termed 'evaluative audiences'. It has already been argued that the exercise of professional judgement, because it is relatively subjective, needs to be tempered by being shared with other professionals. One way of reducing the tendency of subjective judgement to become unself-critical is to build into evaluation procedures a commitment to collecting judgements from a range of perspectives, from a range of people associated with a development; that is, to submit the development to a variety of evaluative audiences.

There was considerable variation in the extent to which a development was offered for evaluation to a range of audiences, even when all four stages identified earlier are considered together. The audiences may be thought of as those within school and those outside it. Within the school were the head and the postholder, the working group of staff developing the programme, a specified staff group with particular interests (for example year-group leaders, or all the infant teachers), and the whole staff group. Outside the school were teachers in liaison schools, teachers who had had experience with a similar development in their own schools, local-authority advisory staff, and university or college lecturers.

Perhaps it is worth drawing attention to the fact that no programme was offered to governors, parents or other such external groups, a fact suggesting that school-based curriculum development in practice seems to run counter to the general pressure in education for greater community involvement.

The range of evaluative audiences in each development can be seen from Table 5.1.

Table 5.1 *Evaluative audience in each case study*

| | Case study | | | | | | | | | | Frequency as audience |
	A	*B*	*C*	*D*	*E*	*F*	*G*	*H*	*I*	*J*	
Head and/or postholder	x	x	x	x	x	x	x	x	x	x	10
Working group of staff	x	x	x	x	x	x					6
Specified staff group (e.g. year leaders, year group)	x			x		x	x				4
Whole staff group	x		x	x		x		x			5
Teachers in liaison schools	x										1
Teachers experienced in similar programmes					x						1
LEA advisers					x	x	x				3
University/college lecturers	x				x	x					3
Number of audiences in each case study	6	2	3	7	4	5	2	2	1	1	

An initial point needs stressing. The table provides only a crude index of evaluative range. Direct quantitative comparison between developments is not justified because in some developments some audience categories were not appropriate. (For example, in Case study B, the only teachers directly involved were the team of four staff and the head; there would have been no point in an evaluation exercise with other staff, whose work was unaffected by the team-teaching innovation restricted to the fourth year.) Thus the variation between developments is partly a product of the nature of any particular development.

However, it is the case that in two developments (both using teachers as specialists) the only evaluators were the postholders and heads, that teachers from other schools were involved in only two developments, that in five of the ten cases no more than two audiences were involved, and that six programmes used no 'external' audience. On the face of it, more could have been done to provide greater plurality of perspectives on the effectiveness of the developments. This comment has more point when it is considered that no development involved 'objective' testing, and only two used a pre-specified set of criteria for judgement. The heavy reliance on subjective evaluation restricted to very few professional audiences, sometimes only the development leaders, suggests a need for schools to find ways to 'objectify' their evaluation procedures more systematically.

In case studies A and E two characteristics stand out: the developments were planned to include evaluation *from the outset* and to build into it views from groups inside and outside the school. The postholder in Case study A made the point explicitly in reference to the review stage of the programme, where one of the criteria for evaluation of the programme had been that it should lead to 'the development of skills in a systematic way'.

A starting point had been provided on an in-service course on the Schools Council History, Geography and Social Sciences 8–13 project, where progression in skills had been discussed.

> We (the working group) felt though that we should be more specific about the skills we were aiming at with our children. A list of skills was drawn up and all staff were invited to circle those they thought it reasonable to introduce during, say, the second year of the school . . . Staff were also invited to add to the list or delete skills they thought inappropriate . . . All views were drawn together and put up for discussion in a staff meeting. After consolidation within the school the scheme was discussed at meetings between schools, both the receiving secondary school and the other primary schools who feed into it.

This programme was one in which planning, implementation and evaluation were integrated in a natural way. A thread of evaluation ran through the texture of the whole development exercise. But the linking of planning and evaluation did not obscure the need to collect a range of judgements from those associated with, or affected by, the implementation of the programme, and to employ explicit criteria for judging the development from the start. It is the latter point that needs elaboration, for drawing on a range of evaluative perspectives need not imply only *people*. There are published sources also.

Externally referenced sources of criteria

One feature that stands out in the schools' approaches to evaluation is the absence of reference to external checklists, guidelines and other written forms of criteria for evaluating aspects of school life in general, as well as the curriculum in particular. Many local authorities have produced such guides, following the example set by the Inner London Education Authority's (1977) *Keeping the School Under Review*. One such document, for example, published by the Metropolitan Borough of Solihull Education Committee (1980), was produced by a working party of teachers and local-authority advisers. It contains a comprehensive, if somewhat daunting, array of items, comprising a list of statements requiring written answers, and kcy questions designed as thought-provoking items for staff reflection and discussion. The document, which was distributed free to all schools in the authority, includes items on management and organisation, the curriculum and relationships, and the preamble makes clear that it could serve a variety of purposes.

The following 'key' questions, referring to the planning, implementing and evaluating of the curriculum, serve to illustrate the approach:

41. When are checks made on the implementation of agreed schemes of work?
42. When are checks made on the interpretation of agreed schemes of work?
43. IIow arc checks made on the implementation of agreed schemes of work?
44. How are checks made on the interpretation of agreed schemes of work?
45. By whom are checks made on the implementation of agreed schemes of work?
46. By whom are checks made on the interpretation of agreed schemes of work?
47. Do schemes of work allow for continuity from one year's work to the next?
48. Do schemes of work preclude repetitive overlap from one year's work to the next?
49. Is there opportunity for assessment of 'match' in schemes of work?
50. How is the assessment of 'match' achieved —
    a. through experience of headteacher
    b. through experience of holder of post of special responsibility
    c. through experience of class teacher
    d. according to age and ability of children
    e. by talking with children
    f. by observation of children and their work
    g. by book collections and other resources
    h. by any other methods?
51. What assistance is provided by the following to enable teachers to implement and interpret the school's schemes of work —
    a. Head teacher
    b. holder of post of special responsibility
    c. other colleagues within school
    d. colleagues in other schools
    e. LEA inspectorate
    f. support services (e.g. remedial service)
    g. professional literature
    h. in-service courses —
        school-based
        LEA based
        National?

Likewise, at national level, the reports by the Assessment and Performance Unit and HMI's *Primary Education in England* (DES 1978a) have also been using and publishing checklists for evaluating aspects of the curriculum. The latter provided in its appendices checklists used by the inspectors to appraise the quality of work in the major curriculum areas. For example, in respect of language and literacy the following items were used about 'Reading' (Annex B, p. 212):

Reading
  8 Evidence, where appropriate, that children's own speech is used to provide early reading material.

9 Evidence that the children's own writing is used as part of their early reading material.
10 The emphasis given to reading practice with main reading schemes and supplementary readers.
11 The emphasis given to the reading of fiction and non-fiction related to curricular work and other reading not related to curricular work.
12 The emphasis on the use of extended reading skills and children's comments on the material read.
13 The emphasis on the selection of books by the children themselves.
14 Evidence that children learn to turn readily and naturally to books for pleasure and that they use books with ease and confidence as a source of information.
15 Evidence that the children read poetry and that some of the children discuss books at more than a superficial level.

These examples have been quoted to illustrate two points. First, they represent criteria statements that derive from professional experience (teachers, advisers, inspectors), but are none the less 'external' to an individual school or teacher. They are therefore particularly appropriate as a basis for constraining subjectivity in evaluation, even though they are not technically 'objective'. Second, and irrespective of the original intentions of their producers, these kinds of checklist provide a rich source of material which teachers can exploit for evaluation, but which are currently under-used to the point of neglect.

The important thing from a professional viewpoint is that teachers should *use* such material, rather than passively accept it. Three obvious uses are:

(a)   to take selected items, unaltered, where the original is considered appropriate for a school's purpose;
(b)   to adapt existing items to suit the school's purposes;
(c)   to use existing items as models for developing school-specific checklists.

In all three uses the published checklists or guidelines both save teachers' time (they do not have to re-invent the evaluative wheel every time they develop the curriculum) and provide an externally derived reference for teachers. Thus, not only do they provide a useful check on undue teacher subjectivity, but they are especially helpful if a curriculum development programme is being reported to, or discussed with, outsiders to the programme, for example advisers, governors or parents. It would illustrate clearly and convincingly that the development and its evaluation had proceeded by taking account of authoritative professional judgements and incorporating them where appropriate into the school's criteria for evaluation. More widespread use of such material would not resolve all the problems of evaluation, for, as Alexander (1984, p. 200) shows, there are still issues of value, and of the control of the evaluation process within schools, but it would make more likely an improvement in evaluation standards without simultaneously making excessive demands on teacher time.

6

Supporting School-based Curriculum Development

PROFESSIONAL SOLIDARITY

Previous chapters have illustrated the complexity and strain in the postholder's role, but it was only part of the picture. Postholders also received advice, help and support from a number of sources, including colleagues, their headteachers, and a variety of people outside the school. The role of the headteacher was seen as especially crucial, and therefore most attention will be focused upon it in this chapter. But a preliminary point concerns the kind of support experienced simply from the groups of colleagues with whom the postholders were working.

Working together in fairly small staff groups, actively participating in the process of hammering out a through-school policy, or of scrutinising the working of a new approach to an aspect of the curriculum, produced its own reward: the spin-off of intrinsic collective satisfaction. One of the postholders put it in the following way:

> It has been useful, even though it's been very hard work, and I did feel like giving up once or twice because there was so much to do. But the nice thing was that everyone did — or nearly everyone — what they promised to do. They did their observation and filled in the evaluation schedule, and turned up to the discussion sessions. Even when things were very hectic we had eight people there, and that was the lowest it got to — and mostly it was the whole ten who started off with the programme . . . I know that it's a slow process, and that we haven't got much concrete change out of it, but working at it together was the most satisfying part of it.

The same feeling was expressed by the postholder in another school, where there had been considerable professional disagreement about how a new course should have been implemented.

> It's been an exciting year, and it's had its frustrations. I even got rather depressed about it once but it's been worth it because of working together on it.

Thus the programmes engendered a kind of professional solidarity amongst their participants, a solidarity supporting the postholders' efforts.

However, warm social feelings, comforting though they are psychologically, are inadequate to sustain curriculum renewal on their own, partly because of their tendency to evaporate after a time if more solid practical support is lacking. In the inquiry schools there were three sources of more palpable support for the postholders: headteachers, the local-authority advisory service, and university/college staff. Of these by far the most significance was attached to the headteachers. The other two, though valued by the postholders, provided one-off, usually ad hoc, advice. The headteachers, on the other hand, were seen as providing the substantial framework, the pervasive school context of values, attitudes and relationships, within which the postholders' initiatives could be encouraged, supported and maintained.

THE ROLE OF THE HEAD

Strategies for support

There was a view amongst postholders and other teachers that the fact that the head had established a 'good atmosphere' in the school was a major factor supporting school-based curriculum development. And it is certainly true that good relationships in a school were regarded as necessary for processes that included teachers discussing each other's professional practice, evaluating policies, giving accounts to colleagues of their own teaching, etc. Without a foundation of good working relationships between the staff involved such enterprises would have collapsed dramatically. For good or ill, headteachers were seen as responsible for creating and maintaining the kind of climate in which curriculum developers could breathe more easily.

However, it was not a case of headteachers wandering benignly round the school with a smile on their face and encouragement on their lips. It is more useful to analyse the headteachers' role in terms of consciously developed *strategies* they used to support school-based curriculum development led by the postholder. Interviews with the heads showed that a number of such strategies were adopted, and they are identified in the following list:

(a) specifying the responsibilities of the post;
(b) delegating responsibility for curriculum development;
(c) recognising opportunities for curriculum development;
(d) providing practical support for an initiative;
(e) occasionally leading an initiative themselves.

Specifying the responsibilities of the post

In terms of strategy for communicating the expectations held of the postholder, four practices were discernible. The difference in these practices were concerned with:

(a) the extent to which expectations were elaborated;
(b) the extent to which expectations were deliberately communicated to the staff.

The four practices are described and illustrated below.

The job specification was elaborated and disseminated to all staff. This strategy involved the head providing a framework of expectations for the postholders in the school which, after staff discussion, became the agreed school policy and was circulated to all staff. An example of such a statement was provided in Chapter 3. The intention of the head was expressed as follows:

> I thought it necessary to provide the job specification for two reasons. First of all, there is the simple matter of communication. People ought to know what is expected of them, and there ought to be as little misunderstanding as possible. Secondly, in primary schools everybody is used to doing everything. If we start to have a little bit of division of labour here, it helps avoid difficulties if we agree about the kind of responsibilities different teachers are expected to take on.

Thus, not only was there a clear specification, but it was also public knowledge.

The job specification was elaborated and diffused to staff. In this approach the job specification was written for a particular purpose and for a particular post. For example, in School 5, a specification was written as part of the 'further details' associated with a vacancy for a Scale 2 post in the school. Thus the postholder knew upon his appointment what expectations the head and governor had of him as a postholder. Other postholders in this school, most of whom had held their posts of responsibility for a substantial period, and many of whom had held them before the appointment of the current headteacher, had no such elaborated specification. In addition, although the responsibilities of the post were known to the staff because the 'further details' of the post were known to them, the specification was not formally circulated as policy to all staff. Expectations for the post were therefore diffused through the staff fairly informally, rather than disseminated formally.

Specification was negotiated and diffused to the staff. A third approach was where the job specification was evolved by the head and the postholder discussing how to conduct a curriculum review. This meant that the head and the postholder worked out their own understanding as a preliminary activity to the curriculum review process itself.

> We decided that Jenny should lead a staff workshop in order to develop a school policy for language. Before I was appointed head here the school had not used curriculum guidelines as much as it might, and I thought that first priority should go to language. In addition to developing the policy in this way, she was to be given time to work alongside staff and monitor the policy.

Since, under this strategy, the specification was unwritten, and the curriculum review was raised in the course of normal staff meetings, there was no guarantee that all teachers had explicit understandings of the postholder's role, or that they shared them.

Job specification was determined privately. In the fourth category the postholders in effect invented their roles for themselves without extensive consultation as they proceeded with their development. In one school the postholder was a part-time music specialist and was able to develop its curriculum relatively independently of the other staff; in the other, the head acted as a postholder for a one-off experiment to enrich the normal curriculum offered in the school over a short, three-week period. The two were thus engaged in the kind of developments where the expectations might need less public elaboration than normal.

It is difficult to know how well the strategies outlined above fit with the little that is known of how responsibilities are understood in primary schools. The Primary Schools Research and Development Group/Schools Council (1983) study at Birmingham University reported that some 75 per cent of 288 postholders in their questionnaire inquiry had been given advice about the nature of their responsibilities informally and 'verbally' and some 70 per cent would have preferred more information regarding their responsibilities. The study also reported the views of 65 headteachers, most of whom considered that postholders were completely or partly responsible to them. Only 20 heads regarded postholders as responsible to the staff as well as to the head. Although the study was not restricted to posts of curricular responsibility as such, it looks as though only a minority of the postholders experienced, and only a minority of the heads adopted, strategies involving elaborated and disseminated job specification. Goodacre (1984) reports teacher ambivalence. Her language postholders apparently distinguished between job *specification* and job *description*; all staff should know what a postholder was doing rather than what she or he was expected to be doing.

Whitaker's (1983) guide for headteachers suggests (pp. 93–4):

> Teachers will only become influential in their specialist role if the head is prepared to give them authority to act, and if other teachers will recognise and accept this . . . Far too often responsibility for mathematics comes down to little more than ordering books and equipment. Until heads are prepared to create conditions in which teachers with responsibility in subject areas are given the authority to make policy as well as executive decisions, there is unlikely to be much improvement in the situation.

For the kind of change recommended by Whitaker to occur in practice, a clearly articulated set of expectations for the postholder is a prerequisite, as is understanding of them by the staff as a whole. Something similar to the first strategy outlined above, i.e. an elaborated specification consciously disseminated to all staff for their consideration, would provide the first step in such a change.

Delegation of responsibility for curriculum development

There is in the mythology of curriculum development the 'charismatic' headteacher who rampages round his or her school enthusing the staff by personal drive and charm. This creature did not emerge in the inquiry schools: on the contrary, the heads in general practised a quiet, low-key style, 'wise but unobtrusive', in Ross's (1960) terms, delegating to the postholder the responsibility for development. It was as though the initiation, implementation and evaluation of curriculum renewal in the area for which the postholder held formal responsibility had to become, and had to be seen to become, her or his responsibility in practice. For this reason the headteachers saw their role as enabling the postholder to take the lead in a development. They did not want to pre-empt the postholder's role by exercising a dominant one themselves. One head put the position in a quite explicit way:

> I try to make every member of staff responsible for something, even the teachers on Scale One. I try to encourage them to feel that they can contribute something to the other staff. Those with special responsibility posts know what is expected of them and know that they will have my support for what they are trying to do. So it would be silly if I gave them responsibility and then took over the running of the working group myself or the staff discussions.

Some measure of the extent of this delegation in the inquiry schools can be seen from the fact that eight of the ten development programmes involved working groups of teachers or staff discussion groups. In six of these the postholder led the groups and chaired all the meetings, and in one the postholder led the small group sessions while the head chaired the full staff meeting. In the remaining development the headteacher was acting as postholder, and therefore chaired the planning sessions.

There were two other reasons voiced by the heads for their delegation, both practical ones. First, the postholder's expertise was seen by the staff and by themselves as superior to that of the head, and they believed that the postholder would make a better job of developing the curriculum:

> She'd been on the OU post-experience course, and she'd done very well on it, and they'd asked her to try out some material for them . . . So she knew what it was all about, she'd got herself up to date . . . I couldn't have done it like she did, nor could the other members of staff — at least not unless we'd gone on the OU course as well.

The second reason was that had the headteachers taken a dominant role in the programmes, their staff might have been reluctant to criticise or comment adversely upon aspects of the programme with which they disagreed:

> We're still at the stage where ordinary teachers are rather too respectful to headteachers . . . If this was seen as my policy, whatever they felt about it, they wouldn't criticise it openly in a staff meeting . . . it may be a shame but it is the way primary school teachers behave, they're respectful in public to their head . . . This way, if I stand back a bit from it, they can feel freer to take part in discussion without worrying about whether they're offending me.

This was, however, a matter of fine judgement. Heads did not simply throw inexperienced postholders in at the deep end and let them sink or swim. In School 3, the head explained that although the postholder had had no previous experience of leading a staff group, she had had experience of being a member of such a group. This was because he had deliberately encouraged policy-making through staff groups over the previous two years.

> It is a bit of a risk, however good she is, but it's less of a risk if the staff are used to working in this way . . . and I wouldn't encourage someone to do it unless I thought they'd be alright.

One head had chaired a staff meeting rather than let the postholder chair it, because it was going to be a complex and difficult meeting for a relatively new, young and inexperienced teacher to handle, even though he had led planning meetings of smaller groups. In the event, as may be seen from the range of questions raised (Chapter 9), the head's judgement was probably correct, in that by chairing the meeting himself he was able to allow the postholder to deal with most of the issues raised, but could control the extent of probing and criticism offered. Similarly, the head in Case study C intervened in the monitoring of the school policy in order to protect the postholder from the charge of 'inspecting' her colleagues' work.

The heads participated in group discussions or staff meetings, but the style of their participation was 'low profile', with relatively little active contribution to discussion. If we look, for example, at Case study D (Chapter 8) we see no intervention in the discussion by the headteacher. When asked how he saw his role he stressed the symbolic importance attached to his presence. He needed to demonstrate the significance he attached to this form of development by giving his own time over to it, even though he did not wish to appear to be running the show. The question also came up in this case, as in most others, of the allocation of official staff meeting time for the curriculum development activity:

> It's important to give official time for this kind of thing not simply so that people can guarantee to be available — they book the staff meetings into their diaries so they know they're not available for, say, games coaching after school that evening. But more important is the fact that by giving official time over to it, you show that you, the head, regard it as important for the school.

Thus the general practice of delegation was tempered by judgement of a particular postholder's strengths. Moreover, the manner of the heads' delegation, by personal involvement in a low-key manner, and by ensuring that the activity of curriculum renewal was officially recognised as important in the professional life of the school, accorded it significance that it would otherwise have lacked. Heads were also thus providing an opportunity for the standing of the postholder among her or his colleagues to be enhanced.

There is scant literature on delegation of responsibility in primary education, possibly because it occurs so rarely. One theme that has emerged is the idea of heads appearing to delegate, but in reality preventing other teachers from appropriating 'their' authority. Coulson (1976) summarised the position thus:

> At present where delegation does occur it is usually of a limited, ad hoc, nature which restricts the occupants of the other supervisory positions in the school to the status of heads' 'aides'. The performance of delegated tasks is frequently accompanied by interference from the head, and deputy heads and holders of posts of responsibility complain that little action is taken on their decision until teachers have sought and obtained the head's endorsement.

There are some alternative reports of heads effecting delegation, such as Johnston and Elliott's (1981) account of the gradual devolution of curricular responsibility in a primary school and Razzell's (1979) brief but glowing account of collective decision-making in his primary school.

The reports, however, tend to polarise possibilities: either the head makes decisions or the general democratic collectivity of the staff does. For this reason, none of the reports, except possibly Johnston's and Elliott's, precisely matches what was happening in the inquiry schools, for delegation was not being made to the whole staff, but to individuals in intermediate positions with identified responsibilities — Scale 2 or 3 postholders for curricular areas. It is from members of this intermediate group that leadership was sought, and to whom authority and responsibility were delegated. It is this kind of teacher, sometimes alarmingly referred to as middle management, more appropriately characterised as the career teacher or the 'extended' professional, with higher-than-normal qualifications and expertise, who might most reasonably be expected to take on in-school development, as Coulson (1976, p. 106) has argued. This seems to have been supported by the teachers involved in the Primary Schools Research and Development Group/Schools Council study (1983), where a view of the desirable relationships between postholder and the head emerged.

> An important theme is the role of the Head Teacher in determining the effectiveness of the teacher 'expert'. It is not an exaggeration to say that the role of the head is crucial . . . The consensus view is that the Head Teacher should demonstrate his respect for the knowledge, skills and enthusiasm of the teacher expert, but is not expected to abdicate his authority in maintaining balance and cohesion. (p. 9)

Recognition of opportunities

There was in five of the developments a clearly intuitive element in that they depended very much upon the head's recognition of the potential worth of the postholder's ideas for development. In School 3, for example, it was the head who realised that an approach from the Open University for the postholder to test some trial materials was also an opportunity for staff development. In School 6 the opportunity arising from the fact that a newly appointed deputy had a record of innovation in CDT in his previous school, allied to an existing interest in CDT on the part of the art/craft postholder, was identified by the head as the basis for development in the school. In School 8 recognition of the potential interest in steel band music, following a visit from a representative of the Commonwealth Institute, was necessary for the development that followed, and so on.

This ability to recognise the potential of what were often accidental, or at least unplanned, beginnings to a development was an important quality in heads, though rarely explicitly acknowledged by postholders. Only two of them realised the significance of the head's early decision to encourage them in this development. One of these said:

> It was Mr Brown (the head) really, at the beginning. I just mentioned to him once that I thought we ought to be making more connections between art and the topic work, and then a couple of days later he suggested that I should start making the links by talking first to June (the social studies postholder) and then to the other third- and fourth-year teachers.

Such initial judgements were not always wise. The head of one school, for example, had two of his staff following an external course in research methods and when they wanted to analyse the role of postholders in the school he thought that it would provide a good chance for an in-service course for all staff. However, it had to be quickly abandoned when the two teachers concerned expressed an interest in carrying out the study without informing the rest of the staff! A head, apparently, has to learn to discriminate between ideas to be encouraged and those to be discouraged.

The importance of the intuitive judgement in school policy-making processes has not been reported in other studies, except for one by Garland (1982), who noted that efforts at school-based innovation were characterised by 'opportunism' as well as planning. However, the significance of the initial judgement itself by the head has been recognised by Whitaker (1983), p. 43:

> In a primary school it is usually only the head who is in a position to take an overall view, to see the school as more than a combination of its parts. Consequently it is likely that many of the problems submitted to the decision making process will be done so on the head's initiative.

Providing practical support for an initiative

For most postholders, time was a major factor in the extent to which they could fully exploit the opportunities for in-school development. One response of headteachers was to take over themselves the performance of a range of apparently routine tasks in order to free the postholders to engage in curriculum-development activities. For example, one headteacher organised experimental science work, testing the equipment and trying out the experiment, so that the postholder would not have to spend time doing it.

In another school the head taught the postholder's class occasionally as the need arose for her to work alongside one of her colleagues to demonstate a teaching technique; in yet another the head provided priority for the postholder's use of secretarial support so that the typing and duplicating of agenda and papers for the working group could be expedited, without the postholder having to spend her own time on it. In another school the postholder needed to spend two days out of school at the Open University and the head, having failed to persuade the local authority that supply cover should be provided, decided to teach her class himself, so that she could be released. His own responsibilities as head had to 'tick over', as he put it, while this happened.

Heads had a further important function, in relationships with external agencies such as teachers in other schools, universities, local-authority advisers, teachers' centre wardens and others, with whom they negotiated advice, information and resources on behalf of the postholders. Presumably the postholders were perfectly able to do this themselves, but professional protocol, access to phones and flexibility of time were on the head's side, and by establishing such apparently bureaucratic contacts, the heads saved the postholders much valuable time and effort. None of these activities was particularly dramatic or public; indeed they may all be seen as routine or even rather mundane 'backstage' aspects of curriculum development, with the limelight focusing on the postholder's performance in front of the staff meeting. But these unglamorous activities had to be carried out, and took time. In organising them, and carrying them out efficiently and unshowily, the heads were providing immensely important practical support for the postholders' somewhat more visible activities.

Two postholders made explicit how much they had been helped by this kind of support from their heads. One of them said:

> He's not made a big thing about it. He's just said that if I needed anything at all I should let him know, and really he's been terrific about it. I needed this stuff typing and you know what it's like in primary schools . . . anyway we normally have to type our own work sheets for example, if we want them typed. But he organised it so that it was almost as if the working group had its own secretary. You're probably used to it in the University, but here it's like being given gold to be given secretary's time.

Another postholder, who had found other teachers slow to respond to their revised scheme of work, made a small breakthrough when she was asked to give a kind of demonstration lesson with another teacher's class.

> It was good because the boss said straight away that he'd take my class, and he did so. And on the following week as well when we needed another shared lesson. I think it made all the difference and it doesn't sound much, taking a couple of lessons — but the other teacher knew he'd done it. And all she needed was to see in her classroom the kind of work you

could get with her children, and she knew much more clearly what she should be aiming at . . . We couldn't have done it if the boss hadn't stood in for me. And it meant a bit to me, because it showed that he thought I was on the right lines because he doesn't say much.

Occasional leadership of a school-based initiative by the headteacher

In School 4, the headteacher had taken the lead in the development of what was called an extended experience venture, which was, in brief, a short, sharp enrichment exercise designed as a supplement to the normal curricular diet in the school. Because it was an illustration of a headteacher leading by example, and acting, so to speak, as a post-holder, the case will be described in some detail.

Aims. The main idea of the extended experience venture was that it should provide an enrichment to the curriculum normally offered to the fourth-year pupils, by setting aside three mornings on consecutive Wednesdays in the summer term for all the pupils to be provided with the opportunity to work with specialist teachers on highly special-ised topics in unusually small groups (about ten pupils per group).

Organisation. The venture was organised by creating eight groups from the 75 boys and girls in the three fourth-year classes, and staffing these groups for the three mornings by the four members of staff normally available to the fourth year at this time and involving four other people interested in, and qualified for, the venture. In the event the four extra teachers were three LEA advisers and the headteacher. The groups were formed by pupils opting for a topic they wanted to follow, after receiving an 'advertisement' describing what would be involved. The sessions started at 9.15 a.m. and finished at 11.45 a.m., with a break around 10.30.

Content. The topics offered were as follows:

Topic	Teacher
1. New ideas in mathematics	Maths teacher
2. Codes, ciphers and mathematics	LEA adviser
3. Experiments with material too small to see	Science teacher
4. Pattern and shape in musical composition	LEA adviser
5. Creative design	Fourth-year teacher
6. Drawing and painting from direct observation	LEA adviser
7. Communications: animals, humans and technology	Headteacher
8. Materials and design	Craft teacher

As an illustration of the approach, Option 2 included the following:

Codes, ciphers and mathematics
Session 1   Introduce codes, ciphers, letter frequency counts.
Session 2   Continuation of work on ciphers, whilst simultaneously having some
                children starting trachtenberg multiplication.
Session 3   Continue, for those who wish, with cipher work, e.g. introducing digraph
                frequencies, continuation of trachtenberg multiplication and introducing
                palindromic numbers. (One pupil did pictographs as a change.)

Evaluation. The original staff dicussion document produced by the head contained an
expression of the need to evaluate the programme:

> In addition to the necessary discussion between group leaders before the scheme starts
> there will, of course, need to be opportunity for exchange of views during the three weeks. A
> report should be compiled at the end as a guide to further action. Amongst other things
> criteria against which the project may be evaluated shall be established before starting.

The criteria agreed upon included: teachers' judgements of pupils' interest, motivation,
quality of response, and variety of response; teachers' judgement of the worth of the
programme; and pupils' views of the programme. These were measured by questionnaires completed at the end of the programme and submitted to the headteacher, and by
teachers' comments after the event. For example, in the case of the codes, ciphers and
mathematics group, the teachers' comments after the three sessions stressed the pupils'
excitement when 'they realised that they really could crack a cipher without knowing
the "code" word'. Their responses to the work were 'not stereotyped once they were
shown possible ways of proceeding', and some pupils quickly organised themselves into
small groups of two or three, 'intelligently dividing labour to speed up their progress'.

The role of the head. The head had taken the initiative for the programme by
introducing the idea to the staff, through the preparation of a brief paper with some
suggested selected reading. After initial staff discussions he had further consultations
with a local university lecturer who had specialised in the field of gifted children. He
drafted a suggested scheme, involved the local-authority advisers, obtained participants' commitment to the scheme and identified the topics they would offer as options,
and held a staff meeting to agree to the general approach. For a relatively brief exercise,
the amount of preparatory organisation was considerable, and it is unlikely that a
normal postholder would have been able to take it on unaided. A second point is that
the programme itself was 'across the curriculum' and would not normally have been an
area identified with a single postholder. For these two reasons it was particularly
appropriate that the head should have acted as postholder in the development.

There is also the symbolic importance attached to the head's leadership of curriculum
development. For him to engage in it, with all the implications for the use of his time and
energy, was in itself a token of the significance he attached to in-school development,
and this transmitted messages to staff about the kind of role he was encouraging them to
adopt.

Headteachers as vicarious curriculum developers

If we combine the five strategies described above, headteachers emerge in supporting, rather than starring, roles. They recognise initiative, encourage postholders, provide useful back-up support of a practical kind and in a number of ways confer official approval and significance upon school-based curriculum development. But they play, or appear to play, a subordinate role in order to highlight respect for the specialist knowledge residing in the postholders, and an emergent sense of their extended professionalism. They are facilitators of development rather than leaders of it, developing the curriculum vicariously, not directly. The headteachers, of course, had formal responsibility for the curriculum in their schools, and none of them had abdicated from it. In specifying responsibilities, allocating posts of responsibility, providing practical support, recognising some initiatives and not others, they were exercising control over the form and direction of development in their schools, in the style characterised by Nias (1980) as 'positive leadership'. They would be neglecting their own contractual responsibilities if they did not apply such a regulating influence. However, their attitude to curriculum development by their staff was not simply a game in which the postholder and head contrived to disguise the latter's ultimate power over the curriculum and his or her control of change. If school-based curriculum development were to graft itself onto the life of the school in a permanent and authentic way the forms of its encouragement had to embody real respect for specialist expertise and an acknowledgement of teachers' potential for shaping and adapting programmes by reference to their professional judgements. In the last resort, the teachers in their classrooms were the real arbiters of change. Perhaps for this reason the style of participation encouraged by the heads in the Warwick inquiry, with its emphasis on decision-making devolved to staff groups informed and led by teachers with specialised knowledge and skills, appeared to be very different from what Nias (1972) discerned in other educational institutions as 'pseudo-participation'.

A further comment is required mainly because of the current emphasis on training headteachers in techniques of management and helping them prepare themselves to deal with the 'management of change'. The dominant model in many training programmes is of a set of techniques to be applied by a manager (the head and senior staff) to the managed (subordinate teachers or pupils) in order to regulate change in a direction considered appropriate by the senior staff. As a representation of the relationships between heads and staff in the inquiry schools, such a model is extraordinarily inappropriate. Given their commitment to delegation, to behind-the-scenes support, and to facilitating programmes developed in staff groups, it is more apt to describe the heads as servicing change rather than managing it.

Deployment of staff: the headteachers' dilemma

One major, and unresolved, dilemma in headteachers' support for school-based curriculum development emerged in the inquiry. The heads in all but two schools were faced with contraction in pupil numbers and some reduction of staffing. This posed for heads a critical choice about the deployment of staff, which had consequences for the encouragement of school-based development. The general decision facing heads was whether to have more class groups of single-age, or nearly single-age, composition, and thus manage without a 'floating' teacher, or to restrict the number of class groupings by having mixed-age compositions and thus retain some flexibility in staffing. This flexibility was a prerequisite for some aspects of in-school development, for example freeing postholders to work with other teachers, to visit other classes or schools, to act as subject teachers for part of the time with small groups in specialised facilities, and so on. In most cases, though to differing degrees, the heads had chosen as far as possible to avoid mixed-age classes, and a consequence was that they were less able to support aspects of curriculum renewal than they would have liked, because of reduced flexibility in staffing.

Their decisions were not easy, and mixed-age grouping may generate substantial anxieties on the part of pupils and parents, as well as administrative complexity. Moreover, official advice is conflicting, Her Majesty's Inspectorate (DES 1978a) warning against it and the Plowden Report (1967) positively encouraging it. However, a major casualty of reduced flexibility was simply the amount of time in school a postholder could spend on a development. In two of the cases the head and the postholder made clear that lack of time was having an adverse effect on a development. It was not time to initiate a development that was lacking, but time to work alongside colleagues, to revise initial ideas in the light of staff comments, and to consolidate the early changes. This issue is returned to in Chapter 10, but an example shows up the difficulty. The example of the dilemma is taken from the staff deployment in School 1 as it became an 8–12 middle school.

Table 6.1 *Staff deployment in School 1*

Classes		Number of pupils	Teacher	Responsibilities
First year	1A	34	Ms A	Year leader; class teacher
	1B	34	Mr B	Class teacher; mathematics co-ordinator
Second year	2C	31	Mr C	Year leader; class teacher
	2D	33	Ms D	Class teacher
	2E	32	Mr E	Class teacher
Third year	3F	28	Ms F	Year leader; class teacher
	3G	27	Ms G	Class teacher
	3H	27	Ms H	Class teacher; French co-ordinator
Fourth year	4IK	28	Ms I	Year leader; class teacher; deputy head; combined studies team; remedial co-ordinator
			Mr K	Class teacher; music co-ordinator; combined studies team
	4L	27	Mr L	Class teacher; social studies co-ordinator; combined studies team
	4M	27	Ms M	Class teacher; combined studies team

Notes
1. Eight children in 2C were actually first-year children. This mixed-age grouping enabled one teacher to be available as a 'float' (Ms I).
2. Ms I, the deputy head and 'float teacher' worked with remedial groups in Years 1, 2 and 3, shared class responsibility for 4IK and led the combined studies team in the fourth-year group.

Table 6.1 represents only a point in time of what was a changing situation, so it would be inappropriate to draw too many inferences from it. However, two facts affecting staff deployment were clear. First, class groups in the first and second years were larger than those in the third and fourth years, and one of these larger groups contained children of more than one age group. Second, there were somewhat fewer children of first-year age than in each of the other years and, since children are not born annually in neat class sizes, the now common pattern of intakes of varying sizes was being experienced in the school.

The headteacher could have retained three first-year class groups of 25, 25 and 26, at considerable cost to the 'floating' element in the deputy head's timetable, or he could have made the decision that he did in fact make to preserve the flexibility in staff deployment by increasing the size of first-year and second-year class groups. The consequence was that, since Ms I and Mr K shared class responsibility for 4IK, more flexibility in both their deployment and that of other staff was possible. Again, of course, there was a cost. Class 4IK had not one, but two form teachers. There were other elements to weigh in the balance, most particularly the use of the two teachers as 'specialists' (remedial and music) for part of their time.

Staff deployment decisions were not taken simply with an eye to curriculum renewal, but the potential for staff to engage in those aspects of it that required time in school (e.g. working with other teachers) was affected by such decisions. For the heads in the schools affected to some extent by falling rolls, the decision about how to use staff was a difficult one, and the majority of heads facing this situation had taken the decision to reduce class sizes rather than accept mixed-aged classes as part of a deliberate staffing policy.

SOURCES OF EXTERNAL SUPPORT

Local-authority advisers

Local-authority advisers were involved in some of the developments in the inquiry schools, as can be seen from the following list.

Case study A   Adviser organised in-school course in some aspects of a social studies project.
Case study B   Adviser was consulted about aspects of the combined studies team teaching programme.
Case study D   Adviser participated in final evaluation discussion group.
Case study E   Advisers were involved as tutors in the programme.
Case study F   Adviser was consulted on the first draft of the scheme of work in science.
Case study G   Adviser was consulted about CDT course for postholder.
Case study J   Adviser encouraged postholder to develop steel bands and helped to arrange special initial funding.

An important characteristic of the role played by local-authority advisers was its highly specific nature. They were consulted for particular advice or help at particular times, usually in the early stages of development. What the postholders needed, given the kinds of insecurities and uncertainties associated with their role, was constructive and sensitively provided advice from advisers who could 'point them in the right direction' at the time they needed it. In Case study F, for example, the postholder had drafted his initial scheme of work in science, which included work for the infant age range, of which the postholder had no experience.

> I wanted to know whether I was on the right lines — not even that, because I was basing it on Science 5–13 anyway. I needed reassurance from the adviser that what I was proposing to the staff was OK. So he came in and we talked about what I was trying to do, and he pointed out something that was obvious — we had this nature trail in the school ground, and the wild area all around it, and I hadn't taken account of the school environment — I'd relied too much on 5–13. And also he suggested ways I could try to integrate the science with other curriculum work. So it was very helpful, and he was nice with it.

This kind of role, though apparently not demanding in terms of the adviser's time, was of very great benefit to postholders in a psychological, as well as a practical, sense. If you are going to lead a staff discussion on your draft scheme of work, it is comforting to know and, if necessary, to indicate that at the very least it has the passive approval and even the active backing of the county adviser.

A further point was mentioned by headteachers: it was that when it was known that an adviser had 'taken the trouble', as one of them put it, to show interest in a scheme, the very act of his or her coming to the school gave added importance to the scheme itself. It showed, as another head said, that 'the advisory service is taking in-school development seriously, not just paying lip service to it'. Interestingly, this symbolic significance, seen by heads to be conferred on a development by the adviser's involvement, was an echo of the symbolic significance attached by postholders to the head's involvement, as was suggested earlier.

By the same token, perceived lack of support from the local authority for a particular project was interpreted as lack of commitment by them to the idea of school-based development generally. In three cases heads had requested, but not obtained, supply cover to release a postholder (to visit other schools, and to attend a relevant university briefing session and conference). These heads all reported that an LEA policy to provide supply cover for postholders occasionally to leave school in connection with curriculum development would have enabled the development to be supported more easily. All three commented also that, besides causing irritating internal adjustments to other teachers' timetables, the lack of a positive policy to provide cover gave the impression that school-based development was not valued highly enough by the authority.

University and college staff

University and/or teacher training college staff had been involved in three of the programmes. In Case study A, the postholder had been given advice by a college lecturer who was running an in-service course on the History, Geography and Social Sciences 8–13 project. In Case study E, the head had used as an informal consultant a lecturer at a local university for guidance about the appropriateness of his proposed approach to able children, and for advice about what to read in the field. And in Case study D, the Open University had been involved in providing materials, advice and one-day conferences, because the materials being used in the programme were trial materials for the Open University. With the exception of the last, the involvement of university/college staff was therefore rather similar in manner to that of the advisory service, i.e. one-off, highly topic-specific, and fairly short-lived, and in these terms it was valued by the heads and postholders.

Thus, in general, support for school-based curriculum development was sought and received from colleagues, headteachers, local advisers and university or college staff. However, the nature of support from within the school differed from that outside it. Heads and colleagues supported the postholder throughout the programme both by their participation in it and by appropriate forms of practical services they provided. The external agents in general provided limited, specific and short-term guidance, which was none the less considered valuable, even though it was different in kind from the internal support. The overall picture therefore fits in general with other studies, by Steadman, Parson and Salter (1978), Taylor, Reid, Holley and Exon (1974) and the Primary School Research and Development Group/Schools Council (1983) report, all of which showed the relatively high importance attached to support from within the school. However, they tended to attach little significance of any kind to external agencies, whereas the postholders and heads in these schools regarded them as useful, though in a different way, and for different purposes, from help looked for within the school. This is perhaps a point worth stressing because of the danger associated with school-based development by Henderson (1979) and others, that it may become too parochial and inward-looking.

CONCLUSIONS

There are four conclusions that can be drawn about support for the kind of school-based curriculum development that occurred in the inquiry schools. First, the headteacher had a powerful role to play in creating the kind of climate for the growth of in-school development, simply because of the pressures of time and uncertainty operating upon the postholders. In developing overall support for them, sensitively applied and explicit strategies for the whole school were critical to their effectiveness. Second, the role of senior people, such as heads, advisers and others, was conceived of as servicing rather than managing such development, in order to ensure authentic devolution and enhanced respect for postholders' expertise. Third, school-based curriculum development did not rest exclusively upon the skills and talents of the school staff: external sources of ideas, materials and advice were drawn upon, in order to give authoritative backing to an often fragile and vulnerable undertaking.

A final point concerns the perceptions of teachers about support or lack of support for their initiatives. Even apparently mundane practical support conveyed meanings to teachers about how their efforts were valued 'officially'. If the head gave his or her time it was read as meaning that he or she valued the activity; if the local authority withheld cover, it was construed as lack of interest in a programme. The accuracy of such perceptions is irrelevant at this level. It is a fact that the teachers interpreted support or its absence as a signal from their seniors about the value to be placed upon the enterprise itself. Teachers engaged in initiatives that are demanding of their time and energy are not sure of any tangible reward for their efforts; if in addition they become unsure about the extent to which such efforts are valued by those nominally superior to them, they are unlikely to persist in them and even less likely to be able to convince hesitant or reluctant colleagues to participate in further forms of curriculum renewal. Supporting school-based curriculum development is like administering justice. It must not only be done, but be seen to be done.

PART TWO

THREE CASE STUDIES

INTRODUCTION

Three school-based curriculum development programmes are presented in this part of the book. The report on each programme is preceded by background material, comprising brief factual data on school size and facilities, catchment area and pupil intake characteristics, staffing responsibilities and a short description of the school atmosphere and the postholder's professional biography. Asterisks identify staff directly involved in the particular programme.

Three general factors require introductory comments: variations in the *school contexts*, variation in the *programmes*, and the *particularistic* quality of case studies.

Differences and similarities in the school contexts

There were some obvious differences in the school background; the three schools differed in respect of age range, size and facilities, in the social mix of their catchment areas, and in general level of attainment amongst their pupils. But three features were common to the schools. First, the teachers generally had a substantial record of participating in in-service courses outside the school, and curriculum review groups inside it. Secondly, despite the experience of contraction in the system overall, there were quite high levels of morale amongst the staff. Third, staffing policies within the three schools had led to scale posts being allocated for clearly identified curricular and organisational responsibilities, with very few 'odd job' responsibilities.

Differences and similarities in the curriculum development programmes

There were some obvious similarities in the programmes; they all relied on specialist expertise and staff collaboration, they embodied the 'gradualism' identified in Chapter 2, and they all involved leadership by the postholder. But there were two features in particular to which it is worth drawing attention. First, the three programmes were all designed to lead to greater 'vertical' or 'through-school' continuity (that is, progression in the curriculum year by year rather than, or in addition to, consistency *within* a year group). Second, to refer to Skilbeck's 'rational-interactive' analysis (Chapter 2), the programmes exemplified the practice of adapting materials and ideas from *outside* the school (in these cases from the Schools Council, the Open University and HMI Primary Survey) in order to develop the curriculum from within it.

One difference represented is that each case study concentrates upon a different *stage*, or phase in the curriculum development process, if we assume as loose stages, *planning, implementation* and *evaluation*. Case study A is mainly about planning, Case study D mainly about implementing a programme, while Case study F focuses upon evaluation of a revised programme after it had been implemented. (It does not, of course, follow that the other stages did not occur.)

The particularistic quality of case study

It would be inappropriate to look to the individual case reports for *generalisations* about the relationship between a school's context and curriculum development initiatives. The factors in school contexts that generally inhibit or facilitate such initiatives cannot be demonstrated from particular cases; the cases are being used here to *illustrate* themes and issues as they emerged in the unique setting of a particular school, with specific individuals at a specific time. Take, for example, the issue of the match between the postholders' training (main subject) and the subject for which they held a responsibility post. In each case reported here, there was a strong match between the two. This fact does not 'prove', and is not intended to demonstrate, that such a match is generally necessary for effective school-based curriculum development. The evidence here is that the good match occurred, and was regarded as a significant factor, in *these programmes, by the particular teachers involved.*

This particularistic quality is emphasised by two further points. First, the contextual data are not fixed and stable. Information on staffing, size of school, etc. was subject to annual change. They provide, so to speak, a snapshot of the school at a particular time. A year earlier and a year later the contexts looked different. Second, the programmes themselves were highly 'personnel-dependent', having been developed by particular teachers with specific skills and personal qualities. Without them the programmes would have been different. Thus the case studies provide differentiated and particularistic illustrations of themes; they are not offered as a basis for generalised statements.

7

Case Study A: Revising a Social Studies Scheme

BACKGROUND

The school

Size. Group 5, Church of England voluntary controlled junior school (7–11) with approximately 320 pupils.

Facilities. A Victorian redbrick building houses the main part of the school, with seven closed classrooms and a hall. A more recent extension has provided four more classrooms.

The catchment area

The catchment area is a Midlands commuter-belt small town, and some outlying villages. There is a broad social mix among the occupations of the parents, with roughly half the employed parents in professional or white collar/supervisory jobs, and half in skilled, semi-skilled or unskilled jobs.

The pupils

The pupils included a wide range of ability and attainment, with scores on the Schonell Silent Reading Test B providing a roughly normal distribution.

Staffing: organisation and responsibilities

The school had previously been a three-form entry, but was beginning to experience falling rolls. Staffing was headteacher and eleven full-time staff, all of whom were deployed as class teachers. PTR is 26.7:1.

Responsibility posts were allocated for a combination of year group and subject co-ordination as shown in Table 7.1.

Table 7.1

Age group	Scale post	Responsibility
Year 1	Sc. 2	Social studies, class teacher*
	Sc. 2	Year leader, class teacher
Year 2	Sc. 2	Year leader, art/craft teacher*
	Sc. 1	Class teacher*
	Sc. 1	Class teacher
Year 3	Sc. 2	Year leader, class teacher*
	Sc. 1	Class teacher
	Sc. 2	PE, class teacher
Year 4	Deputy head	Remedial work, PE, class teacher*
	Sc. 3	Mathematics, class teacher
	Sc. 2	Music, class teacher

The school atmosphere

The atmosphere is detectable fairly soon upon entering the school. It is calm, ordered, and yet bursting with lively examples of children's work. The staff attributed this partly to the sense of purpose and direction given by the head, who had clear ideas about the curriculum and 'leads firmly, by example'. (When an expected appointment for science in the school failed to materialise, he took on the extra responsibility himself, for instance.) They also valued highly the role fulfilled by the deputy head, who took a major part in actively developing various aspects of the curriculum, and whose enthusiasm and good classroom practice carried the staff involved in these developments along with her. The particular combination of the two provided the kind of atmosphere in which change was not entered into for its own sake or lightly, but when a development was encouraged, it generated a lot of staff commitment. The staff themselves had a record of active participation in in-service training both inside and outside the school.

The postholder

The postholder had trained with geography as his main subject. He had six years' teaching experience, and had attended a variety of substantial in-service courses run by the local authority, a nearby university and a college of education. In addition, the school had been involved in trials of the Schools Council 'Home and Family' project materials, and the postholder had played a leading part in the trial. He had thereby achieved considerable familiarity with the somewhat amorphous subject area called social studies and was recognised within the staff as the 'expert' in the field. As one of the staff said:

> Gordon goes to every course that's going, and if we want to know anything about social studies or environmental studies, he's the man to talk to.

In addition to the importance of this knowledge base for the group within the school, the confidence and competence it gave the postholder in discussions with other schools was significant. This was especially the case in discussions with the secondary school, where some degree of disagreement about the aims and nature of the subject area itself emerged, and the rationale for the school's approach had to be articulated and justified.

THE SCHOOL-BASED CURRICULUM DEVELOPMENT

The revision of the scheme was the result of a process involving five teachers from the school, with the postholder acting as co-ordinator. They reported back regularly to whole staff meetings, and from time to time met representatives of the secondary school and its other feeder school. The process itself stretched over an eighteen-month period, and included considerable preparatory reading and reviewing of materials. The resulting scheme was seen as a set of 'planning guides', able to be, and expected to be, modified in the light of experience. The focus of the case study is upon the attempts made to ensure that the revision fully incorporated the views of participating staff. The process could be seen as moving through six stages, though in practice the stages were not discrete.

Stage 1: Review of existing practice

In one sense the staff thought that the existing scheme, called environmental studies, had considerable merit. There was a degree of progression in it, and it enabled those who followed it to avoid repetition. But generally speaking the practice had been that teachers had devised their own schemes, which resulted in lack of progression in content and skills, and some unnecessary repetition.

The review identified six criteria which the staff group hoped the new scheme would meet. They were:

(a)   clear progression in content;
(b)   avoidance of repetition from year to year;
(c)   a balance between various curriculum areas, such as geography, history, etc.;
(d)   systematic development of inquiry skills;
(e)   effective record-keeping;
(f)   effective use of resource materials.

Stage 2: Review of possible approaches and materials

The team of teachers did not try to develop detailed content to begin with, but worked at broad outline coverage of 'key concepts'.

> Although we did not want to get too involved with the details of content until we had a workable conceptual framework, we decided from the start we wanted to utilise materials, approaches and concepts from, and develop skills relevant to, the traditional curriculum areas of history, geography, environmental science, home economics (as interpreted by the Schools Council 'Home and Family' project) and health and social education (as outlined by the Schools Council project 'Think Well').

In addition to considering published materials from Schools Council projects, staff attended courses and workshops and produced some suggested approaches in a preliminary format to indicate the contribution that could be made by particular subjects or topics to whatever overall scheme was finally arrived at.

At this early stage also, there were staff discussion groups, and an inter-school group examining the implications of adopting the five key concepts of the 'Home and Family' project (development, interdependence, management, nutrition and protection). The minutes of one of these inter-school meetings showed some measure of agreement between the schools and the general principle that the curriculum content would need to be decided upon by staff in each school. The outline of the main ideas to be covered in each year group was to be seen only 'as a guide to providing all pupils with a common background on which the secondary school could build'.

Stage 3: Creating an agreed framework

The next stage involved the production of an overall conceptual framework within which the earlier reviews of material could be examined and, where appropriate, integrated. The group developed what they referred to as a 'matrix', setting basic themes from environmental studies against broad themes from the 'Home and Family' materials. The matrix, which was a kind of planning grid for each age group, was as follows:

Year Group	Development and change	Interdependence and relationships	Protection	Nutrition
Man in his personal environment				
Man in his physical environment				
Man in his social environment				
Man in his economic environment				

Each of the teachers involved completed, as far as he or she could, suggested topics or content in the matrix boxes for each year of the school, and then pooled their drafts. The drafts illustrated in detail how effectively the matrix was used as a device for getting the teachers to put down ideas within an overall scheme and in a manageable form, even though the scheme covered four years' work. Of course the teachers were not starting from scratch: they had been involved in the previous stages and therefore the background to the 'Home and Family' (the vertical line on the matrix) and to the existing 'Environmental Studies' scheme (the horizontal line) was familiar to them. But this was seen as a disadvantage as well as an advantage, since there was a built-in tendency to reproduce the existing scheme in its entirety. The co-ordinating teacher summarised the dilemma neatly:

> We allowed the conceptual areas to be fairly 'self-defining'; this was easier since most members of the initial working party had participated in the 'Home and Family' pre-publication workshop and were used to the terms. When the staff meeting looked at the matrix, it was necessary to stress that concepts were broader than the limitations of traditional subject divisions. For example, 'Development and Change' should not be redefined as 'History' since on this matrix it could (and does now in fact) include things like the development of children before and after birth (personal environment) and old and new houses in the town (physical environment).

A discussion paper that resulted from processing the draft matrices embodied the ideas generated by the staff group, and was seen to be genuinely its own school-specific scheme. As the co-ordinating teacher explained it:

> The working party tried out the matrix in terms of possible content, and the whole thing was brought together in a discussion document. This showed well that it was possible to develop a conceptual framework *meaningful to us* which would help us to organise and integrate the material we as a staff decided was important.

Stage 4: a minimum content

The discussion paper itself made clear to staff that there was a need to ensure continuity and progression throughout the school, and to maintain a balance between various areas in the proposed content. A series of working parties, involving at different times all members of staff, established what was a required minimum coverage for each year group. The original conceptual areas of the matrix were collapsed into four thematic areas (namely society and self, place, development and change, and the natural order) and to ensure balance staff in each year were asked to take as a starting point a theme in each of these areas. A description of the four areas, in the terms agreed to by the staff, is as follows:

Society and self
Themes which originate in this conceptual area should aim to make the child aware of his existence as a social being. First, by helping him to discover his bodily functions, his emotions and feelings and his physical, mental and moral development and then lead him by stages to an understanding of his changing role in, relationships to, and responsibility towards, society as a whole.

Place
Themes originating in this conceptual area should aim to acquaint the child with the man-made aspects of his environment, their function and design. They should aim to give the child an understanding of the physical context of his social environment.

Development and change
Themes originating in this conceptual area should aim to make the child aware that he is a changing, evolving being; that the institutions of the community have evolved out of past beliefs and decisions and past as well as present needs; that the common artefacts of life (buildings, roads, clothes, etc.) have a historical development. They should encourage the child to have an awareness of the past. They should demonstrate to the child that change is an on-going process affected by choices made and actions taken in the present.

The natural order
Themes originating in this conceptual area should:
1. aim to make the child aware of his natural environment;
2. increase his understanding of the interdependence of living things;
3. demonstrate the ways in which human life has been, and still is, affected by natural phenomena and the availability of the earth's resources.

The intention of using thematic areas was to restrain to some extent the diversity of approach that had previously prevailed, without discouraging individual initiative and flair:

> Having chosen the theme, the required content can be fitted in any way the year team thinks appropriate *alongside content of their own choosing.* The year group (or individual teacher) retains by this formulation considerable initiative in terms of content and total freedom as to methods, techniques and approaches.

Stage 5: The checklist of skills

The skills that pupils should practise and acquire over the four years had been given consideration at an early stage in the discussions about the new scheme, and the staff had been influenced by the kind of skills progression illustrated in the Schools Council's 'Time, Place and Society' project. A list of more than 60 skills was drawn up and staff were invited to identify which skills they considered should be taught in which year of the school. Staff were also asked to add or delete skills if they thought it necessary to do so. As a result of this exercise, the staff were able to agree upon a checklist of skills that should be taught in each year of the school.

Stage 6: The draft scheme of work

The final draft scheme of work provided a year-by-year sequence of basic concepts as the minimum 'required content', with suggested approaches, resources, visits, etc. Each year also had its list of skills. It was not a syllabus in the conventional sense that it indicated in detail the content to be covered, but was, in the postholder's words, a 'structured framework of concepts and skills', which left detailed planning to the year group teachers.

In its draft form, it provided the basis for further discussions between the secondary school and the other main feeder primary school. The minutes of one of these meetings indicated some agreement, and some points of difference, about the social studies scheme. The secondary school staff present expressed their support, and willingness to give advice on matters they could help with, despite reservations about the coverage of the scheme. At the same time all three schools agreed to exchange completed schemes — the secondary school providing its 11+ year (first year) course in humanities — and all expressed interest in maintaining and extending the professional contacts established through the discussions.

8

Case Study D: Increasing Teachers' Awareness of Pupils' Language Difficulties

BACKGROUND

The school

Size. Group 6, county middle (8–12) school, with approximately 350 pupils.

Facilities. The school is housed in an old aluminium sectional building, designed as an infant and junior school some thirty years ago, and now contains the hall, seven closed classrooms and the head's and secretary's rooms. There was also an extension CLASP building added in 1976, comprising semi-open class areas for seven groups, and specialist science/craft areas. Two temporary classrooms were also in use.

The catchment area

The catchment area is the less affluent part of a Midlands town. It includes a large community of Punjabi-speaking families, mostly Sikhs. Nearly 40 per cent of the school's pupils came from this community, and most of them were born in this country and spent four years in the feeder first school. About 20 per cent of the pupils came from single-parent, mostly indigenous English, families. The majority of employed parents work in the nearby engineering and appliance assembly firms, in semi-skilled or unskilled occupations.

The pupils

The pupils included a small number whose language skills did not enable a valid reading age to be derived from standardised tests, but data provided by the school showed a wide span of reading ages in the school (from below seven to above thirteen). A more important feature was the wide span within each year group. Since the class groupings were not set by attainment, each class group contained at least a five-year span of reading ages.

Staffing: organisation and responsibilities

1. Full-time equivalent staffing was 18.4, including the head, and 2.5 teachers allocated under s. 11 of the Local Government Act 1966. PTR is 19 (including s. 11); 22.0 (excluding s. 11).
2. The school was organised very much on the conventional primary-school lines, only one full-time teacher not having a class responsibility. This meant relatively small class groups (about 25) and little specialist teaching.
3. Responsibilities were as in Table 8.1.

Table 8.1

Age group	Scale post	Responsibility
Year 1	Sc. 1	Class teacher*
	Sc. 1	Class teacher
	Sc. 3	First-year co-ordinator, language development, liaison with first school, class teacher*
Year 2	Sc. 1	Music, class teacher*
	Sc. 2	Library, class teacher*
	Sc. 2	Needlework, class teacher
	Sc. 1	Class teacher
Year 3	Sc. 3	Science, audio-visual aids, class teacher*
	Sc. 3	Games, class teacher
	Sc. 2	Games, class teacher
	Sc. 2	Art, class teacher*
Year 4	Deputy head	Class teacher
	Sc. 3	Maths, class teacher*
	Sc. 2	Social studies/school visits, class teacher*
	Sc. 1	Class teacher
Additional 'floating' teachers	Sc. 2 (temp.)	Remedial work*
	PT 0.6	French
	PT 0.4	Science, music
	PT 0.4	General studies

The school atmosphere

The atmosphere in the school played a very important part in this programme. In the first place the staff were used to working together in groups to examine aspects of the curriculum in the school; scrutinising each other's practice was not unusual to them, for it had been encouraged and built into the working life of the school by the headteacher over the previous two years. Thus the programme inherited constructive attitudes to the process involved, and extensive experience of them. It is probably difficult to overstate the importance of staff relationships in a programme such as this. Collective scrutiny of their own professional practice can be a risky business. It can only be done authentically in an atmosphere of trust and respect for one another. The school staff was in general lively and enthusiastic, with a long record of active involvement in their own in-service education. The school had more than its fair share of difficult pupils, and life was not easy for the staff, but morale was high. There was a kind of pride and high-spirited professional pleasure amongst the staff just because they knew that they were doing a difficult job well. It was epitomised by the comment of one of the staff to me:

> You have to be hard and tough — you mustn't stand any nonsense, and you have to know when they're trying it on, and when they're really upset and disturbed. But you know that if you can teach here, you can probably teach well anywhere. And the staff are good here — well most of them anyway — you know that in the staffroom you'll get a lot of support.

The postholder

Beth had trained as an infant teacher, and thus had particular preparation for work in language. She had eleven years' teaching experience. She had recently followed the Open University Post-Experience Diploma in Reading Development, and had been released by the head to attend a briefing conference on the materials to be used in the programme. A consequence of this was the confidence and assurance with which she was able to prepare, present and lead the programme, even though she had not previously led staff groups.

The teachers engaged in this programme valued particularly highly the way this assurance had made itself felt in the postholder's producing relatively simple versions of the course materials, jargon-free and more easily applicable to their classroom activities. This ability, to produce an 'idiot's pack' as they put it, was a very important spin-off from expertise, and without it this fairly demanding and full programme would have progressed much less easily than it did.

THE SCHOOL-BASED CURRICULUM DEVELOPMENT

The information on the school and its pupils has provided an indication of the special role that language development had to play in the school. The school had been invited to try out some school-focused in-service materials being developed by the Open University to help teachers observe and assess children's reading and language in everyday classroom contexts.

The draft materials were not a curriculum project in the conventional sense of a pack of teaching material to be tried out with pupils. They were aimed at teachers, and they comprised a set of worksheets for private study and a set of notes for group discussions. One of their aims was:

> . . . to provide a series of starting points for observing and evaluating reading and language as a normal part of everyday classroom activities.

The head of the school realised the materials' potential for school-based in-service work with a substantial number of teachers in the school, and in particular was anxious that at least one teacher in each year group should be involved with the materials.

The materials were adapted by the language postholder to provide a term-long programme, involving three sequences of activities, one to do with children's comprehension of classroom language, one with their use of classroom language, and one with their ability to extract information from resources. Each sequence involved the teachers in:

(a)   reading some 'study notes';
(b)   participating in a planning session;
(c)   observing a small number of children as they set about their learning tasks; and
(d)   reporting back to the staff group in an evaluation session.

The sequence of the programme overall was as indicated in Table 8.2.

Table 8.2

Group sessions	Private study	Classroom activities
1. Introductory briefing	Study notes 1	
2. Planning session		Observation and assessment (activity 1. 'How well do they comprehend the language?')
3. Evaluation session	Study notes 2	
4. Planning session		Observation and assessment (activity 2. 'How well do they cope with language?')
5. Evaluation session	Study notes 3	
6. Planning session		Observation and assessment (activity 3. 'How well do they extract information from resources?')
7. Evaluation session		
8. Evaluation of whole course		

Of the seventeen full-time members of staff, ten were actively involved in the whole of the programme, including the head, the language co-ordinator, the remedial specialist, and teachers in each of the four year groups. None of the sessions was attended by fewer than eight teachers. The programme itself lasted just over ten weeks, including a school half-term.

The first sequence

The first of the three sequences in the programme was concerned with observing and assessing how well pupils comprehended passages they had been required to read or to listen to. The teachers used normal routine classroom learning tasks to observe, and these included pupils modelling from a text, pupils answering questions from a written text and illustration, and answering questions from a worksheet. The co-ordinator's notes on the evaluation session indicated the conclusions reached by the teachers, which included the following:

(i)   Purposes for reading/listening need to be quite specific in order to assess understanding.

(ii)   Children can often express understanding of reading 'between and beyond' the lines orally in a way they cannot write — to what extent is this mostly true? The teachers discussed the implications if it is.

(iii)   The group agreed that 'comprehension' questions after passages were 'largely useless' in enabling the teachers to assess the extent of the pupil's real understanding and to promote it.

(iv)   Many participants felt 'shattered' by what they had been doing up to now. But what are the implications of 'heightening awareness' if there is not a substitute readily available for consideration?

The second sequence

The second sequence of activities was concerned with observing and assessing how well pupils coped with the language of normal classroom learning tasks set for them. The language co-ordinator had prepared, as she always did, an overhead transparency for the discussion groups (both planning and evaluation sessions) that focused the group's attention on specific classroom activities.

The co-ordinator's notes on the discussions record again the teachers' expression of some anxiety about increasing their awareness of the need for developing skills, without supporting ideas for satisfying such a need. 'We can see the need for change/development. What can we do about it?'

(At this stage the group agreed that the arrangement of the discussion sessions (over lunchtime) was limiting the effectiveness of the sessions, and from this time onwards the sessions were allocated a scheduled (fortnightly) time in the programme of staff meetings.)

The notes on the evaluation sessions centre upon the teachers' reports of their classroom activities, and the common realisation that they often had broad, and even ill-defined, intentions in the tasks they had set for pupils, and the difficulties that follow for both teachers and pupils, if the intentions of the learning tasks were not specified. The discussion also raised the problem of knowing whether learning had really occurred, or whether, for example, pupils successfully completing the tasks set, already had the knowledge or skill required. The teachers began to discuss the notion that setting tasks where pupils have to apply a skill or idea might be the best way of establishing that they have learned it. 'Opportunities for transference of concept acquisition must be given before learning can be said to have taken place.'

This particular discussion session seems to have been a critical stage in the programme as teachers began to recognise that they themselves had some of the solutions to the needs they had identified, and moreover, that what they were engaged in, was not merely heightening their awareness of pupils' language needs, but raising some more fundamental issues of general curriculum practice. The co-ordinator noted:

> More and more this course seems to be highlighting problems to do with the evaluation of curriculum process in general, as much as heightening awareness of language in the classroom.

The third sequence

For the third sequence it was planned that the teachers should observe one pupil, or a small group of pupils, using resources as part of their normal curriculum assignments and assess the extent of their difficulties in this aspect of their work. The teachers were under considerable pressure at this stage, from other, legitimate, demands upon their time, and a less-involved group, and one which did not have the guidance and support of a committed and positive co-ordinator, might have given up. The co-ordinator's notes may have understated the stress in the situation.

> We are now in the middle of the Joseph musical (a production of Joseph and his Techni-colour Dream Coat) and the Richmond tests. I feel that the group is tired though still interested. Time-keeping not v. good and this must be a factor in in-school INSET. Between-session support and encouragement needed at this stage.

Despite all these competing demands the teachers continued with the programme, and the nature and quality of the group discussions were sustained. To illustrate the way the group had been working, a fuller narrative account of the evaluation session in this third sequence is provided below. There were eight members of staff from the school present and a visiting teacher who had been working with the programme in her own first school. The session was introduced and led by the language co-ordinator. It started at 3.45 p.m. and finished at nearly 5.00 p.m.

The discussion group

The language co-ordinator introduced the session with an OHP which reviewed a list of skills, and focused upon two, namely the ability of children to use 'signposts' in the layout of books (she instanced conjunctions such as 'therefore' and 'but') which indicate the direction that language is taking; and skills concerned with reading for different purposes (she instanced skimming, scanning, and reading carefully for note taking). The meeting progressed with each teacher reporting her/his observation of one or two children responding to tasks that required them to use some of these skills, and raising issues for discussion or comment.

A third-year teacher reported on his observation of ten-year-old Brian ('not the slowest in the class') who had not known where the Isle of Wight was or how to find out. The teacher had set Brian the simpler task of finding out about the River Avon. Brian had gone to the encyclopaedia and not found it there. When pushed to say where he would look for it next, he had said 'the library'. The teacher had, as he put it, 'fixed it' so that an appropriate book was standing out a little from the rest, but to no avail. Brian had looked for 'Avon' on the shelves and had had to be directed to *Know How to Use your Library* and had found its system of classification. He then found a book on rivers, but didn't look in the index. Up to this point it would be accurate to describe Brian's search skills as 'undirected' without any clear strategy, and without much success. The teacher had set him a new task to see what he had learnt in the process of looking for the River Avon. Brian was required to find a book entitled *An Easy Way to Understand Photography*. Once again, he 'trundled round' the library looking in an undirected way until reminded about the *Know How to Use your Library* book. He proceeded to look up 'a', but with hints from the teacher looked up photography. Finally, the teacher reported that Brian, when asked to look up Astrology in the *Know How to Use your Library* book, had looked all through the a's section, rather than use the second letter as an eliminating mechanism.

Told with sympathy and humour, the teacher's report illustrated something of the difficulties that a ten-year-old pupil in the school might encounter if teachers assumed that he or she had the necessary strategies for finding out, from resources, when he or she did not in fact have them.

Next a second-year teacher reported her observation of two pupils sharing a task she had set. The task set was to look at the cover of a book and to pose three questions they thought they would find answers to, in the book. The teacher had been observing how far the pupils were able to generate their own questions and find answers to them, and how far they could use the cover of a book to help them assess its suitability for their purpose.

The two pupils had each responded differently. Harold had opened the book and turned over the pages randomly, until he had lighted on a 'volcanoes' section which dealt with the third of his questions. Marilyn on the other hand had asked first of all if she could use the index; she found 'hot and dry regions', read the relevant section and wrote down a summary of the appropriate information; she got the material very quickly and used previous knowledge. She looked for Sahara under 's' in the index but not for deserts under 'd'. The teacher's discussion of her skills included the views that: 'I think that she decided it was too superficial'; 'It was too general for her purposes.' 'I was surprised how well she did it.'

In the discussion about what the pupils had learned, the teachers said, 'Harold learned scanning, perhaps.' They thought that Marilyn had learned to some extent to be discriminating about books: 'Perhaps she learned some books are superficial!' In addition, the teacher concerned noted that she had been required to discuss with the pupils what was not answered in the material, as well as what was. She herself had learned that the two pupils were able to create their own questions but expressed reservations about how well they could produce answers to them unaided.

A fourth-year teacher reported an observation carried out that morning of the skills used by two children when they used books to answer questions. She was looking for scanning, skimming, use of index and contents page, and use of other clues such as sub-headings, words in bold type, etc. She had given them books related to their topic work, but which they had not used before. One of the pupils had been asked to find out answers to specific questions on fossils: 'What are fossils? Where are they found? What can we learn from them?'

The boy, Martin, had gone to the index, then to the appropriate page, but couldn't extract relevant material from the page, even though he had read through it. Then he went to an encyclopaedia and found material by using the contents page. He didn't use pictorial sources. The teacher gave an example of the way the boy used material without meaning. He had copied down: 'Fossils can be found in many rocks, mainly sedimentary rocks' — but he didn't know, and had not found out, the meaning of 'sedimentary'.

The girl, Ann, had questions on food, including 'Why is milk important in diet?' She used the contents page and found a sub-heading 'Eating for good health'. In the section on 'food for good health' she had scanned the pages and skimmed generally for the word 'milk'. Undeterred by a stage-whispered reference by one of the group to 'skimmed milk', the teacher said of Ann's approach, 'She had all the strategies'. Moreover, Ann had changed the material 'a little bit' into her own words. Martin was, however, seen as 'daunted by the index', a bit 'lost', finding it 'difficult to pick up clues'.

Finally, the language co-ordinator reported a task she set for three children in her first-year group. The task was for them to find out something for presentation to the others in the class about the frog spawn in the school's aquarium. They were to approach their task independently, and tape-record themselves whilst engaged in the activity. Her instructions to them were:

1. Get a note-maker.
2. Decide what you want to find out.
3. Talk about how you will share the information with the rest of the class. (She had suggested some possible ways to them.)

She then assessed how they approached the tasks:

1. They 'talked through' the work card.
2. They agreed on a note-maker.
3. They devised and agreed on questions they wanted to find out information about.
4. They poked about a lot in the aquarium.

Second, she set up some books for them to sort out into those that would help them find out more about the topic and those that would not. They had done that easily, explaining patiently to the teacher that the reason why they'd chosen a book on amphibians was that frogs were amphibians.

From the observation the co-ordinator noted that the pupils didn't work out how to present their material; the ordering of their work was a consequence of her ordering of their activities on the work card, and if children could create questions to be answered, they also created the need to observe and record. They found using the library difficult.

The point developed into a discussion of the use of the library generally, one teacher reporting two pupils expressing surprise on discovering that the school and town library both had the same classification system.

The visiting first-school teacher made a number of points about her experience of a similar programme in her school, for the purposes of comparison.

1. The teachers had decided that the pupils didn't have the skills needed and had developed a checklist of skills, graded in terms of their difficulty.
2. For children to pose their own questions was very important in terms of motivation.

3. Her school had used simplified Alison Uttley type stories/material for children to extract the basic meaning.

The language co-ordinator concluded the session by noting that for most children these skills — scanning, skimming, etc. — did not come incidentally. Perhaps the school and the pupils needed a structure to work with — a checklist for example. She stressed the need for the pupils to have the strategies developed before they left primary school, since it was likely that the secondary schools would assume they had them and make no specific provision. A further point related to this, was the need for pupils to practise note-taking, from a variety of media. The general point of the need for links with the upper schools was made.

The teachers' evaluation of the programme

The final overall evaluation session was attended by nine members of staff and a local authority adviser. The purpose of the discussion was to evaluate the materials that had been used and to discuss their impact upon the teachers involved. The two elements are obviously related, but the summary that follows concentrates upon the teachers' views of the effects of their participation in the programme, upon them as teachers — the extent to which the process of planning the activities in a group, carrying out the observation and assessment and discussing it together, had contributed to their professional development. Their comments may be considered under three headings.

The role of the co-ordinator

Firstly, the teachers said that the discussions 'didn't just happen'. They had needed to be structured and led by someone (in this case the co-ordinator) who could provide overall direction to them, because of her greater knowledge or expertise. 'There would be problems', said one of them, 'if the discussion sessions had just been started cold. They needed someone who's familiar with the material, and who knows the background to it.'

A second related issue was the need for someone to 'translate' the study notes for the teachers who weren't very familiar with the approaches embodied in them. The study notes had been found 'a little off-putting' both in terms of their amount and their language use. The co-ordinator had produced her own version of these, especially for the planning sessions, in the form of an overhead transparency, suggesting very specific learning activities to observe. This had been a considerable help to busy teachers and had made it possible to have shorter planning sessions than would otherwise have been the case.

> It was very efficient. You said, 'You can do this, or that' and it was more to the point than the (study) notes.

> We thought your notes were better (than the OU's) — it was a sort of translation, a simpler version, an idiot's pack.

The role of the discussion groups

The teachers regarded the discussion sessions as probably the most useful of the activities.

> They were very useful, you had to think about what you were doing with the kids and why.

> It was especially valuable that there was a planning discussion before we did something, and then to come back afterwards.

One of the teachers related the value of the discussion sessions to the atmosphere in the school generally:

> I think it's worked well here because we don't mind being shown up — you know, we don't mind coming in and saying 'It's been a disaster.' There's no point in doing this kind of thing if you're not going to be honest with one another — pretending you got perfect results would be just a waste of time.

Another of the teachers was more specific about the advantages to her:

> It's not only that you pool ideas and problems, it's that when you've sorted out something specific to observe (in the discussion groups), you observe differently. You know you normally notice the troublemakers a lot, and keep an eye on them. But this has made me watch pupils I just assume are getting on OK. It's not the discussion sessions individually — it (the programme overall) has brought out how we make assumptions about what they know, and how clearly we tell them. Now I think more about the assumptions I make. I've been surprised really about how I assumed lots of the kids had no difficulty in say using resources — and yet it's obvious that they have, and would have.

It should be remembered that the discussion sessions were well organised, well structured, and focused on specific practical problems. And it was this characteristic that the teachers found helpful. A number of them contrasted it with discussion groups they had experienced elsewhere which were vague and open-ended.

The group sessions therefore were seen to have the effect of sensitising the teachers to the pupils' difficulties and needs in a way that the materials read and applied in isolation, or discussed in unstructured groups, would not have done.

A realistic programme

A third element in the programme that teachers wanted to stress was that it was realistically limited. Its intention was to raise their consciousness, heighten their awareness of children's problems and difficulties in developing advanced reading skills. Although this was to some extent frustrating initially, in the final discussion the teachers saw it as a sensible limitation, a kind of first stage in which the group explored and discussed their assumptions, and that, *as a first stage*, this was enough for busy teachers. Part of the final session was given over to a discussion about 'where we go from here', and a number of possibilities were raised including developing a school-wide checklist, and some suggestions for teachers who had not been involved about skills associated with topic work, and the production of some worksheets building up advanced skills, and changes in library procedures. However, the teachers concerned thought this particular programme was about right in terms of length. To prolong it over another term to look at solutions to the pupils' problems would be difficult. The solutions might be produced in a variety of ways, but this particular programme was judged successful partly because of the realistic limits on time and energy it involved.

> If you were to prolong it, it would get to be a drag. It's up to individuals now to develop their own answers.

> It's got to be like this – short and sharp, and then it's up to the individual.
> We've obviously got to go on and develop something out of this, and I'd like to be involved in it if there is another group for something, but really from now on it's up to us in the classroom to sort it out.

9

Case Study F: Evaluating the Implementation of a Science Scheme

BACKGROUND

The school

Size. Group 5 combined school (5–12) with approximately 280 pupils.

Facilities. Semi-open-plan design with eight class areas, specialist facilities for craft and science, an enclosed music room and an open-access library/resources area.

The catchment area

The majority of pupils lived in the medium- to high-priced private houses in the school's neighbourhood, although twenty or so were brought in by bus from a village some seven miles away. The majority of parents were in professional, white-collar and skilled manual occupations.

The pupils

Very few pupils, 'only a handful' according to the head, were slow learners, and tests of reading and mathematics administered in the school indicated that the majority of pupils were of average or above-average attainment for their age.

Staffing: organisation and responsibilities

1. Full-time equivalent staffing was 11.9, including the head. PTR = 23.5:1.
2. The main organisational principle was class teaching, with some limited opportunities for the postholders to work alongside class teachers, by using one 'floating' teacher and having two classes of mixed-age groups with a two-year spread.
3. There were nine classes, and the staffing responsibilities were as shown in Table 9.1.

Table 9.1

Class	Scale post	Responsibilities
8	Sc. 2	French, drama, class teacher*
7	Sc. 2	Science, PE, class teacher*
6a	Deputy head	Mathematics, class teacher*
6b	Sc. 2	Library/resources, class teacher
5	Sc. 2	Home economics, needlework, class teacher*
4	Sc. 2	Language, class teacher*
3	Sc. 2	Music, class teacher
2	Sc. 1	Class teacher
1	Sc. 2	Girls' PE, class teacher
–	Sc. 2	Environmental studies*

There were part-time teachers amounting to 0.9 f.t.e.

The school atmosphere

The atmosphere in the school was lively and bustling, with children's work spreading into display areas throughout the building. Relationships among staff were good, with coffee breaks characterised by noisy and good-humoured banter and there was some effective co-operative teaching in the semi-open areas. Many staff regularly became involved in in-service training of various kinds, so the curriculum practice in the school benefited from informed and critical discussion. The head had been appointed to the school five years previously, and saw his role as providing a framework for the further development of an already effective school.

The postholder

There was a good match between the postholder's initial training — in geography and science — and his responsibility for science throughout the school. Since qualifying, he had had four years' teaching at another school before being appointed to his present post. Before his arrival there had been considerable activity in science, especially with a nature-study emphasis, focused on a 'wild area', nature trail and rural crafts, which had contributed a lively and visible part of the school environment. There was therefore a genuine base for development in science: at the same time there was the possibility that teachers already doing their own kind of science might be inclined to resist attempts to redefine the subject by a new member of staff. Part of the intention was to extend work in science into the infant/first-school age range, and this was a particular challenge to the postholder, Philip, who was relatively young and without infant experience. An important part of the postholder's role therefore was to build upon and extend the existing interest and activity, without appearing to devalue it.

THE SCHOOL-BASED CURRICULUM DEVELOPMENT

The process of designing, implementing and evaluating a revised approach to science in the school went through three stages. First, there was a review of existing work, which coincided with a vacancy enabling the postholder to be appointed to a Scale 2 post with responsibility for science and PE. Second, there was the production and implementation of a new scheme of work in science, with particular emphasis on progression and integration with other curricular areas. And third, there was, at the end of its first year, a collaborative evaluation of it by the staff concerned.

The review of existing work

The main impetus for review came from the headteacher, who made clear that in doing so he had been influenced by what HM Inspectors had had to say about science in *Primary Education in England* (DES 1978a).

> In the light of the Primary Survey and various meetings and publications on science, it was felt that a more structured approach was desirable. As a vacancy occurred from 1st January, it was decided that a Scale 2 post be offered for responsibility for science throughout the school.

The specification of the science component of this post included among its responsibilities the development of science throughout the school and the requirement to encourage other teachers and to assess the effectiveness of science 'at regular intervals'. The head indicated that where science had been done in the school it was of good quality, involving projects providing first-hand experience of the environment. It had, however, depended very much on the enthusiasm of individual staff members, and had to some extent lacked regularity and sequence. The new scheme was intended to develop and spread this interest within an overall framework.

The head also identified a stumbling-block for any such development: the anxiety that some staff had about doing science. He summarised his view as follows:

> It should be said that I as headmaster had every confidence in their ability, but the mere mention of 'science' made a few of the staff turn pale. If we had used another description — 'Investigations' or 'Topic involving discovery and observation' — the staff would have realised that they had for many years been teaching science, though perhaps not in a structured way or on a regular basis. The first task, therefore, was to reassure teachers and to provide clear guidelines and resources with which to form starting points.

Producing the scheme

In the first term the new postholder produced a first draft for discussion with the head, deputy and local-authority adviser. Following this the revised scheme, based on the Schools Council Science 5–13 project, was discussed in staff meetings, and amended in the light of them.

The scheme provided themes and progression covering the eight year groups, and provided further detail for the first six class groups, where science was taught by the class teachers. (Pupils in classes 7 and 8 were taught science by the postholder.) A characteristic of the scheme was that, in addition to references to resources and suggested themes, it stressed the importance of developing research skills and helping pupils to acquire and use scientific language, especially an appropriate scientific vocabulary. In addition, it attempted to link work in science with the school's topic programme.

Although the formal meetings about the scheme were seen by the head and science co-ordinator as significant, not least because they represented an official recognition of the need for the development, other, less formal contacts, in which teachers followed up points with the science co-ordinator, were seen as more important. The head summarised the process as follows:

> At the meeting with all the teachers, aims and development, including scientific concept development, were discussed. However the most important meetings took place informally at break times and after school, when individuals and small groups of teachers saw the science co-ordinator, and problems of lesson content, resources and methods of approach were sorted out. By September (i.e. after two terms) the teachers were primed and ready to go.

The role of the science postholder in the first year of the development

The science postholder's role in the first year included four activities: subject teaching, providing teachers' resources, consultation and teaching alongside colleagues.

Subject teaching

During the year in which the science scheme was implemented an important contribution to it was his subject teaching with Classes 7 and 8. He felt that the potential quality and the nature of his approach to science should be visible in the school, and this would give a lead to other teachers.

Providing teachers' resources

The postholder built up sets of resources for teachers, and these were kept in the staffroom. They comprised teachers' handbooks for the Science 5–13 scheme and other reference sources. In addition, he had produced a 'resources pack' for one of the infant teachers, on the topic of electricity, comprising a set of circuits, batteries and cells.

Consultation

There was the regular and informal activity of being consulted by teachers who needed help or advice in putting some of the themes into practice. A particular issue here was his help for teachers attempting to integrate science material into their more general topic work.

Teaching alongside colleagues

A fourth element in his role was co-operative teaching, with the deputy head, of the latter's class. This was possible because the deputy and the science co-ordinator were able to work alongside one another, and because the class concerned was physically close to the specialist area. Thus the deputy was able to be involved in his class's science and to be aware of the pupils' progress.

The staff's evaluation

After the first year of the scheme's implementation a staff meeting was called after school, to evaluate the way it had been working and to explore possible improvements in the next stage. The meeting was attended by the head, the postholder, the deputy and five other class teachers, and lasted just over an hour. The head chaired the meeting and started it off by indicating that its purpose was to evaluate the appropriateness of the science scheme in the school, and to consider the practical and other difficulties that had arisen during the year. He suggested that this might include the extent to which the scheme had been found unduly constraining upon individual teachers' freedom. He quoted from HMI's *Primary Education in England* (DES 1978a, paras. 5.66 and 5.72) to stress that the school had started from a base in science teaching which was probably better developed, even before the introduction of the current scheme, than in most primary schools. The science co-ordinator followed up the head's introduction by commenting that his scheme might have included too much 'straight content'. He had attempted to provide a structure and sequence of science concepts but also to take some account of what other work teachers were engaged in:

> I knew I'd put a lot in it, but I did try to link it with existing work in topic for example.

The class teacher of Class 5, a split age-group class, commented on the way she had used the scheme. She had been selective about content, partly on the basis of personal preference — 'I chose the things I especially liked and was interested in' — and partly on her judgement about which topics were difficult for her age group:

> I covered colour, food and smell, but not water and air. Water and air aren't quite right somehow — when I did them (last year) with class 7 they were fine.

She also pointed out that early on in the year all pupils had covered much the same work, but some of the later work, on the topic of food especially, had been very appropriate for enabling her to develop individual work more. The theme of colour had been linked naturally to the work she did in art, and she felt she had been able to integrate these elements well.

> Teaching the theme of colour was great fun. We did colour collection, mixing colours, colour preferences, simple chromatography, and colour wheels. It worked very well with them.

She made three points which she thought deserved rethinking. In the first place she wondered whether the considerable energy and time that even partial coverage of the scheme involved might be giving undue priority to science over other subjects, such as geography for example. Second, she felt that some of the virtues of the 'nature study' style of the old primary-school approach were being lost. She gave examples of ways in which previously her pupils would have observed and known that different plants had different root systems, whereas this was not the case now. A third issue was the extent of possible overlap between different classes, since there were a number of common themes.

Another teacher raised the general point of how far the actual content in the scheme should be seen as 'required' content: 'Are we trying for a methodology of science or a content?'

The teacher of Class 5 added that it might be useful to develop a framework showing a progression of skills, rather than, or alongside, the framework of content.

The teacher of Class 4 made favourable comments on her experience with the scheme. She had covered air, wind, flight and electricity with her pupils and said how useful she had found the resource pack on electricity made for her by the science co-ordinator:

> It was very useful because it was all there for me. I didn't have to run about sorting my own things out.

At the same time she raised two further issues for consideration. In the first place, the whole area of language in relation to science needed fuller examination. Although there was a component of language in the scheme, she thought it needed fuller treatment. Another problem she identified was the limited amount of time the teachers had to talk to one another about what they were doing in science, and to plan together the details of the work, especially in the lower part of the school.

Responses to the problems raised so far came from the science co-ordinator, the head and the deputy head. The deputy head agreed with the need for specified progression in skills, especially skills of observation. The head and the science co-ordinator stressed the need, as they saw it, to avoid the possibility of duplication in content also. The latter acknowledged the need to incorporate more fully the important skills of 'collecting and classifying', instanced by the reference to the nature-study approach.

The teacher of Class 8 reported that from her point of view the science had become very discrete, with very little linking with the pupils' topic work. The major reason for this was an organisational one: that she was unable to be involved in her class's science because at the time they were having science, she taught French, and thus was unable to help realistically in any follow-up work or to integrate it with the topic work that she did with them: 'It's becoming secondary-based because I don't know what's going on'. Moreover, the arrangement whereby the postholder taught her class science was preventing her from developing her own skills in science. As she put it, coining a splendid neologism: 'You are devoiding me of all science competence'.

She also raised the issue of the subject's gender image, saying that the pupils were beginning to see science in gender terms:

> I've got some very good girls — they're better at science than a lot of the boys — but they're already seeing 'science' equals 'men'. Even within science — Dorothy does domestic science and I do health — the women's kind of science.

The head questioned the assumption that for eleven- and twelve-year-olds science ought to be integrated, and referred to the organisation of science teaching in some secondary schools. He also raised the issue of the form in which children's recording of science activities should be encouraged. His own view was that some of the recording could be more suitably expressed in the pupils' own terms and language, rather than in the formal 'secondary-school' style.

The staff then raised possible practical improvements for the coming year. These included:

(a) further resource packs to be produced by the postholder;
(b) fuller use of pre-recorded TV programmes;
(c) time given to the postholder to work alongside the infant teachers;
(d) devising a list of skills from the specification of skills in the Science 5–13 handbook.

Appendix to Part 2

COMMENTARY: CENTRAL THEMES AND PROBLEMATIC ISSUES

The reports on each curriculum development programme enable the main themes of the preceding part of the book to be seen in a more 'holistic' way. Thus the theme of the exploitation of specialist expertise can be seen in all three cases, but the way such expertise has been exploited differs in each, because of differences in the programmes, the role of the head, the forms that teacher participation took, and so on. Case study A illustrates most clearly the process of staff collaboration and staff participation in a working group that reported to the larger staff meeting for the purposes of collective decision-making. Case study D illustrates the nature of supportive relationships that enable scrutiny of colleagues' professional practice to occur in staff meetings. Case study F reveals a collective approach to evaluation as part of the process of developing a through-school continuity in an area of the curriculum.

A number of other themes are clearly in the programmes. They include the following:

(a) the complexity of the postholder's role (see Chapter 3);
(b) the strain in the 'educationalist' context (see Chapter 4);
(c) the gradualism of school-based development (see Chapter 2);
(d) the head 'servicing' change (see Chapter 6);
(e) the adaptation of externally developed ideas and materials (see Chapter 2);
(f) the combining of specialist expertise with teacher participation (see Chapter 2);
(g) formative evaluation using a wide range of 'evaluative audiences' (see Chapter 5).

Thus it would be easy to pick up the central themes of Part 1 and illustrate them by detailed reference to the material in the case studies, and it would be useful for readers to do so. However, because all the case studies provided source material for the analysis in Part 1, the process of illustration would become something of an exercise in tautology. An alternative approach has been adopted, which involved bearing the central themes in mind, but focusing on *problematic issues* associated with them in particular cases. I use the term 'problematic' to mean perplexing or puzzling, because the way an issue should be resolved could not be taken for granted by those involved. Three such issues have been identified, and each is raised briefly as a kind of extended question for readers to consider themselves.

Raising issues of a problematic kind about a programme should not be read as a criticism of the school, the teachers, or the programme itself. The point has already been made that the programmes were regarded by the participants as effective, and we saw something of the commitment and involvement of postholders in Chapter 3. Most worthwhile educational enterprises embody uncertainties and, as was indicated in Chapter 4, these programmes were no exception.

ISSUE 1: COLLABORATIVE WORKING GROUPS OR SYLLABUSES BY COMMITTEE?

The postholder in Case study A, anticipating HMI's (DES 1983b) idea that schemes should be thought of as 'working documents' designed for regular review, characterised the social studies scheme as 'planning guides' intended to help teachers to structure their teaching around a set of concepts and skills that provided coherence without imposing uniformity in terms of detailed classroom content. The intention of the lengthy process of working parties regularly consulting whole staff meetings was that teachers should be closely and actively involved in the production of the scheme, and there is little doubt that the process was thoroughly and effectively brought about.

However, two questions are raised by the process. First, would the classroom practice of those teachers not directly involved in the small working party be more influenced by the scheme than by the previous one? And second, did the process of collaboration bring about a scheme incorporating material that was a kind of compromise reflecting the interests of its participants, much as the Agreed Syllabus for Religious Education does at local-authority level? The skills list, for example, included some degree of arbitrariness that appears to reflect the needs of particular contributors rather than an interrelated grouping of skills. The list included:

Fourth year
1. Extrapolate data to make predictions.
2. Recognise contour pictures.
3. Devise route, given variables.
4. Understand the globe and implications of spherical earth for travel.
5. Construct a transect e.g. land use, dwelling type, etc.
6. Distinguish differences and similarities in two views of an event.
7. Trace a line of historical development noting important steps.
8. Use a cooker.
9. Devise a balanced meal.
10. Use a sewing machine.
11. Use an iron.
12. Suggest factors relating to site of settlement.

The group process helped to build in consensus and create a commitment to continuity through school at the level of the scheme. And because the scheme provided concepts and skills in an overall framework, its basic approach was coherent overall. But how far any syllabus, scheme or planning guide can capture the commitment of teachers not directly involved in its production is difficult to tell. Equally, how far some degree of internal consistency and logical relationships in the content of a scheme will have to be sacrificed as a consequence of the collaborative process itself is an open question.

ISSUE 2: MAINTENANCE-FREE CURRICULUM DEVELOPMENT?

The aims of the programme in Case study D had been to increase teacher awareness of pupils' language difficulties arising from the routine classroom assignments, and to encourage teachers to look for solutions to such difficulties by exploring them with their colleagues in the discussion sessions. During the programme these sessions had been characterised by considerable commitment, openness and good-natured public analysis of the classroom practice of the teachers concerned. It was a good illustration of teachers engaging in peer-group accountability with each other.

At the conclusion of the programme the teachers were anxious to limit any further commitment of their time, for example to its evaluation or maintenance, in subsequent terms. The participating teachers felt they had done as much as they needed to as a working group. Given the pressure to meet other demands in school, such anxiety is understandable. However, the consequence of not maintaining the programme, or evaluating it collectively, possibly by group discussion, leaves uncertainty about its long-term impact, and therefore about how worthwhile the expenditure of energy and effort had been.

Thus we are left with a series of questions about the programme's effectiveness. Would Brian's teacher (Chapter 8) give similarly vague instructions to Brian (and other Brians) in the future? Would the teacher who acknowledged the ways she had ignored the needs of pupils she had assumed were competent continue to ignore them? Would pupils with differing needs be catered for in a more consistent way throughout the school by the participating teachers? One answer to these kinds of questions is that if you leave it to the teachers, with no systematic follow-up, the impact of the programme will evanesce. Another is that, because the programme has been developed co-operatively and has been focused on teacher consciousness, it will take root in the stock of teaching techniques common to the school.

ISSUE 3: LESS PROCESS, MORE PRODUCT?

The main thrust of the programme in Case study F was to involve staff in understanding the revised scheme in science, in order to create greater continuity and consistency in the way the subject was treated in the school. And something of the impact of the scheme and the process of teacher involvement in it can be gauged from the wide-ranging and serious nature of the evaluation session. If, as the head said, the staff had initially been fearful of science, little of such fearfulness was in evidence in the confident and even assertive way in which the teachers talked of their experience over the year and the questions it had raised with them about the through-school implications.

Valued though the process was, reflection on the outcomes of the evaluation session raises the question of whether some teachers in the school would have preferred an initiative in which less process and more products — in the form of packs of material and equipment such as the one on electricity — were created for classroom use. The evaluation session examined principles underlying the new scheme, but the priorities established for the following year emphasised *utility in the classroom*, further resource packs, more planned use of TV programmes, time for the postholder to work with the infant teachers in their classrooms, etc.

The emphasis on product usability can even be seen in the format adopted by the postholder for rewriting the scheme after the evaluation session. The original document simply listed topics and resource books. For example, the topic of 'soil' was simply presented as one of a number of possibilities and teachers were directed to relevant resources. Though this approach seems to have been useful for the assured teachers (e.g. of Class 5), others wanted a more detailed, prescriptive and directly usable scheme. The postholder's new treatment of 'soil' therefore took the following form:

1. Looking at soil. What is it made up of?
2. Shaking soil in jar of water to settle into layers. What is soil made up of?
3. Burning soil — observation — what is it made up of? How much water is in the soil?
4. How much air is in the soil?
5. Make a soil profile.
6. Analysing different soils with above tests and for acidity and drainage.
7. Acidity using soil-testing kit.
8. Testing for different elements such as calcium and phosphorus.
9. Which soil drains the quickest?
10. Which soil produces the best growth?
11. Are different soils preferred by certain plants?

There is probably a subject-specific element here, in that teachers felt they needed directly usable materials for science, in a way they might not for social studies, for example. But given the pressure on teachers' time, were teachers in this school implicitly asking for the postholder to spend more of his time producing classroom materials and less of his (and theirs) in meetings discussing the scheme?

PART THREE

TOWARDS THE COLLEGIAL PRIMARY SCHOOL

10

Towards the Collegial Primary School

INTRODUCTION

Previous parts of this book have been very much concerned with empirical reality — with how things are in particular schools and in the school system. In Part 1 we saw the political pressures on the schools to develop their curricula by stressing subject expertise and collective decision-making, and we examined the strains experienced by postholders in the schools themselves. We identified approaches to evaluation and sources of support. In Part 2 the three case studies illustrated this form of curriculum development from the practice in particular school settings. This chapter is very different because it is not primarily concerned with actual practice, but with *images* of 'good practice'.

The chapter is frankly speculative, exploring possibilities rather than realities. First, it examines previous images of good primary school practice, followed by a projection of an image of the 'collegial' primary school. Second, two obstacles to the development of collegiality are discussed. These are teacher relationships and attitudes, and the working conditions in primary schools. Third, a model of professional accountability — of teachers being able to give curricular accounts to each other — is explored. The conclusion is drawn that teachers' working conditions in primary schools are the major obstacle to more widespread adoption of the approaches to curriculum development analysed in the preceding parts of the book.

ICONOGRAPHIES OF THE PRIMARY SCHOOL

Images of 'good practice' are nothing new. In the period since the Education Act 1944, the primary school profession has had transmitted to it a number of images of what have been often called 'good practice'. These images have conveyed to teachers definitions of the way that the primary school curriculum should change. Images of this kind serve to portray in vivid, condensed and potent form the values that schools should adhere to, rather as icons in Eastern Orthodox churches help worshippers to concentrate their devotion on the central figures of their belief system. The groups in the education system who have been able to create and propagate such images have included government committees, such as Plowden, Bullock, Cockcroft, etc., HMIs, writers such as Marshall (1963) and Blackie (1967), teachers' unions and other professional associations and teacher training institutions. There has been no shortage of image makers for the profession, and no shortage of iconographies of the primary school.

There have been some recurring themes in these images. The needs of able children figured large in the Ministry of Education's (1959) report on primary education as they did in HMI's survey (DES 1978a). A broad curricular coverage rather than the narrow 'basic skills' approach has also been a constant feature, according to a recent survey reported by the Schools Council (1983). However, the dominant images have varied at different times, reflecting different emphases in values about what schools should be like. At least three are detectable, viz., 'humane-meritocratic', 'emotional-integrative', and 'community-oriented.'

The 'humane-meritocratic' style of the 1950s, was portrayed in the Ministry of Education's (1959) *Primary Education*, and the NUT's (1958) *The Curriculum in the Junior School*. This style highlighted respectful relationships between pupils and teachers, through which the former could learn moral and social values experientially, by being part of a 'democratic' school society. At the same time, since the schools fed mainly selective secondary systems, their internal organisation was shown cultivating intellectual merit, with arrangements such as streamed or setted groupings of pupils. The tension between these values was reflected by urging the schools to avoid giving pupils a premature sense of rejection by unduly rigid grouping practices, or offering what a White Paper (1958) called a 'cramped and distorted' curriculum, in order to increase selective pass rates. The NUT's picture included children 'approaching' their teachers,

> consulting them and feeling confident of their interest . . . school is not now a place where a child feels he is continually wanting, but a place where he is acceptable as a personality . . . In the liberal yet orderly atmosphere of a good junior school, the children will make progress in one of their important lessons — the art of living together. (NUT 1958 pp. 35–6)

Despite all this, the schools had to take account of meritocratic considerations, and the NUT could not imagine the schools without some form of grouping by ability:

> the slower child might suffer from the prominence and superior quickness of the more gifted children . . . A child may work with an A group in some sections of the curriculum, and a B group for others: or the school may be streamed in the more basic skills only . . . (op. cit. p. 40)

A second style, the 'emotional-integrative' school, was shown in considerable detail in the Plowden Report (1967). It laid stress on the social and emotional impact on children, especially deprived children, of their immersion in the school community.

Rounded pictures were presented of good practice in a part of the report (para. 277ff.) where 'composite' schools were seen through the eyes of an 'imaginary visitor'. The image offered was concrete, detailed and suffused with light and joy, showing a school world of emotional security and wellbeing for pupils, combined with a range of artistic and cultural activity apparently unconstrained by time, or the pupils' age, or intellectual shortcomings among staff or pupils:

> The nursery class has its own quarters and the children are playing with sand, water, paint, clay, dolls, rocking horses and big push toys under the supervision of their teacher. There is serenity in the room, belying the belief that happy children are always noisy . . . Learning is going on all the time but there is not much direct teaching.
>
> Going out into the playground, the visitor finds a group of children, with their teacher, clustered round a large square box full of earth. The excitement is all about an earthworm, which none of the children had ever seen before. Their classroom door opens on to the playground and inside are the rest of the class, seated at tables disposed informally about the room, some reading books that they have themselves chosen from the copious shelves along the side of the room and some measuring the quantities of water that different vessels will hold. Soon the teacher and worm watchers return except for two children who have gone to the library to find a book on worms and the class begins to tidy up in preparation for lunch. The visitor's attention is attracted by the paintings on the wall, and as he looks at them, he is soon joined by a number of children who volunteer information about them. In a moment the preparations for lunch are interrupted as the children press forward with things they have painted, or written, or constructed to show them to the visitor . . . The sound of the music from the hall attracts the visitor and there he finds a class who are making up and performing a dance drama in which the forces of good are overcoming the forces of evil to the accompaniment of drums and tambourines.
>
> As he leaves the school and turns from the playground into the grubby and unlovely street on which it abuts, the visitor passes a class who, seated on boxes in a quiet, sunny corner, are listening to their teacher telling them the story of Rumpelstiltskin. (Plowden Report 1967)

Happiness is a curriculum called Plowden!

A third dominant image was the 'community-orientated', often multi-ethnic, primary school, briefly sketched by Plowden, and forcefully projected by Midwinter (1972) and analysed by Halsey (1972). In it the school is turned outwards, opening itself both to community use of its facilities, and community participation in its management. In its later versions it welcomed and respected the cultural diversity of its catchment area, seeing in them strengths where others saw weakness and problems. Linguistic and cultural differences, defined as 'deprivation' elsewhere, would become powerfully incorporated into the curriculum of the community school, by the adoption of mother-tongue teaching, multi-faith RE, and other local and sub-cultural imperatives. In Midwinter's version the boundaries between school and community dissolve:

> it (the school) attempts to relate fluently and productively with the ethos, character and values of the community it serves . . . it constructs a stable basis upon which a three cornered partnership of parent, teacher and child might harmoniously operate . . . The shopping precinct pram park might run into the nursery unit; the school clinic and the civic group surgery might be one; and the children might eat their school dinner in what is also the local cafe and snack bar . . . The community school requires a highly socialised format because it has a social rather than an academic aim. Its long term aim is to equip the critical parent, worker, consumer and citizen of the next generation in the hope that they might respond creatively to the challenge of deprivation . . . (op. cit. p. 22)

When these images were set against reality in schools and classrooms, there was only a limited match. Jackson's (1964) study of streaming in primary schools reported the divisive and alienating impact it had had on pupils and teachers. Although there is some evidence from Barker Lunn (1970) that pupils in progressive schools have more positive attitudes towards school, both the extent and efficacy of the Plowden ethic have been brought into question by studies quoted in Chapter 1 (pp. 26–7). Programmes of community education may have effected significant changes in parents' involvement in young children's reading, according to research by Tizard and Hewison (1980), but it is doubtful whether they have begun to live up to the ambitious aims of their proponents in respect of regenerating their environments, or altering the life chances of their pupils.

However, to demonstrate by empirical research that classroom reality does not match ideal images is to miss the point about such images, which are designed to represent values not reality. Images of 'good practice' are offered as concentrated ideals to a profession whose vision is often obscured by the hectic, draining and pragmatic demands of their everyday contexts. When Plowden claimed that 'a school is not a teaching shop' it was making a moral and ethical assertion, despite its use of the indicative mood; it meant that a school *should* not be a teaching shop. Thus, although images of good practice are often presented as though they were *descriptions* of reality, there is not normally much doubt that they are *prescriptions*, pictures of the way a report's authors think professional practice should develop.

Any professional practice is based on values, even if they are only partly articulated to the profession as a whole, because it is intended to serve some aim or purpose, is supposed to conform to some standard of behaviour, and to have a relationship to society as a whole. Thus a primary function of such images of good practice is to reflect fundamental values to a profession so that the assumptions upon which its practice is founded may be reaffirmed, and to some extent, confronted. (It is why such images have been widely used in teacher training courses, attracting recent criticism from those who expect training to be more rooted in classroom practice, and less addicted to examination of underlying values.) It is, of course, of very great interest to investigate empirically the influence of such values, or their lack of influence, upon practice, but educational values cannot be 'disproved' by demonstrating that they are difficult to realise, or have not been realised as Bennett (1976), amongst others, acknowledged.

AN IMAGE OF THE 'COLLEGIAL' PRIMARY SCHOOL

The contemporary image of good practice has been promoted by the Inspectorate since 1978, and has been illustrated in the practice of the Warwick inquiry schools. It is of the 'collegial' primary school, predicated on the two values of *teacher collaboration* and *subject expertise*. The political background and the value position of this image have been analysed previously (Chapters 1 and 2) but the image itself needs fuller elaboration. It has a number of characteristic features. It shows small working groups of teachers reporting back recommendations for school-wide change to the collectivity of the whole staff meeting for decision-taking. These groups are led and organised by the curriculum postholders, who draw upon expertise from outside school as well as upon their own professional knowledge, in order to enable the staff to develop the curriculum as authoritatively as possible. Occasionally the postholder works alongside class teachers to illustrate ideas in practice, and to become aware of progress throughout the school. The skills involved in these processes are not only academic; considerable sensitivity, personal enthusiasm and charm are required in order to maintain good working relationships in schools where professional practice is being subjected to the scrutiny of colleagues. The teachers involved become used to tolerating uncertainty and working under pressure of time and conflicting demands. Supporting this collaborative effort is the headteacher who has committed himself or herself to devolving responsibility to the staff group; servicing their activities by putting appropriate school facilities, and where possible his or her time, at their disposal.

The image also shows an atmosphere, ethos or climate distinctive to collegiality. The teachers exist in a school in which constructive and critical scrutiny of each other's practice and ideas is the normal expectation. There is a continuing commitment to professional development through in-service activities both within the school and outside it. Although the teachers are not insensitive to the implications of such involvement for their own career prospects, the major focus of in-service training is the whole school, and there is an open understanding that teachers will feed back into school implications they see for their colleagues of off-site in-service courses. The ethos is not created simply by encouraging teachers to feel solidarity with one another, but by deliberate strategies that make role expectations explicit to all staff, and by the head's involvement in school-based development in practical and supportive ways that do not undermine the authority of teachers with special expertise. The overt commitment to evaluate their initiative collectively accustoms the teachers to giving accounts to each other of the reasons and justifications for particular approaches to the curriculum, and so helps them to anticipate representing their subject or subject area to people outside the school, to parents, other teachers in feeder schools, to advisers, and governors and others. The school thus becomes collectively accountable for its curriculum. The teachers committed to collegiality see the atmosphere in the school as the element most critical to its maintenance, and derive strong personal and professional satisfactions from their involvement in, and contribution to, its continuance. They see the creation and maintenance of such an atmosphere as the responsibility not just of the headteacher, but of the whole staff group. Collegiality will survive the departure of the head.

It is obvious that the foregoing is a projection from empirical reality, not a description of it. It differs from previous images in one particular way: its dominant focus is upon *teachers*. In the foreground of this image is not the school's organisation, or children's emotional adjustment, or community relationships, but working groups of teachers engaged in the process of developing school-wide policies and practices for the curriculum.

There is some evidence from the USA that the cluster of in-school variables depicted above as collegiality, is related to effective change. Goodlad (1975) analysed a five-year action research programme designed to encourage primary schools to improve their curriculum from within. He characterised the processes involved as DDAE — dialogue, decision-making, action and evaluation — and reported on a 'league' of schools co-operating in the research. In those schools scoring high on DDAE, there were more 'co-operative teaching groups, more friendship networks amongst staff, and more task-oriented communication networks amongst staff. Teachers had more influence in decision-making, especially in areas affecting schools as total units' and heads of such schools were more 'apt to see teacher influence in schools as a desirable condition'.

There is an element of tautology in the defining characteristics of the schools, but Goodlad concluded that high DDAE was associated with high teacher morale, a high sense of professionalism and a high sense of the teacher's own power amongst staff, especially where there were effectively functioning 'sub-groups' of staff. If these characteristics were combined,

> they helped us . . . to describe a school's propensity for change, a school's readiness for and ability to work towards self improvement. (Goodlad 1975, p. 135)

IN-SCHOOL OBSTACLES TO THE DEVELOPMENT OF COLLEGIALITY

Drawing an ideal picture, however helpful it is as an expression of values, nonetheless immediately raises questions, especially perhaps for teachers who find the values attractive. These questions are about obstacles to change, and the extent to which practice in contemporary primary schools may be hindered from moving to a better match with the image, if teachers become committed to the values it embodies.

Two features of the culture of contemporary primary schools may particularly hinder the development of collegiality; *role relationships* between teachers, and the *conditions* in which teachers work. The former has been seen in much of the literature as the overriding factor. Until very recently, the latter has been virtually ignored. I believe that the evidence for the problems associated with role relationships is rather insubstantial and to some extent dated, and that the major stumbling block for collegiality is no longer teacher relationships, but some of the conditions in which primary school-teachers have to work, which are not conducive to curriculum development of a school-based kind.

Role relations in primary schools

Studies of role relationships in primary schools by Lortie (1969), Taylor, Reid, Holley and Exon (1974) and by Coulson (1974, 1976, 1978) have drawn attention to the relationship between heads and class teachers, noting the dominant power position, both in law and in convention, of the former in the structure of school staff roles (see Chapter 2, pp. 42–5). However, the important common feature of these studies is not the relative *positions* in the structure of schools, but the complementary sets of *attitudes* that heads and teachers have towards each other. The attitudes support the conventional power positions and give them life and meaning.

On the part of the headteacher, these attitudes combine into 'paternalism', according to Coulson's (1976) analysis, and include influencing teachers to adopt his own aims and methods, filtering information from outside the school, and protecting teachers from parents, and pupils from moral contamination. The explanation for this set of attitudes is the 'ego-identification' of the head with 'his' school, and the historical roots of the moral character of the role, according to Bernbaum (1976) and Peters (1976). On the part of the class teachers, the characteristic attitude set is 'acquiescence' in subordination to the head's dominance, partly because of 'immersion in teaching tasks', according to Coulson, to such an extent that they are 'relatively indifferent to organis- ational matters involving the school as a whole'. These attitudes preserve a kind of mutual autonomy in preferred professional activities. Heads are in charge of what they like to call 'their' school, and teachers are in charge of 'their' class. By a proprietorial and implicit gift exchange, the head offers not to interfere in the classroom and the class teachers accept as their part of the bargain not to expect to participate in school-wide policy-making. Thereby, both parties gain *de facto* control over what gives them most professional satisfaction.

From the point of view of collegiality, these studies, which have helped to create the prevailing view of primary teaching, have identified three major problems. First, class teachers get very great personal and professional satisfaction from the arena most in their own control — their classroom. Leese (1978) illustrated the point in graphic terms:

> a teacher's real gratification comes from what her pupils do and learn with her . . . There is I think, no greater reward for my daughter, a first grade (i.e. reception class) teacher than the evidence that those who come to her unable to read can do so when they leave. There is a strong interpersonal transaction and subsequent bond between her and each child. It is her individual influence upon her client which makes her professional . . . Consequently she deeply resents and resists those who would stylize and interfere with that intimate art upon which her ego rests . . .

To put those satisfactions at risk by subjecting them to a more public scrutiny, and to allocate energy and commitment to more collaborative endeavours outside the class- room, is not self-evidently seductive for already effective teachers, and not at all so for ineffective ones.

Second, for all concerned in the primary school, the conventional role perceptions are comfortable. They function to insulate class teachers and headteachers from each other and thus from the considerable opportunities for conflict that might arise if they stepped outside the normal role expectations into the less clearly defined authority territory of 'whole school' activities. These arrangements make for what Hanson (1977) has called predictability in role relationships. Activities involving collective discussion and decision-making reduce predictability and require tolerance of ambiguity and conflict in relationships, and this is not a very comfortable experience, especially in relatively small organisations, where daily and frequent face-to-face contacts require that friction be avoided as far as possible. Thus there is in the conventional role relationships a subtle but potent pressure to settle for what you know you can do well rather than enter the high risk enterprise of school-based development.

A third problem derives from teacher attitudes to authority; according to Lortie, primary school teachers are disinclined to recognise any authority intermediate between themselves and the head. Coulson (1976) and Coulson and Cox (1975) showed that class teachers did not accept decisions arrived at by deputies and postholders, but sought clearance from the head before going along with them. Curriculum postholders trying to lead staff groups and basing their leadership on their post of responsibility, or on their expertise, will thus be operating in what is perceived as no-man's-land, where territorial rights are in question, and boundaries in dispute.

Alexander (1984), in a major critical re-working that questions the Lortie/Coulson thesis, illustrates the persistence of paternalism and acquiescence by means of a metaphor that the modern consciousness will find provocative. According to it, primary school relationships are like those in a Victorian family, with its dominant male head and its submissive and subordinate, mostly female, members, each happy to perform her allotted function at the head's behest. Alexander acknowledges the problem posed by female heads of infant schools (though not by the ubiquitous overly deferential male teacher in junior schools) but the metaphor itself encapsulates the prevailing cultural analysis in a potent manner.

This analysis shows the primary school world pressing upon class teachers to settle for restricted professionality of the classroom practice, leaving the extended role of curriculum policy-making to the head; it sets the sure and personal satisfactions of the private classroom experience with pupils, against the uncertain and stressful public arena of staff meetings and collaborative groups. It leads heads and classteachers to seek comfortable roles of relative independence from, rather than inter-dependence upon, each other. In the prevailing view, the primary school culture is predicated on individualistic, not collective, endeavour. As Lawson (1979) has suggested about the primary school world from the pupil's point of view, fraternity is not a dominant value. For the pursuit of collegiality, a more daunting scenario would be difficult to imagine.

A re-appraisal of the prevailing view

The view of the professional culture of the primary school as massively oppositional to the development of more collegial relationships, needs to be questioned on two grounds; the nature of the evidence upon which it has been based, and some very recent studies that suggest that teacher roles, or at least teacher perceptions of their roles, may be changing in the direction whereby collegiality could become more feasible.

The empirical basis for the prevailing view is rather insubstantial for making any general statement about teacher relationships in contemporary primary schools. Lortie's study was of US elementary schools in the late 1960s. Taylor and his colleagues used questionnaires from 120 teachers in twelve schools rated as typical by local-authority advisers. Although it is unclear precisely when the questionnaires were completed, the study itself was published in 1974. The authors were careful to describe the study as 'exploratory', and urged the need for more real-life detail created from case studies of actual schools. Coulson's (1976, 1978) analyses were derived from his Master's thesis, presented in 1974, which investigated the conceptions of the deputy head's role held by heads and deputies, again by questionnaire although with a large (more than 600) sample. He argued for administrative change in the direction of expertise and collegiality and the use of flexible working groups led by 'the best qualified and expert person in the subject area the group is to tackle, regardless of his position in the school' (1976, p. 105).

The first point therefore is that the influential studies were using material gathered in the late 1960s and early 1970s, so that none relates to teachers' perceptions since the Great Debate, or more importantly, to the time following the publication of the Primary Survey. Wicksteed and Hill's (1979) survey suggests that teacher attitudes to classroom autonomy have changed, in ways that may soon make the earlier studies period pieces. Secondly, strictly speaking, the studies were of what teachers wrote about primary school teaching on questionnaires, not of teaching itself as experienced in the real worlds of classroom, staffroom and playground. Such a methodology loses out on the diversity and complexity of the real-life situations from which they are abstracted. Thirdly, there is no claim that the samples were representative, either of schools generally, or of good practice, or of anything else, with the ambiguous exception of Taylor's 'typical' or 'modal' schools (which seems to mean that they were not regarded by advisers as unusual in terms of intake, resourcing, degree of innovation and quality of home–school contacts). Thus, strictly speaking again, the studies tell us only what an identified number of particular teachers perceive, or believe about the culture of a particular number of schools, and relationships in them. Finally, both the English studies concluded that the existing teacher–headteacher relationships were anachronistic and in need of modification. Alexander's (1984) commentary on the issue goes further and sharply points out the 'fine line' between a class teacher's insistence on classroom autonomy for personal satisfactions, and 'mere self indulgence or professional irresponsibility'.

None of the above should be seen as criticising the early studies for claiming to be more than could be justified. Their authors were scrupulous in indicating the nature and quality of their basic data. But the clarification of the nature of the evidence raises questions about how generalisable, how reliable, and how dated the analysis conveyed in the studies is, in respect of contemporary primary schools. Some more recent studies suggest that primary school culture has begun to allow a little more flexibility than the somewhat tightly-prescribed roles discerned in the earlier studies, while others suggest that teachers' perceptions and beliefs about the legitimacy of intermediate authority roles, such as postholders, are undergoing change.

Bassey's (1978) survey of Nottinghamshire teachers included the responses of 114 heads to the question 'Who decides on the outline syllabus: head, a teacher with special responsibility for the subject, a group of staff or individual teachers?'. The replies are subject to the methodological problems associated with questionnaires, and there is the specific problem that what was meant by 'outline syllabus' probably varied from respondent to respondent, but 46 per cent of heads said that the mathematics syllabus was decided by groups of staff, and for other subjects the percentages for group decisions were: English 40 per cent, physical education 27 per cent, music 28 per cent, art/craft 21 per cent, and topic 20 per cent. Of Bassey's 281 infant teachers, 28 per cent had 'regular' assistance from another teacher in their classrooms, and around a third of junior and infant teachers 'meet with other staff' when their class is in assembly. What happens at these times is not specified. Although Bassey's survey provided evidence that was in a number of respects problematic and difficult to interpret, on the face of it his primary teachers appeared to operate in less isolated contexts, and his heads in less monopololistic decision-making worlds, than those envisaged in the previous studies.

A study sponsored by the Schools Council and the Primary Schools Research and

Development Group at Birmingham University (1983) examined 'responsibility and the use of expertise' in primary schools using a range of methodologies, including questionnaires, interviews, discussion groups, free accounts and diaries, in order to obtain both range and depth in teacher perceptions and experience of the use of teacher expertise in schools. The study captured in a welcome and unusual way, a diverse and even contradictory range of teacher perceptions about the issues. It revealed teachers' unease about terms like 'expert' and even 'influence', whilst recording their readiness to seek advice from postholders, especially in informal ways. Non-postholders seemed more ready to acknowledge a distinctive role for 'experts' in school, at least in interview. Headteachers on the whole welcomed the idea of making fuller use of teacher expertise, with 80 per cent of the 65 heads who completed a questionnaire approving of the Primary Survey's suggestions to that effect (though they did not, ironically, seem to acknowledge their own self-interest, recognised by class teachers in interviews who felt that postholders were still seen as 'instruments of the head; to do his bidding, to realise his vision.') The heads also commented on the 'need for staff to be engaged in a common enterprise. To co-operate as a team, perhaps through small committees co-ordinated by staff with special curricular interests . . .' The 465 teachers who responded to a questionnaire perceived as very or extremely important sources of their own professional development, 'help from colleagues with special knowledge and experience' (89.7 per cent), and 'help from teachers with scale posts of responsibility' (82.6 per cent).

Paradoxically, although these teachers strongly supported the idea of school-based in-service activity, they did not expect teachers with posts of responsibility to be engaged in 'chairing a group of colleagues working in a curriculum area'. An important finding was that there were subject differences in the extent to which teachers would wish to draw upon subject expertise of colleagues, and in the kind of help that would be sought. There was more readiness to look for help in drawing-up schemes of work, than in teaching methods, resource management, and methods of assessment, possibly because the first area is seen as school policy, whereas the other three are seen as classroom practice. The teachers on the whole thought the wider use of teacher expertise would be mainly beneficial to the school, and judged that its effectiveness would depend to a great extent upon school-wide support. The ambivalent nature of support for the idea in general was summed up by the authors:

> One way teachers had of seeing the teacher expert was as an agent of change, alert to innovations in primary education and determined to make a contribution to the professional development of his colleagues. Another, as a quietly concerned colleague, ready to help if asked.
>
> In the main it was the last way of seeing teacher expert that was most generally supported. The former found more support among teachers with posts of responsibility and among teachers who belong to a teaching association. But this support, though evident, was not strong. (Primary Schools Research and Development Group/Schools Council 1983, p. 98)

The evidence from the Birmingham study does not reveal a profession wholeheartedly committed to changing conventional authority roles and relationships; in many ways it could be used to demonstrate that teachers are divided about the consequences for in-school relationships of implementing the recommendations of the Primary Survey. I interpret it, tentatively, as a record of a profession at a transitional stage, aware of the potential benefit to a school of a shift in exercise of authority to teachers with subject expertise, but perceptive about the repercussions on the quality of staff relationships, and fearful of a loss of informality and reciprocity in professional exchanges. But the study cannot easily be used to argue that teacher perceptions of their roles are fixed in the immutable 'class-teacher–headteacher' division of earlier studies.

A study at Durham University by Rodger et al. (1983) comprised case studies of teachers with posts of responsibility built up collaboratively by the postholders and Rodger, by self-monitoring, triangulated interviews with the postholders and their headteachers, diaries, analysis of critical incidents and a questionnaire. The case studies are rich in personal detail and embedded in the contextual minutiae of postholders' working worlds, offering fascinating source material for examining the potential and problems associated with changing teacher roles in the contemporary primary school. There is naturally great variation in the case studies but the general picture gained from them supports the view of a professional culture being slowly and with difficulty modified in the direction of greater collegiality with some enlightened headteachers enabling postholders to attempt to influence the work of other class teachers, without challenging the principle of class teaching itself. The conclusion of Rodger's study noted the interdependence of the roles of postholder and head and the increase in 'corporate' approaches to managing aspects of the curriculum. He concluded, as the Birmingham study did, that postholders preferred informal 'consultant' roles to more directive ones, because they were uneasy at the prospect of being required to operate as a 'leader' in contexts where their colleagues felt themselves equally competent.

Finally, indirect supportive evidence for a shift in actual attitudes and role relationships has come from a very recent study at Sheffield Polytechnic by Gray (1984), in which headteachers reported that, in 'key' areas of language and mathematics, postholders were exercising a fully 'professional' role in their schools: this role included 'the broad oversight of one sector of the primary schools activities, requiring substantial delegation of powers from the headteacher' (p. 50). Furthermore, the heads identified, as their main criteria for promoting teachers, 'curricular knowledge and skills' and 'personal qualities and attitudes'. Gray quotes heads as explaining their priorities in the following terms (p. 57): 'It used to be for long service, but the climate is now right for curriculum posts' and, more directly, 'The postholders have been told that they've got to become curriculum experts and earn their money.'

All the recent studies are subject to limitations, especially in respect of how far their tentative findings may be generalisable. The Warwick and Durham studies were of small numbers of probably untypically committed postholders, and the Sheffield study is of what 29 headteachers reported as happening. The multi-methodological Birmingham study used samples ranging from 7 (the diaries kept by postholders) to 465 (the questionnaires from teachers), although the ways the samples were reported does not permit us to know what larger populations they were representative of, if any. Caution is necessary, given small, untypical samples, but all these recent studies have findings about role relationships in primary schools that point, albeit uncertainly, in the direction of collegiality and away from individualistic roles in private and autonomous classrooms.

Teachers' conditions of work

A second obstacle to collegiality is a more practical one, and concerns the conditions in which teachers work. For the purposes of this analysis I am restricting the definition of working conditions to (a) the provision of *time*, and (b) access to *facilities* and *ideas* for in-school development.

The use of teacher time

There is hardly any comparative evidence about the 'educationalist context' in primary schools, but it has been shown in Chapter 3 that postholders in the inquiry schools were expected to deploy a wide range of curricular and interpersonal skills, many of which assumed that time was available for exercising such skills, over and above those required for the mainstream teaching. The major problem in adequately meeting these demands was identified by the teachers as a matter of the time available.

Likewise, Rodger et al (1983) comment of one of their postholders:

> *Organisation of non-contact time.* Fiona was never anything but totally dissatisfied with this aspect of her role. She either had no non-contact time due to circumstances in the school, or it was taken up with the remnants of her previous post, e.g. games and coaching. Accordingly she never felt able to devote enough time to her curricular leadership function. (p. 108)

In the conclusions of this study, Rodger indicated ways in which his postholders had 'won' time from other activities. These included such strategies as doubling up classes with another postholder and using hymn practices, assemblies, visits from outside speakers, etc., as well as team teaching and having the head teach classes (p. 136). Whatever their immediate effectiveness, such strategies required the teachers to remove themselves from school activities in which they would normally participate. The assumptions about teacher time underlying curricular leadership activities thus appeared to clash with assumptions about teacher time underlying 'normal' teaching and teaching-related activities.

A fuller consideration of the issues raised by this kind of clash is offered below, where the use of teacher time is discussed under four headings, '*other contact*' time, '*group* time, '*snatched*' time, and '*personal*' time.

'*Other contact*' *time.* The first kind of time is what is normally (and inappropriately) referred to as 'non-contact' time. This is time formally provided in the school to enable the teacher to be free of class teaching. It is the same time as secondary school teachers call 'free' time, although in primary schools staffing tends to be organised on the basis that teachers need, or should be allowed, less 'free' time than secondary school teachers. The basis for this distinction has not been articulated or justified, and a recent report from the National Association of Schoolmasters/Union of Women Teachers (1984) calls for up to 20 per cent of primary school teachers' time to be of this kind. It is perhaps unfortunate that this kind of time is most often seen as either a rest period or a period in which marking and preparation may be carried out. From the point of view of curriculum development, this time might most usefully serve two purposes, namely working alongside colleagues to develop ideas in practice or monitoring work through the school, and visiting other schools, or resource agencies in the LEA and elsewhere, in order to increase expertise. For these reasons it might be useful to designate it as 'other contact' time.

There are two points to make about the 'other contact' time. First, if the Warwick inquiry schools were even remotely typical, there is very little of it available for through-school and outside-school activities of this kind. Ignoring the head and the part-timer, the average time available to the other eight postholders was some 37 minutes per week, though there was great variation in individual schools. Four of the eight had no 'free' time at all. (See Appendix, Table A2, for details.)

The second point is that the non-contact time was a strangely inflexible arrangement, since it meant that the postholder was free at a given time each week, whereas through-school development requires a much more flexible response. Some weeks there will be no need, from a curriculum development point of view, for postholders to be freed from teaching their classes. Some weeks they will need to work alongside teachers at quite different times from other weeks, and on occasions they will need to be out of school for a morning or a day. It is thus not merely shortage of time for this role that is the problem, but arrangements that are inappropriately inflexible to suit the curricular leadership function. 'Non-contact' time for marking and preparation is, or could be, adequately provided for by the current assumptions of how teachers' time should be organised, but through-school developments call for different, more flexible assumptions.

Group time. A second category is 'group time', i.e. time spent in working groups, of varying size, including both the smaller review and development groups producing guidelines, etc. and the whole staff groups which arrive at decisions about through-school policies. The current conditions mean that teachers have to organise these activities, obviously, outside the times when pupils are being taught. This means either at lunchtimes or after school, when most children have gone home, or on 'occasional' days given over to in-service training.

There are two problems with this use of time. First, many primary schoolteachers conventionally give time both over the lunch break and after school to pupils, for example by organising clubs, music, sports and games coaching, extra reading and language work, etc. This means that curriculum working groups may interfere with these activities, or that some teachers, often the most committed ones, will be unable to participate in them, or will do so intermittently. Although this problem can be mitigated to some extent by advance planning, there would be understandable resistance among primary school teachers if in-school development was to be implemented at the expense of time devoted to these other kinds of professional activities. The other problem is to do with teacher perceptions. Group time is perceived as a voluntary activity, a 'moral' obligation, not a 'contractual' one, in Becher, Eraut and Knight's (1981) terminology. Because it is seen as voluntary, it is vulnerable both to the vagaries of industrial relations in education and differential levels of teacher involvement.

'Snatched' time. A third time category is what can only be called 'snatched' time. Much school-based work involves informal discussion and consultation, and one part of the empirical picture of the postholder's role emerging from the Warwick inquiry is of brief and rushed consultations with other teachers, and with advisers and heads often at times such as lunch or coffee breaks. Such discussions also occurred.whilst the postholder was actually engaged teaching a class. One postholder told me of being called out of her class to discuss the school scheme with an adviser whose help had been sought, whilst two others referred to discussions occurring in the classroom. No doubt this has to happen, given the time constraints upon both the advisory staff and primary teachers, and it is clear from both the Birmingham and the Durham studies that class teachers value very highly curricular leadership exercised informally, but the use of snatched time for considering curricular issues must look to outsiders as an amateurish way for professional affairs to be conducted. It is probably necessary to make distinctions according to the nature of such consultations; a brief word over coffee about how to start pupils off on using pastels may be sensible and desirable given the informal and friendly nature of most staffroom contacts, but discussion of possible problems and approaches in a suggested scheme of work needs a less harried, more thoughtful context than a school corridor or classroom.

In many ways the use of snatched time is not unexpected; it is how much time of primary teachers is used in the routine of school days — mending plugs for equipment, dealing with interruptions of lessons by requests for administrative information, going along the corridor to borrow work cards or teaching materials, helping children find things they have lost or mislaid, taking assembly at unavoidably short notice, and so on. But snatched time sits uneasily with a rhetoric about extended professional behaviour and raising the quality of in-school decision-making.

'Personal' time. The final category is 'personal time', i.e. time used by individuals for curriculum development, entirely out of school, either for reading, attending courses, and time used for discussion with external 'experts' such as university and college tutors. This was not a serious problem amongst the postholders in the Warwick inquiry, partly because of their history of involvement in such activities, and partly because it is the only time category under their own control. Moreover, they were unusually well-matched in terms of their initial training and the subject for which they held responsibility posts. In the situation where a postholder is required to acquire familiarity with a relatively new subject, as was the case in some of Rodger's postholders, much more personal time will be used up.

Official recognition of the problem of teacher time

The Primary Survey noted that some time would have to be available in school if postholders were to influence the work in their subject throughout the school, and thus went a little way towards recognising the need formally to allocate time for in-school development. There were strongly held views about this in the Warwick inquiry schools, to the point where, as has been shown in Chapter 6, assumptions about teacher time took on a *symbolic* as well as practical significance, with teachers interpreting lack of recognition for time spent on in-school development, as lack of interest in it by local authorities. To illustrate the point tendentiously, if a head has to spend a lot of time negotiating with the local authority for cover for the release of a teacher for a morning, as happened in one school, and if the teacher has to spend a lot of what little free time in the day she has negotiating with a nearby school to arrange a visit for observation and discussion, and if at the end of it all there is no cover supplied, so that the teacher feels guilty about leaving her class for the head to teach, they may both begin to ask whether their priorities in use of their time are shared by the local authority.

This is not just a local difficulty. Evidence from national surveys is beginning to identify teacher time as a major problem. It emerged clearly in two recent reports by HMI (DES 1983a, 1983b), one concerned with 9–13 middle schools, and one with secondary schools.

In the middle schools, postholders had on average 3¼ hours per week for curricular and other responsibilities, allocated free from teaching. Despite this, HMI raised teacher time as an issue for discussion, seeing the level of staffing in the schools leaving

> little margin of teacher time for purposes other than the teaching of a class . . . While it is reasonable to expect teachers to give some personal time to planning work, managing resources and keeping up to date with developments, they also need sufficient opportunities, while the schools are in session, to observe the work the children are doing and to guide and support other teachers. A very heavy teaching load inevitably limits their effectiveness as consultants or co-ordinators. (DES 1983a, para. 8.13)

In the secondary schools report there had been a co-ordinated attempt to adopt 'curriculum appraisal' in some 34 schools in five authorities. The Inspectors found that 'radical thinking about the curriculum was difficult to realise because teachers had to maintain the necessary daily routines', and in an explicit reference to teacher time, pointed out both the conflict of priorities and the resource implications.

> Much of the discussion and group planning had to take place at the end of a full day's teaching, and this was not the best time for the considered discussion of important issues . . . teachers were often prevented from giving a full commitment to the work (of curriculum development) because of the routine pressures associated with their normal duties. Problems of communication within the schools have been accentuated by the limited time which is available for this work in the normal context of school life. If LEAs wish to sponsor work of this kind there are implications for staffing and in-service work. (DES 1983b, p. 16)

The enterprise developed out of thoughtful and well resourced collaboration between HMI, LEAs, and teachers in schools that are staffed, as are 9–13 middle schools, more favourably than primary schools. If it partly foundered upon the problem of teacher time, it shows how important an issue it is for the profession as a whole to face up to in extending the movement for in-school development to the less formally resourced and supported context of the normal primary school.

Access to facilities and ideas

By facilities and ideas for in-school development I mean access to secretarial help, to reprographic processes, and to ideas and materials relevant to a particular programme.

Facilities

In most primary schools provision of facilities for reproducing notes or minutes of working group meetings, to ensure distribution of them in time for proper consideration, is antediluvian. To struggle for half an hour to get an antiquated Banda machine to provide even rough and ready versions of a manuscript original is a common experience; to have a secretary to type out and photocopy such matter is 'like gold', as one postholder said.

Conventional assumptions about the work of primary school teachers are that they will teach — they will be the 'teacher as teacher', and for that role all they will need is teaching materials, felt-tip pens for their work cards, and a ready supply of chalk. However the 'teacher as educationalist' role requires of them that they produce working drafts, discussion papers, guidelines, and all the documentary trappings that flow from more collective forms of decision-making. In most of the schools in the Warwick inquiry, there had been cuts in the hours of the school secretary, and it was difficult to argue that priority should be given to the work of postholder-led teacher groups over 'normal' administrative functions. The facilities in general were inadequate to cope with the kind of demands that in-school development has to make on secretarial and clerical services. For the purposes of my own inquiry I needed copies of working drafts, group papers, and guidelines etc., and in every case I had to have the material typed and copied at the university because it was not in a state that met normal reprographic standards. When I offered to make available to the schools some extra copies of their own schemes, typed and photocopied, I was made to feel like some modern version of a cargo cult carrier.

Ideas and materials

A second problem is one of access to ideas and materials that can help in the curriculum development programme itself, and in the teachers' own professional development. Some schools were trying to build up staffroom copies of books, reports and materials relevant to a particular programme, but on the whole teachers do not have easy access to recent thinking, relevant research and reports of practice in other schools, or even to information about where such ideas might be available. The Schools Council (1983) has attempted to remedy the latter problem by identifying a list of 26 books for the staffroom — a kind of curricular version of 'Your 100 Best Tunes' — although the list seems somewhat arbitrary. The idea of a professional reference library in primary school staffrooms may sound a little pretentious, but easy access to major reports on the curriculum, together with teachers' handbooks on the major curriculum projects and materials in the normal curriculum areas, and subscription to one or two professionally-oriented journals might go some way towards reducing the professional isolation of primary school staff. Even if it only mildly dented the monopoly of the local authority job circular for teachers' attention in the staffroom, it would be worth it.

Teachers also need access to specialised advice on ideas and materials from outside the school, from advisers, university staff and other people. At the present time such access is difficult to arrange, mainly because it has not been given attention. It would be a considerable boost to schools involved in curriculum development if they knew that they could get access legitimately and quickly to the kinds of information and ideas necessary to its initiation and maintainance. At a time of reduced expenditure, discriminating advice at an early stage would help in decisions about priorities for spending what is available.

There is no single person, agency or institution that has a monopoly on specialised ideas and materials relevant to in-school development. LEA advisers, teachers' centres, other schools, publishing houses, university and college of education tutors, field centres and a range of other agencies are within the range of most teachers. What is required is that it should become normal, or expected, for teachers to have access to them. Without time and access to ideas, curriculum development will be less effective than it could be as Sutherland's (1981) comments on larger-scale projects reminded us (Chapter 1, p. 28).

PROFESSIONAL ACCOUNTABILITY: A MODEL AND A PRACTICE

Up to this point, teacher role relationships and work conditions have been treated separately for purposes of analysis. But they are not independent of one another; in a collegial school they converge in the practice of 'professional accountability' — the delivery by postholders of 'curricular accounts' to their colleagues and the developing of such accounts with them. This kind of accountability to one's professional peers, illustrated in Chapter 4, includes providing statements justifying policies and practices, preparing material for discussion groups, recording and reporting their decisions, dealing with doubts and disagreements in staff meetings, handling inter-school liaison meetings, and representing the subject to advisers and others from outside the school. For most postholders this was a central, and to some extent stressful, aspect of their role, and to be effective it requires both appropriate working conditions and appropriate working relationships. There is in the literature both a model for and a report of professional accountability in practice.

A mutual accountability model

A sustained analysis of this kind of accountability (in two institutions of higher education) by Adelman and Alexander (1982) characterised their 'mutual culpability', or mutual accountability, model as requiring that:

> all participants regardless of role or status, see themselves as equally accountable to each other for their particular contributions to the educational process. (p. 26)

Despite differences in the institutional contexts, Alexander (1984) has persuasively argued for the application of the mutual-accountability model to primary schools, pointing to its congruence with through-school curriculum development, and with the values that primary teachers hold up to their pupils.

> A 'whole curriculum' as we have considered it (i.e. as having a vertical dimension as well as the horizontal coherence) can exist only in a climate of mutuality, openness, sharing and

comparing of ideas, dovetailing of schemes and practices. And if primary schools are serious in their commitment to educational goals for the child like co-operation, the development of empathy, interpersonal skills and so on, they need to acknowledge the force of the hidden curriculum in such matters whereby the behaviour of adults in the school towards each other is as significant a learning resource as, say, group work in the classroom. (p. 185)

Two points about the model shed light upon relationships in in-school development programmes. First, the model assumes an organisational style, stressing *flexibility* and 'organic' relationships rather than fixed roles and mechanistic relationships. We saw in Chapter 2 a similar point made by Henderson and Perry (1981). It assumes that teachers are redefining their roles and relationships in order to cater for change. They render accounts to one another as equals, even though they may occupy different formal positions of authority. Second, it assumes relationships that are mutually *supportive*. This is because teachers opening up their professional practice to the professional scrutiny of their peers, are making both themselves potentially vulnerable, and the emergence of disagreement probable. For this to happen to the benefit of a school requires supportive, not corrosive, relationships between staff.

This was a point commonly made in the inquiry schools to explain why professional disagreement had not degenerated into dispute. As one head said:

In another school, they would have quarrelled — the programme would have collapsed, because it was a serious disagreement they were having. They couldn't resolve it, they just disagreed about priorities. But they worked well as a team, they were very professional, and because their relationship was professional, they kept together as a team and saw it through.

Giving accounts to colleagues, therefore, is not just explaining and justifying educational policies in an educationalist discourse; it is a process embedded in, and simultaneously extending, relationships that permit what Alexander called 'intellectual autonomy' of individuals, but from a foundation of mutual support. Thus the mutual-accountability model translates at primary school level into a climate of relationships of *mutual responsibility*. Such a climate will need to be maintained not only by the head, though his role at the initial stages will be critical, but by the staff as a whole.

The model needs to be elaborated in two respects; one concerns the importance of personal characteristics, the other the importance of efficiency. First, professional accountability depends upon the personal, the idiosyncratic, the human qualities amongst staff. When teachers talked about the postholders' qualities it was these personal qualities that they stressed as much as anything — how well she had managed the meetings, how she had jollied them along, how interesting her style was in discussion groups, and so on. No management style can eradicate these unpredictable personal attributes from affecting a particular programme, any more than curriculum materials in centre–periphery projects were able to be teacher-proof. Conventional management techniques may see such unpredictability as a weakness, but the teachers in the schools saw it as a strength.

Second, for the climate to embody responsibility as well as mutuality, there is the need for efficiency, which does not sit easily with the long traditions of cosy informality in primary schools. The danger of unduly formalised staff meetings ought not to provide the excuse for unstructured and aimless meetings, which are neither informed by specialist advice nor managed and resourced effectively. This would lead to the legitimation of what Alexander (1984) has characterised as 'random chat'. His discussion of meetings shows their potential and their pitfalls:

> Staff meetings can engender a sense of collective commitment; they can help teachers towards an understanding of and involvement in whole school concerns; open up the individual teacher to alternative arguments and ideas; stimulate intellectual engagement; minimise curriculum incoherence and inconsistency: in short, staff meetings are *potentially* one way of realizing both the concept of a 'whole curriculum' . . . and the notion of the (intellectually) autonomous teacher. Equally, staff meetings can consist of headteacher monologues, aimless and trivial anecdote-swapping or opinion-parading, frustrating to staff and head alike.

Professional accountability in practice: a special school

Professional accountability of the kind implied by the above model, appears in a report by Ainscow and Tweddle (1979) of curriculum development in a special school. The Warnock Report (1978) had recommended that curricular guidelines in such schools should be well defined and that all staff should be involved in their production, implementation and evaluation (paras. 11.14–11.16). In this particular school, 'in order to improve the teamwork of the staff', short daily staff meetings were held to deal with administrative matters, and a more substantial programme of formally planned and serviced meetings was implemented to carry out curricular reviews. The 'guiding rules' for these meetings were:

(a) a programme agreed in advance with set time limits on meetings;
(b) a clear brief for each meeting, with a discussion document presented by the relevant member of staff;
(c) an agreement to move towards decision-taking in each meeting and to record decisions in circulated minutes.

Ainscow and Tweddle argue that 'in the long run' this format would lead to greater continuity and consistency through the school, and that it provided two further advantages. First the staff could 'collectively decide upon their own in-service needs and then together . . . pool their ideas, experience and expertise to meet these needs'. Where necessary 'outside expertise' could be imported to the meetings for specific purposes. Second, there would be an increase in informed decision-taking about the curriculum, because each member of staff had participated in the discussion leading up to it. They summarised the school's practice as follows:

> the collective strength of staff expertise used in a consistent and continuous manner, an organisational procedure relying heavily on discussion meetings and consensus decision making . . . formed a basis for school based curriculum development and in-service training.

Although this might read to some like a dauntingly formal set of arrangements, they appear to have been created from assumptions about teacher working conditions, use of teacher time, and access to facilities and ideas far more appropriate for curriculum development than those operating in most mainstream schools, for while part of the explanation for the realisation of professional accountability in the school must lie in the development of staff relations, another part may lie in the levels of resource and staffing in special schools.

CONCLUSION

Obstacles to the full realisation of collegiality in the professional life of primary schools have been examined in this chapter under the two headings of role relationships and working conditions. In the early 1970s it was the relationships between teachers that were seen as the major obstacle to change, whereas the working conditions of teachers were not given much attention. If the very recent studies prove reliable guides, problems of teacher relationships and teacher perceptions of their roles appear to be reducing (though by no means disappearing) as the profession responds to pressure from HMI and others, and begins to accord recognition to the intermediate authority of postholders.

Teacher working conditions however seem stuck on the anachronistic assumptions that there is no need to provide time, facilities and ideas for curriculum development. It is this aspect of primary school life that requires urgent re-appraisal, especially in the light of findings of the most recent HMI surveys (DES 1983a, 1983b). At the present time expectations for school-based curriculum development of the kind called for in the stream of documents from the DES are probably only realisable in those schools that have a fortunate combination of an enlightened and supportive headteacher and unusually talented and hard-working postholders. What is now required is that such development should become routinised in the system; it should be translated from the pioneering schools into the normal ones. For this purpose the kinds of change in teacher working conditions hinted at earlier need to be implemented.

This is not the place for a full examination of what should happen to teacher working conditions, which are properly a matter of negotiation between employers' and teachers' representatives. There is, however, a basis for such negotiation. Teacher time as a problem could be alleviated by an additional allocation of a fixed (annual) amount of staff time to each school for in-school development, INSET, and other related activities, with the understanding that the school could decide in detail how the time should be used. Within the school the time might pass from one postholder to another in the light of school needs. This would provide for the desired flexibility in the use of postholders' time and give an extended professional role the symbolic recognition it needs. If this were done it might be easier to move to a position where teachers would accept that some of their working day after teaching could be rightly reserved for group planning of through-school practice.

Second, an additional element in the resource given to schools could be made available for flexible use of secretarial/clerical time, again to be used at the discretion of the individual school to service in-school development. Access to ideas and expertise also needs resourcing, and a small element of the school's budget for a professional library in the staffroom, or for teacher release to travel to appropriate agencies, could also be provided.

This is not a claim for more of everything in an indiscriminate way. It is a claim that in-school development has sufficient potential to make a fair bid for some of the budget nationally allocated for teacher INSET, and that what is required for using the resource wisely is a re-examination of the assumptions commonly made about the nature of primary school teachers' working conditions.

This has been an unusual book about primary schools in the sense that it has hardly mentioned pupils. Its focus has been upon teachers and their role in school-based curriculum development. Arguing for an increased commitment to the values of collegiality in primary schools, however, is not fundamentally about improving the professional experience of teachers. In collegial schools the teachers will co-operate to develop the curriculum more firmly and consistently upon the imperatives of subject expertise; they will collectively review their policies, and openly commit themselves to evaluating their practice, and they will develop and sustain a climate in which peer group accountability for the curriculum can grow. In such schools, the quality of the professional life of the teachers will undoubtedly be enhanced, but because the curriculum is constantly being developed and consistently being implemented, the ultimate beneficiaries will, quite properly, be the pupils. Improvement of the curriculum as it is offered to them, is the purpose of school-based curriculum development, and the main justification for expending time, energy and resources on it.

Appendix

A COMMENTARY ON THE TYPICALITY OF THE SCHOOLS AND THE CURRICULUM POSTHOLDERS IN THE WARWICK INQUIRY

The schools were not selected as a statistically representative sample of primary schools in the authority concerned, or, of course, of primary schools generally. None the less, the question of the typicality of the subject of the inquiry has to be raised, at least in the minimal form 'Were the schools so untypical of primary schools in general that the inquiry would produce little of interest or relevance to teachers other than the participants?'. In this kind of inquiry the question has to be examined after the event, because the major criterion for their inclusion was the fact that they had been, or were, engaged in school-based curriculum developments. There are a number of different ways of answering the question, and five are discussed below.

Staffing in the schools

First, except for the transitional school 1, Case study A, and the combined school, Case study F, the schools were middle schools 'deemed primary', catering for children up to 12, and were staffed marginally better than some junior or junior and infant schools. The extent to which middle schools 'deemed primary' are staffed more favourably than other primary schools varies but is not generally very great, according to Hargreaves and Tickle (1981) and Taylor and Garson (1982). This issue is difficult to resolve with certainty because the pupil:teacher ratio is given by local authority, not by school, in the official statistics, and there is considerable variation by school within each authority. This is because divisional officers of the local authority have some limited discretion to enable the particular circumstances of a school to be taken into account, and because of staffing for identified special needs, as for example under s. 11 of the Local Government Act 1966. There is also the fact that the extent of non-teaching duties varies by school. Individual school PTRs were provided in Table I.1 so that specific comparison with other schools may be made.

However, two comparisons of PTRs in general are possible, and of some help in forming a judgement about the typicality of the schools as primary schools. There are comparisons of PTRs in the inquiry schools with those in the local authority as a whole, and comparisons of PTRs in the authority with those in other comparable authorities nationally.

PTRs in the authority and in the inquiry schools (School 1 treated as in Case study B)

The basic data are given below:

(a) Mean primary PTRs in the inquiry authority:

1979–80	22.7	(actuals)
1980–81	23.0	(actuals)
1981–82	22.9	(actuals)

Source: CIPFA Education Statistics

(b) Mean PTRs in the eight inquiry schools in 1980–81: 22.4.
(c) Mean PTRs in the six inquiry schools without substantial s. 11 staffing in 1980–81: 23.8.

Direct comparison between the means is not appropriate, partly because the means in (b) and (c) are part of the mean in (a), and because the authority mean includes staffing not attached to particular schools, staff on secondment, etc. The figures are provided to show only the general relationship of the staffing in the inquiry schools to that in the authority overall. If the schools with s. 11 staffing are excluded, as in (b), the inquiry schools were not staffed better than the county average; if all eight inquiry schools are considered, the staffing was marginally better than average. The figures suggest that on the whole the inquiry schools were not staffed in a substantially more generous way than other comparable schools in the county, given some allowance for the needs of the multi-ethnic schools.

The PTRs for the particular county set in the national context

These show a similarly middle-of-the-road picture, as is indicated below:

Mean primary PTRs:	1979–80	1980–81	1981–2
(a) in the authority	22.7	23.0	22.9
(b) in English counties	23.3	23.3	23.2
(c) in all LEAs in England and Wales	22.7	22.6	22.5

Source: CIPFA Education Statistics (actuals)

These data show the inquiry authority with marginally better PTRs than the most comparable group, the English counties, and marginally worse than the national average. Again the figures are not offered as a demonstration of any precision, but merely to show that the particular local authority in which the schools were located did not have an untypically generous, or for that matter ungenerous, policy on staffing.

Curricular facilities in the schools

Another definition of typicality refers to the nature of the physical provision of facilities in a school. To develop work through the school in, say, science is probably easier if specialised facilities exist than if they do not. A narrative description of the facilities in the schools has been provided earlier. The most direct comparison is with Taylor and Garson's (1982) survey of middle schools, which showed the primary category nationally as being less well provided for than the eight inquiry schools, as can be seen in Table A.1.

Table A.1 *Percentage of 8–12 schools possessing specialist facilities*

Facilities	Taylor and Garson's sample	Warwick inquiry (eight schools)
Craft	78	100
Music	43	100
Science	56	100
Home economics	58	100
Language laboratory	9	0
Gymnasium	37	100[a]

[a] Includes the hall used as a gym.

In respect of semi-open-plan provision, which was part of the facilities in seven out of the eight inquiry schools, a typical primary school is less well provided for. HMI (DES 1978) found only one in ten classes working in open or semi-open facilities, and the study by Bennett et al. (1980) suggested a similar proportion, while pointing out the problems associated with the term, including problems of how the facilities were actually used. He hinted that the time pupils spend 'on task' might be lower than average in open-plan schools, because of the time spent in transition between areas and activities.

From the point of view of school-based approaches to curriculum development, however, the facilities in the schools were probably untypically advantageous, for they both encouraged the development of specialist skills in particular subjects by a teacher with expertise in them, and they enabled some teachers to work together more easily than if they each taught in enclosed classrooms. Thus, indirectly at least, the physical arrangements in the schools would be particularly helpful if postholders wished to increase their influence in their specialist subject throughout the school.

Age range and size of the schools

The question of typicality in respect of age range and size of schools is fairly easily examined. Six of the schools covered the age range 8–12, one 5–12, and one included

7–11 then 8–12-year-olds. In an obvious sense most were not directly typical of the conventional 5–7, 7–11 infant/junior arrangements. Thus in terms of the organisation of the educational system, and particularly the ages of transfer from one kind of school to another, the schools were untypical. This would be an important limitation if the focus of the inquiry was particularly to do with transfer arrangements, or if the inquiry schools were 9–13 schools 'deemed secondary'. But the focus of the inquiry was how curriculum postholders in primary schools were able to influence other teachers in the schools, and because the schools were staffed and organised on conventional primary lines, with class teaching as the major feature, the actual age of transfer is of relatively little significance. The applicability of the inquiry to small infant-only schools is probably less direct than to junior schools, but even here the recent study by HMI (DES 1982a) has stressed the significance of curriculum postholders.

In respect of size, the schools in the inquiry were as follows:

(a)   five three-form entry;
(b)   two two-form entry;
(c)   one one-form entry.

The problems of small, often rural, schools with less than one form of entry, with classes of mixed age ranges, and with relatively few staff, especially the problems of adequate coverage of the curriculum, are very considerable, and particular to such schools. They account for 9 per cent of infant and junior schools according to HMI (DES 1978, p. 13). The findings of the inquiry can have only indirect relevance to the problems of curriculum development in them. There is, on the other hand, no obvious reason why the findings may not be applicable to larger schools than those in the inquiry, and to 9–13 middle schools.

The workloads of postholders

The previous three aspects of typicality have referred to the typicality of the *contexts* in which the curriculum developments occurred. Although such aspects impinge to some extent upon discussions of the relevance to other primary schools, they are not the central issue. The central issue is how far the role of the curriculum postholder in the school was untypical of the role of teachers generally, and if so in which ways. For the curriculum postholders were key figures in the developments. Thus the critical questions about typicality are about their workloads, formal responsibilities, extent of free time, etc. Put simply, were their workloads untypically light so that they were able to spend more time and energy than is usually available for school-based curriculum development? Some data to help answer this question are provided in Table A.2.

The picture emerging from the table about the postholders is far from standardised, but a number of points can be made. If the headteacher and the part-timer are excluded, seven of the remaining postholders have responsibility for general class teaching; only in Case study I was a postholder freed from class teaching and used as a specialist teacher. This latter is distinguished from the others also by the amount of time she had free from teaching, and by the absence of other responsibilities. Of the others all but the postholder in Case study A had substantial responsibilities in addition to one curriculum

Table A.2 *Some characteristics of the postholder's role*

| Case study | Level of responsibility and subject | Other responsibilities | | | Time formally free from teaching duties, in minutes per week |
		Class teaching, with age group and number of pupils in the class	Another curriculum subject	Non-curriculum responsibility	
A	Sc. 2, Social studies	First year (7+), $n = 31$	n.a.	n.a.	nil
B	Deputy head, combined studies	Fourth year (11+), $n = 28$	Remedial work	Fourth-year co-ordinator and deputy head	55
C	Sc. 3, Language	First year (8+), $n = 32$	n.a.	First-year co-ordinator	60
D	Sc. 3, Language	First year (8+), $n = 25$	n.a.	First-year co-ordinator and liaison with first schools	nil
E	Head	n.a.	n.a.	Headteacher	n.a.
F	Sc. 2, Science	Third year (10+), $n = 32$	Physical education	n.a.	50
G	Sc. 3, Art/craft	Second year (9+), $n = 34$	n.a.	Second-year co-ordinator	nil
H	Sc. 3, Social studies	Fourth year (11+), $n = 30$	Religious education	n.a.	nil
I	Sc. 3, Art/craft	n.a.	n.a.	n.a.	130
J	Sc. 2, Music (part-time, 0.5)	n.a.	n.a.	n.a.	nil

subject and class teaching. Three had another subject, and four had co-ordination of a year group. The implication of this spread of responsibilities for school-based development has been examined in Chapter 4 but it is important to note that on the whole the postholders in the inquiry had a very full range of responsibilities, as have most primary school teachers.

In terms of time formally free from teaching duties, the position varies considerably. Apart from Case study I, which is, in this respect as in others, distinctive, only three postholders had time allocated for, amongst other things, curriculum development. Of these, the deputy head, who was responsible for two subject areas as well as a year group co-ordination, had the equivalent of eleven minutes a day. The other two postholders had twelve and ten minutes a day respectively. No other postholders had time freed from teaching to develop their subjects in the school, or for other more routine purposes.

Again there is no direct basis for comparison, though work by HMI (DES 1983a) on 9–13 schools offers some help in making judgements. According to them, teachers holding curriculum posts in 9–13 schools tend to have on average some three and a quarter hours a week free from teaching duties, although they also found considerable variation.

Curricular responsibility and curricular expertise

A final point concerns the allocation of special responsibility posts themselves. In this respect the schools seem somewhat untypical in the extent to which they have identified postholders with responsibility for areas of the curriculum. The data for the inquiry schools have been given in Table A.3. The national picture was provided by HMI (DES 1978a) in the Annex to Chapter 4 of their survey of primary education. Their figures are given by size of school and show the percentage of schools having teachers with special curricular responsibility. Some relevant percentages are given in Table A.4.

Table A.3 *Curriculum subjects for which a post of responsibility was allocated by school*

	School								
Subject	1	2	3	4	5	6	7	8	Total
Art/craft		√	√	√		√	√	√	6
English/language		√	√	√	√	√	√	√	7
French	√	√	√	√	√	√	√		7
Home econ./health/n'work		√		√	√		√		4
Mathematics	√	√	√	√	√	√	√		7
Music	√	√	√		√	√	√	√	7
Physical education		√	√	√	√		√	√	6
Remedial work	√	√						√	3
Resources/library/AVA		√	√	√	√		√	√	6
Science		√	√	√	√	√	√	√	7
Social studies	√		√		√		√	√	5
Others	√	√			√		√	√	5
Total	6	10	10	8	10	6	11	9	

Curricular responsibility	Primary survey		Inquiry schools
	Two-form entry	*Three-form entry*	*Inquiry schools*
Music	78	84	88
Language/reading	58	63	88
Mathematics	49	65	88
Science	20	30	75
Environmental studies	20	27	63
French	16	14	88

Of course there was a time difference between the national survey and the Warwick inquiry, and certainly in the case of French, a locally agreed policy was influential, but the general picture of the inquiry schools is that they were ones in which more posts of responsibility were formally allocated for areas of the curriculum than is the case nationally. The schools were probably untypical in the policies they had adopted about the use of staff expertise. This would make sense given that the schools were selected because they were known for their interest in curriculum development.

A related issue concerns the *match* of expertise of the postholders. Of the ten postholders in this inquiry, seven had followed an initial teacher training course in which their main subject had been the curriculum subject (or a cognate one) for which they held special responsibility, and in which they had developed a school-based programme. Of the remaining three, two (Case study B, and Case study E) had developed programmes — in team teaching and in an enrichment experience — for which the main subject at initial level was not available or appropriate. The other postholder (Case study H) had trained in RE as her main subject, but was following an in-service BEd. specialising in environmental studies, the area for which she had a responsibility post (with RE). Thus there was a very strong 'match' between the professional training of the postholders, their curricular responsibility posts, and the nature of their school-based curriculum development activity. No data exist for comparison, but it is unlikely that the match of posts to expertise is as good generally as it was for these particular postholders.

Conclusions

Five aspects of the typicality of the inquiry schools have been explored above in a way that is designed deliberately to enable readers to judge for themselves the extent to which, if at all, the schools and the postholders deviated dramatically from current primary school conventions. My own judgement is that the schools are typical in respect of pupil:teacher ratios, and the postholders' workloads, except for the postholder in Case study I, whose load was untypically light. The size and age range of the schools, whilst not typical, place only limited restrictions upon the inquiry's applicability to the general potential for school-based curriculum development. The inquiry schools seem to have enjoyed advantages that are probably untypical in respect of their physical facilities, which would encourage the development of specialist expertise, and, because of the commonness of the semi-open-plan features, would ease its application to classes other than the postholder's. A second advantage, again untypical in all probability, is the number of special responsibility posts devoted to curriculum areas, and the good match between the postholders' expertise and the curricular responsibilities allocated to them.

The above comparison has been spattered with phrases like 'in all probability' because, given the indirect basis for comparison between the inquiry schools and other primary schools, judgement about typicality has had to be tentative. The 'case studies' were not studies of schools, but of curriculum development programmes led by teachers holding posts of responsibility. My subjective judgement after the inquiry was that despite individual differences, these postholders were untypical in the critical matter of their expertise (both academic and in terms of their interpersonal skills) and in their commitment and energy. Two years after the inquiry, some indirect evidence emerged to support my judgement. If the headteacher and the part-timer (Cases E and J) are excluded from consideration, 4 of the 8 remaining postholders had been promoted, one to a headship, one to a teacher training institution and two to deputy headships. There may be no general connection between merit and promotion, but it does suggest that in the particular cases educational virtue has not gone unrewarded.

Bibliography

Adelman, C. and Alexander, R. (1982) *The Self Evaluating Institution: Practice and principles in the management of educational change*. London: Methuen.

Ainscow, M. and Tweddle, D.A. (1979) *Preventing Classroom Failure*. London: John Wiley.

Aitkin, M., Bennett, S.N. and Hesketh, J. (1981) 'Teaching styles and pupil progress: a re-analysis'. *British Journal of Educational Psychology*, 51, 170–86.

Alexander, R. (1984) *Primary Teaching*. Eastbourne: Holt, Rinehart and Winston.

Auld, R. (1969) *Report of the public enquiry into the organisation and management of the William Tyndale junior and infants school*. London: Inner London Education Authority.

Barker Lunn, J. (1970) *Streaming in the Primary School*. Windsor: NFER.

Barker Lunn, J. (1982) 'Junior schools and their organisational policies'. *Educational Research*, 24(4), 250–61.

Bassey, M. (1978) *Nine Hundred Primary School Teachers*. Windsor: NFER.

Bealing, D. (1972) 'Organisation of junior school classrooms'. *Educational Research*, 14, 231–5.

Becher, A. and Maclure, S. (1978) *The Politics of Curriculum Change*. London: Hutchinson.

Becher, A., Eraut, M. and Knight, J. (1981) *Policies for Educational Accountability*. London: Heinemann.

Bennett, S.N. (1976) *Teaching Styles and Pupil Progress*. London: Open Books.

Bennett, S.N. and Jordan, J. (1975) 'A typology of teaching styles in primary schools'. *British Journal of Educational Psychology*, 45, 20–8.

Bennett, S.N., Andreae, J., Hegarty, P. and Wade, B. (1980) *Open Plan Schools: Teaching, Curriculum, Design*. Windsor: NFER for the Schools Council.

Bernbaum, G. (1976) 'The role of the head'. In Peters, R.S. (ed.) *The Role of the Head*. London: Routledge and Kegan Paul.

Bernstein, B. (1973a) 'Class and pedagogy: visible and invisible'. In Bernstein, B., *Class, Codes and Control*, Vol.3. London: Routledge and Kegan Paul.

Bernstein, B. (1973b) 'Open school, open society?'. In Bernstein, B., *Class, Codes and Control*, Vol.3. London: Routledge and Kegan Paul.

Blackie, J. (1967) *Inside the Primary School*. London: HMSO.

Blyth, W.A.L. (1965) *English Primary Education*, Vol.1. London: Routledge and Kegan Paul.

Blyth, W.A.L. (1968) *English Primary Education*, Vol.1. London: Routledge and Kegan Paul.

Blyth, W.A.L. and Derricott, R. (1977) *The Social Significance of Middle Schools*. London: Batsford.

Bornett, C. (1980) 'Staffing and middle schools'. In Hargreaves, A. and Tickle, L.

(ed.) *Middle Schools: Origins, Ideology and Practice*. London: Harper and Row.

Boydell, D. (1975) 'Pupil behaviour in junior classrooms'. *British Journal of Educational Psychology*, **45**, 122–9.

Boydell, D. (1980) 'The organisation of junior classrooms: a follow up survey'. *Educational Research*, **23**, 14–19.

Brown, M.R. (1971) *Some Strategies used in Primary Schools for Initiating and Implementing Change*. MEd. dissertation, University of Manchester.

Bruner, J.S. (1963) *The Process of Education*. New York: Vintage Books, Random House.

Bullock Report (1974) Committee of Enquiry into Reading and the Use of English. *A Language for Life*. London: HMSO.

Burgess, R.G. (1983) *Experiencing Comprehensive Education*. London: Methuen.

CIPFA Annual statistics of the Chartered Institute of Public Finance and Accountancy, London.

Clift, P. (1982) *Case Study 1. An Oxfordshire School*, E364, *Curriculum Evaluation and Assessment in Educational Institutions*. Milton Keynes: Open University.

Cockcroft Report (1982) Committee of Inquiry into the Teaching of Mathematics in Schools. *Mathematics Counts*: report of the committee under the chairmanship of W.H. Cockcroft. London: HMSO.

Coulson, A.A. (1974) *The deputy head in the primary school: the role conceptions of heads and deputy heads*. MEd. dissertation, University of Hull.

Coulson, A.A. (1976) 'The role of the primary head'. In Peters, R.S. (ed.) *The Role of the Head*. London: Routledge and Kegan Paul.

Coulson, A.A. (1978) 'The politics of curriculum reform'. In Richards, C. (ed.)

Coulson, A.A. and Cox, M. (1975) 'What do deputies do?'. *Education 3–13*, **3**(2), 100–3.

Cox, C.B. and Boyson, R. (ed.) (1975) *Black Paper 1975*. London: Dent.

Cox, C.B. and Boyson, R. (ed.) (1977) *Black Paper 1977*. London: Temple Smith.

Cox, C.B. and Dyson, A.E. (ed.) (1969a) *Fight for Education: A Black Paper*. London: Critical Quarterly Society.

Cox, C.B. and Dyson, A.E. (ed.) (1969b) *The Crisis in Education: Black Paper 2*. London: Critical Quarterly Society.

Cox, C.B. and Dyson, A.E. (ed.) (1970) *Goodbye Mr Short: Black Paper 3*. London: Critical Quarterly Society.

Davies, B. and Bernstein, B. (1969) 'Some sociological comments on Plowden'. In Peters, R. (ed.) *Perspectives on Plowden*. London: Routledge and Kegan Paul.

Davis, E. (1980) *Teachers as Curriculum Evaluators*. Sydney: George Allen and Unwin.

Dearden, R. (1969) 'The aims of primary education'. In Peters, R. (ed.) *Perspectives on Plowden*. London: Routledge and Kegan Paul.

Dearden, R. (1976) *Problems in Primary Education*. London: Routledge and Kegan Paul.

Dearden, R. (1978) 'Reflections on Plowden'. *Education 3–13*, **6**(1), 27–30.

Dearden, R. (1980) 'The Primary Survey: an assessment'. In Richards, C. (ed.) *Primary Education: Issues for the Eighties*. London: A. and C. Black.

DES (1970) *Towards the Middle School*. London: HMSO.

DES (1977) *Curriculum 11–16* (Working Papers by HMI). London: HMSO.

DES (1978a) *Primary Education in England* (A survey by HMI). London: HMSO.

DES (1978b) *Making INSET Work*. London: HMSO.

DES (1979a) *Local Authority Arrangements for the School Curriculum*, Report on the Circular 14/77 Review. London: HMSO.

DES (1979b) *Aspects of Secondary Education in England* (A survey by HMI). London: HMSO.

DES (1980a) *A View of the Curriculum*. London: HMSO.

DES (1980b) *A Framework for the School Curriculum* (Proposals for consultation by the Secretaries of State for Education and Science and for Wales). London: HMSO.

DES (1981a) *The School Curriculum* (Guidance by the Secretaries of State). London: HMSO.

DES (1981b) *Curriculum 11–16*: A review of progress (joint study by HMI and five LEAs). London: HMSO.

DES (1981c) *Report by HMI on the effects on the education service of local authority expenditure policies*: financial year 1980–81. London: HMSO.

DES (1982a) *Education 5–9*: An illustrative survey by HMI. London: HMSO.

DES (1982b) *Report by HMI on the effects on the education service of local authority expenditure policies*: financial year 1981–82. London: HMSO.

DES (1983a) *9–13 Middle Schools*: An illustrative survey by HMI. London: HMSO.

DES (1983b) *Curriculum 11–16*: Towards a statement of entitlement. London: HMSO.

DES (1984) *The Organisation and Content of the 5–16 Curriculum*. London: HMSO.

Donoughue, C., Ball, S., Glaister, R. and Hand, G. (ed.) (1981) *In-Service: The Teacher and the School*. London: Kogan Page/Open University.

Dottrens, R. (1962) *The Primary School Curriculum*. Paris: UNESCO.

Eggleston, J. (ed.) (1980) *School-Based Curriculum Development in Britain*. London: Routledge and Kegan Paul.

Elliott, J. (1981) 'The Cambridge Accountability Project'. *Cambridge Journal of Education*, **11**(2), 146–66.

Elliott, J., Bridges, D., Nias, J., Ebbutt, D. and Gibson, R. (1981) *Case Studies in School Accountability*. The Cambridge/SSRC Accountability Project.

Ellis, T., McWhirter, J., McColgan, D. and Haddow, B. (1976) *William Tyndale: the Teachers' Story*. London: Writers and Readers Co-operative.

Evans, P. and Groarke, M. (1975) 'An exercise in managing curriculum development in a primary school'. In Taylor, P.H. (ed.) *Aims, Influence and Change in the Primary School Curriculum*. Windsor: NFER.

Fisher, R. (1972) *Learning How to Learn: The English Primary School and American Education*. New York: Harcourt Brace Jovanovich.

Galton, M. and Simon, B. (1980a) *Inside the Primary Classroom*. London: Routledge and Kegan Paul.

Galton, M. and Simon, B. (1980b) *Progress and Performance in the Primary Classroom*. London: Routledge and Kegan Paul.

Galton, M. and Willcocks, J. (1983) *Moving from the Primary Classroom*. London: Routledge and Kegan Paul.

Garland, R. (1982) 'Curriculum policy making in primary schools'. In Richards, C. (ed.) *New Directions in Primary Educa-*

tion. Brighton: Falmer Press.

Ginsburg, M.B., Meyenn, R.J., Miller, H.D.R. and Ranceford-Handley (1977) *The Role of the Middle School Teacher*, Aston Educational Monograph 7, Department of Educational Enquiry, Aston University.

Gipps, C. and Goldstein, H. (1983) *Monitoring Children*. London: Heinemann.

Goodacre, E. (1984) 'Postholders and language assertiveness'. *Education 3–13*, **12**(1), 17–21.

Goodacre, E. and Donoughue, C. (1983) *LEA Support for the Language Postholder in the Primary School*. School of Education, Middlesex Polytechnic.

Goodlad, J.I. (1975) *The Dynamics of Educational Change*. New York: McGraw-Hill.

Gray, J. and Satterly, D. (1976) 'A chapter of errors'. *Educational Research*, **19**(1), 45–56.

Gray, J. and Satterly, D. (1981) 'Formal or informal: a re-assessment of the British evidence'. *British Journal of Educational Psychology*, **51**, 187–96.

Gray, L.S. (1984) *Resource Management in Primary Schools*. Sheffield Papers in Educational Management, Sheffield Polytechnic.

Halsey, A.H. (1972) *Educational Priority*, Vol. I. London: HMSO.

Hamilton, D. (1976) *Curriculum Evaluation*. London: Open Books.

Hanson, M. (1977) 'Beyond the bureaucratic model: a study of power and autonomy in educational decision making'. *Interchange*, **7**(2). Quoted in Coulson (1978).

Hargreaves, A. (1980) *Teachers, Hegemony and the Educationist Context*. Paper presented to the 4th Annual Sociology of Education Conference, Westhill College, Birmingham.

Hargreaves, A. (1982) 'The rhetoric of school centred innovation'. *Journal of Curriculum Studies*, **14**(3), 251–66.

Hargreaves, A. and Tickle, L. (1980) *Middle Schools: Origins, Ideology and Practice*. London: Harper and Row.

Hargreaves, A. and Tickle, L. (1981) 'Middle school muddle'. *Times Educational Supplement*, 13 November.

Harling, P. (1980) 'School decision making and the primary headmaster'. *Education 3–13*, **8**(2), 44–8.

Havelock, R. (1982) 'The utilisation of educational research and development'. In Horton, T. and Raggatt, P. (ed.) *Challenge and Change in the Curriculum.* London: Hodder and Stoughton/Open University.

Henderson, E. (1979) 'The concept of school-focused INSET'. *British Journal of Teacher Education,* **5**(1), 17–26.

Henderson, E. and Perry, G.W. (ed.) (1981) *Change and Development in Schools.* Maidenhead: McGraw-Hill.

Holt, M. (1980) *Schools and Curriculum Change.* Maidenhead: McGraw-Hill.

House, E. (1974) *The Politics of Educational Innovation.* Berkeley: McCutchan.

House, E. (1975) 'Accountability in the USA'. *Cambridge Journal of Education,* **5**(2), pp. 71–8.

House, E., Rivers, L. and Stufflebeam, D. (1974) *An Assessment of the Michigan Accountability System.* Washington: NEA.

Hoyle, E. (1975) 'Professionality, professionalism and control in teaching'. In Houghton, V., McHugh, R. and Morgan, C. (ed.) *Management in Education.* London: Ward Lock/Open University.

ILEA (1977) *Keeping the School Under Review.* London: Inner London Education Authority.

Jackson, B. (1964) *Streaming: An Education System in Miniature.* London: Routledge and Kegan Paul.

Jenkins, D. and Shipman, M.D. (1976) *Curriculum: An Introduction.* London: Open Books.

Johnston, D. and Elliott, J. (1981) 'Case study 5, Ballifield School'. In Henderson, E.S. and Perry, G.W. (ed.) *Change and Development in Schools.* Maidenhead: McGraw-Hill.

Jones, K. (1983) *Beyond Progressive Education.* London: Routledge and Kegan Paul.

Joseph, Sir K. (1984a) 'View from the top'. *Times Educational Supplement,* 13 January.

Joseph, Sir K. (1984b) Parliamentary answer to question by L. Stevens MP, quoted in *Times Educational Supplement,* 13 July.

Keddie, N. (1971) 'Classroom knowledge'. In Young, M. (ed.) *Knowledge and Control: New Directions for the Sociology of Education.* London: Collier-Macmillan.

Kogan, M. (1980) 'Policies for the school curriculum in their political context'. *Cambridge Journal of Education,* **10/11**, 122–33.

Lawson, K. (1979) 'The politics of primary school curricula'. *Education 3–13,* **7**(1), 23–7.

Lawton, D. (1975) *Class, Culture and the Curriculum.* London: Routledge and Kegan Paul.

Lawton, D. (1980) *The Politics of the School Curriculum.* London: Routledge and Kegan Paul.

Lawton, D. (1983a) *Curriculum Studies and Educational Planning.* London: Hodder and Stoughton.

Lawton, D. (1983b) William Walker Lecture, quoted in *Times Educational Supplement,* 4 November.

Leese, J. (1978) 'Politics and power in curriculum reform'. In Richards, C. (ed.) *Power and the Curriculum.* Driffield: Nafferton Books.

Levy, P. and Goldstein, H, (ed.) (1984) *Tests in Education.* London: Academic Press.

Lortie, D. (1969) 'The balance of control and autonomy in elementary school teaching'. In Etzioni, A. (ed.) *The Semi-professions and the Organisation.* New York: Free Press.

Macdonald, B. and Walker, R. (1976) *Changing the Curriculum.* London: Open Books.

Marshall, S. (1963) *An Experiment in Education.* Cambridge: Cambridge University Press.

Martin, B. (1971) 'Progressive education v. the working class'. *Critical Quarterly,* Spring.

Metropolitan Borough of Solihull Education Committee (1980) *Evaluating the Primary School.* Solihull Education Authority.

Midwinter, E. (1972) *Priority Education.* Harmondsworth: Penguin Books.

Ministry of Education (1959) *Primary Education.* London: HMSO.

Mitson, R. (1980) 'Curriculum development and staff development at the Abraham Moss Centre'. In Eggleston, J. (ed.) *School-Based Curriculum Development in Britain.* London: Routledge and Kegan Paul.

Naismith, D. (1983) quoted in *Times Educational Supplement,* 2 December.

National Association of Schoolmasters/ Union of Women Teachers (1984) 'Staffing standards in primary schools', quoted in *Times Educational Supplement*, 9 March.

National Union of Teachers (1958) *The Curriculum of the Junior School*. London: Schoolmaster Publishing Company.

National Union of Teachers (1978) *Partnership in Education: the NUT commentary on the Taylor Report*. London: NUT, Hamilton House.

National Union of Teachers (1979) *Middle Schools: Deemed or Doomed?* London: NUT, Hamilton House.

Newson, J. and Newson, E. (1976) *Seven Years Old in the Home Environment*. London: George Allen and Unwin.

Newson, J. and Newson, E. (1977) *Perspectives on School at Seven Years Old*. London: George Allen and Unwin.

Nias, J. (1972) 'Pseudo-participation and innovation in the introduction of the BEd'. *Sociological Review*, May.

Nias, J. (1980) 'Leadership styles and job-satisfaction in primary schools'. In Bush, T., Glatter, R., Goodey, J. and Richer, C. (ed.) *Approaches to School Management*. London: Harper and Row.

OECD/CERI (1978) *The Creativity of the School*. Paris: OECD.

OECD/CERI (1979) *School Based Curriculum Development*. Paris: OECD.

Parlett, M. (1974) 'The new evaluation'. *Trends in Education*, 34.

Parlett, M. and Hamilton, D. (1972) 'Illuminative evaluation: a new approach to the study of innovatory programmes', University of Edinburgh Centre for Research in the Education Sciences, Occasional Paper. Reprinted in Tawney, D. (1975) (ed.) *Curriculum Evaluation Today*. London: Macmillan.

Peters, R.S. (ed.) (1969) *Perspectives on Plowden*. London: Routledge and Kegan Paul.

Peters, R.S. (ed.) (1976) *The Role of the Head*. London: Routledge and Kegan Paul.

Plowden Report, CACE (1967) *Children and their Primary Schools*. London: HMSO.

Primary Schools Research and Development Group/Schools Council (1983) *Curriculum Responsibility and the use of Teacher Expertise in the Primary School*, University of Birmingham Department of Curriculum Studies.

Razzell, A. (1979) 'Teacher participation in decision making'. *Education 3–13*, **7**(1), 4–8.

Richards, C. (ed.) (1980) *Primary Education: Issues for the Eighties*. London: A. and C. Black.

Richards, C. (ed.) (1982) *New Directions in Primary Education*. Brighton: Falmer Press.

Rodger, I. et al (1983) *Teachers with Posts of Responsibility in Primary Schools*. Schools Council, University of Durham School of Education.

Rogers, V. (1968) *The Social Studies in English Education*. London: Heinemann Educational.

Ross, A.M. (1960) *The Education of Childhood*. London: Harrap.

Salter, B. and Tapper, T. (1981) *Education, Politics and the State*. London: Grant McIntyre.

Schon, D. (1971) *Beyond the Stable State*. Harmondsworth: Penguin.

Schools Council (1983) *Primary Practice*. London: Methuen.

Scriven, M. (1967) 'The methodology of evaluation'. In Tyler, R., Grane, R. and Scriven, M. (ed.) *Perspectives on Curriculum Evaluation*, AERA Monograph on Curriculum Evaluation. Chicago: Rand McNally.

Sharp, R. and Green, A. (1974) *Education and Social Control*. London: Routledge and Kegan Paul.

Shipman, M.D. (1973) 'The impact of curriculum project'. *Journal of Curriculum Studies*, **5**(2), 47–56.

Shipman, M.D. (1983) *Assessment in Primary and Middle Schools*. London: Croom Helm.

Shipman, M.D., Jenkins, D. and Bolam, D. (1974) *Inside A Curriculum Project*. London: Methuen.

Skilbeck, M. (1972) 'School-based curriculum development', mimeo, University of Coleraine. Quoted in Eggleston, J. (ed.) (1980) *School-Based Curriculum Development in Britain*. London: Routledge and Kegan Paul.

Skilbeck, M. (1976a) Ideologies and Values, E203, *Curriculum Design and Development*. Milton Keynes: Open University.

Skilbeck, M. (1976b) 'School-based curriculum development'. In Walton, J. and Welton, J. (ed.) *Rational Curriculum*

Planning. London: Ward Lock.

Skilbeck, M. (1982) 'School-based curriculum development'. In Lee, V. and Zeldin, D. (ed.) *Planning the Curriculum*. Sevenoaks: Hodder and Stoughton/Open University.

Sockett, H. (1976) 'Teacher accountability'. *Proceedings of the Philosophy of Education Society of Great Britain*, **X**, July, 34–57.

Southgate, V., Arnold, H. and Johnson, S. (1981) *Extending Beginning Reading*. London: Heinemann.

Steadman, S.D., Parson, C. and Salter, B.G. (1978) *An inquiry into the impact and take-up of Schools Council funded activities: a first interim report*. Schools Council.

Stenhouse, L. (1982) 'The conduct, analysis and reporting of case study in educational research and evaluation'. In McCormick R. (ed.) *Calling Education to Account*. London: Heinemann Educational.

Sutherland, A. (1981) *Curriculum Projects in Primary Schools: an investigation of project adoption and implementation in 185 Northern Ireland Schools*. Northern Ireland Council for Educational Research.

Taylor, M. and Garson, Y. (1982) *Schooling in the Middle Years*. Stoke: Trentham.

Taylor, P.H. (1970) *How Teachers Plan Their Courses*. London: NFER.

Taylor, P.H. (ed.) (1975) *Aims, Influence and Change in the Primary School Curriculum*. Windsor: NFER.

Taylor, P.H., Reid, W., Holley, B. and Exon, G. (1974) *Purpose, Power and Constraint in the Primary School Curriculum*. London: Macmillan.

Taylor Report (1977) *A New Partnership for Our Schools*. London: HMSO.

Thomas, N. (1980a) 'The Primary Survey: a beginning to the follow-up'. *Education*

3–13, **8**(1), 28–32.

Thomas, N. (1980b) 'The primary curriculum, survey findings and implications'. In Richards, C. (ed.) *Primary Education: Issues for the Eighties*. London: A. and C. Black.

Timms, S. and Lees, B. (1981) 'Head-initiated INSET activity in a primary school'. In Donoughue, C., Ball, S., Glaister, R. and Hand, G. (ed.) *In-Service: The Teacher and the School*. London: Kogan Page/Open University.

Tizard, J. and Hewison, J. (1980) 'Parental involvement and reading attainment'. *British Journal of Educational Psychology*, **50**, 209–15.

Warnock Report (1978) *Special Educational Needs: A Report of the Committee of Enquiry into the Education of Handicapped Children and Young People*. Cmnd 7212. London: HMSO.

Whitaker, P. (1983) *The Primary Head*. London: Heinemann Educational.

White, J. (1980) 'Teacher accountability and school autonomy'. In Finch, A. and Scrimshaw, P. (ed.) *Standards, Schooling and Education*. London: Hodder and Stoughton.

White, J. (1984) 'The Descent of the Humanities' *Times Educational Supplement*, 19 September.

White Paper (1943) on Educational Reconstruction. Quoted (p. 58) in Ministry of Education (1958) *Primary Education*. London: HMSO.

Wicksteed, D. and Hill, M. (1979) 'Is this you? A survey of primary teachers' attitudes to issues raised in the Great Debate'. *Education 3–13*, **7**(I), 32–6.

Wragg, E.C. (1978) 'A suitable case for imitation'. *Times Educational Supplement*, 15 September.

Index